FINISH WHAT
WE STARTED

FINISH WHAT WE STARTED

THE MAGA MOVEMENT'S GROUND WAR TO END DEMOCRACY

ISAAC ARNSDORF

Little, Brown and Company
New York Boston London

Little, Brown and Company
Hachette Book Group
1290 Avenue of the Americas, New York, NY 10104
littlebrown.com

First Edition: April 2024

Little, Brown and Company is a division of Hachette Book Group, Inc. The Little, Brown name and logo are trademarks of Hachette Book Group, Inc.

The publisher is not responsible for websites (or their content) that are not owned by the publisher.

The Hachette Speakers Bureau provides a wide range of authors for speaking events. To find out more, go to hachettespeakersbureau.com or email HachetteSpeakers@hbgusa.com.

Little, Brown and Company books may be purchased in bulk for business, educational, or promotional use. For information, please contact your local bookseller or the Hachette Book Group Special Markets Department at special.markets@hbgusa.com.

ISBN 9780316497510
Library of Congress Control Number: 2023952555

Printing 1, 2024

LSC-C

Printed in the United States of America

We will not back down. We will not bend. We will not quit. We will not yield. We will press forward with vigor. We will push onward, and we will finish what we started.

— Donald Trump, at the Conservative
Political Action Conference, March 4, 2023

It is necessary for most of us these days to have some insight into the motives and responses of the true believer. For though ours is a godless age, it is the very opposite of irreligious. The true believer is everywhere on the march, and both by converting and antagonizing he is shaping the world in his own image. And whether we are to line up with him or against him, it is well that we should know all we can concerning his nature and potentialities.

— Eric Hoffer, *The True Believer:
Thoughts on the Nature of Mass Movements* (1951)

If all others accepted the lie which the Party imposed, then the lie passed into history and became truth. "Who controls the past," ran the Party slogan, "controls the future: who controls the present controls the past."

— George Orwell, *1984*

Contents

Author's Note

ALL THE NAMES, dates, and places in this story are real. Verbatim quotes are drawn from recordings, direct observation, contemporaneous notes, or, only where those weren't available, the best recollection of the participants. In a few instances, extended quotations have been lightly trimmed for clarity. I have made every effort to corroborate details that could be independently verified and to check information about someone with that person him- or herself. Where my original reporting was augmented by the research of others, I have documented those citations in the endnotes, for ease of reading.

The reporting that became this book is based on hundreds of hours of interviews and travel across the country over three years, in the course of my work for ProPublica, *This American Life*, and the *Washington Post*. Often the questions that most interested me and that friends would ask me about my work were not the type that would be answered in news articles; they involved deeper mysteries about what shaped people's beliefs and drove them to action. I realized there had never been a journalistic account of the rise of the MAGA movement — the movement as distinct from its leader, where it came from, and what it means for the future of American politics.

For the everyday people featured in this book, I have chosen to use first names with the goal of sounding like natural conversation. I met hundreds of people, each with their own unique stories to tell. The relative few whom I was able to focus on in these pages were chosen both because they are representative of thousands, maybe millions more like them, but also because they were in some ways exceptional. I am grateful to them for sharing a lot of their time and a little bit of their worlds with me.

The MAGA King in Exile

THE BALLROOM AT the Mar-a-Lago Club in Florida was modeled on the Palace of Versailles in France, that international icon of being out of touch. ("Let them eat cake.") The Palm Beach imitation is a long gallery that shimmers with gold leaf lit by triple-decker chandeliers and arched windows opposite paneled smoked mirrors. The ballroom wasn't part of the original estate. It was added in 2005 by the reality TV star who'd bought the property and dreamed of making it a winter White House. Once he did, the club's exotic name came to connote everything that people loved or hated about his presidency: his wealth, showmanship, and outsider status, how he smashed all the usual rules and customs of politics; or else his garishness, his way of mingling public service with his own private business, how he ensconced himself with his rich friends and whoever else might have been paying to see him while he launched top-secret overseas military operations over dinner. Just as the White House stood for the Office of the President, Mar-a-Lago symbolized the Court of Donald Trump, self-described MAGA King.

Mar-a-Lago was where *Air Force One* deposited Trump for the last time, after he refused to accept his defeat in the 2020 election, insisting it had been stolen, to the point of piquing his supporters to disrupt the peaceful transfer of power. His self-imposed exile there only increased the club's mystique in Republican politics, as it became a pilgrimage site for leaders and candidates seeking Trump's approval. Kevin McCarthy, Rick Scott, Elise Stefanik, Senate hopefuls in Georgia, North Carolina, Alabama, Ohio, Arizona...they all passed through for fundraisers or to take a photo with the king giving them a thumbs-up. Then Mar-a-Lago became a crime scene: the place where, in August 2022, the FBI executed a search warrant to recover sensitive government documents stashed away in a bathroom, in boxes stuffed with newspaper clippings, a cocktail napkin, and a dinner menu, making the club's name a shorthand for yet another political scandal. And now, precisely three months later, on the night of the 2022 midterm elections, the ballroom was all set up with gold chairs and brocade tablecloths, silver chafing dishes (let them eat burgers?), and a ring of flat-screen TVs to play live coverage of the election results. Outside, the palm trees were flailing, the sky was darkening, and Mar-a-Lago was in a mandatory evacuation zone, as a late-season tropical storm named Nicole barreled directly at it.

But Donald Trump would not evacuate. He would not cancel his election watch party. He would not let the hurricane be a metaphor! This was supposed to be an epic night for Trump. He, like most every Republican alive, was expecting a rout. All the historical and environmental conditions pointed to a banner night for the GOP. A president's first midterm was almost always a disaster for his party (it had happened to Trump, in 2018), and Joe Biden was an unpopular president. His approval rating was in the dumps, and Democrats were running away from campaigning with or even mentioning him. Inflation was soaring to a forty-year high. An overwhelming majority of Americans said the country was on the wrong track, and polls showed surging enthusiasm on the Republican side.

That was not all the night meant to Trump. He had more on the line than partisan pride. This election, even though Trump himself was not on the ballot, was the critical test of a consolidated MAGA slate. He'd handpicked the candidates with his endorsements, which had almost always proved decisive in the Republican primaries, and he'd hosted rallies for them around the country, calling them the Trump Ticket. The candidates had to agree with Trump that the 2020 election had been "rigged and stolen," but he wanted more than lip service. He wanted to put Republicans in office who would use their power to clear his path back to the White House in 2024. In Arizona, gubernatorial candidate Kari Lake was ominously calling this "the last election," and Mark Finchem, the Republican running to be the state's top elections official, had been outside the U.S. Capitol during the riot on January 6, 2021. Finchem's counterpart in Michigan, Kristina Karamo, appeared at events with supporters of the QAnon conspiracy theory and a far-right religious group denounced by both the Catholic Church and the Southern Poverty Law Center. The Republican running for governor of Pennsylvania, Doug Mastriano, promised to decertify voting machines and make every voter reregister (a likely violation of federal law), while the Wisconsin gubernatorial nominee, Tim Michels, proposed dissolving the state's bipartisan election commission and vowed, "Republicans will never lose another election." Nevada's candidate for secretary of state, Jim Marchant, led a nationwide coalition of election deniers whose goal, he said, was to "fix the whole country, and President Trump is going to be president again in 2024." They were all in contention for positions that took part in certifying election results — historically a mere formality, but in their hands a real means of blocking the Democrats from winning the Electoral College. (Let them *eat shit*.)

Assured of his impending triumph, Trump could barely wait to seize on this momentum by declaring his candidacy for president. He came close to blurting it out the night before the midterms, at a rally in Ohio, setting off a scramble among his advisers and other Republican leaders to talk him out of it. They warned him his announcement would get drowned out by election news, it might backfire by motivating Democratic voters, and he could get blamed if Republicans underperformed. Instead he settled on announcing that he was *going to announce* in another week. And he contented himself to rattle off poll results showing him ahead of potential rivals for the Republican nomination, as well as against the incumbent president.

But the Trump who stepped into the Mar-a-Lago ballroom on election night was not Trump Rally Trump. His tie was blue. His MAGA hat was off. And no amount of cheering from his adoring fans who greeted him in the ballroom across a red velvet rope line could budge the dour expression off his face. Trump, for all his deceits, could be hopelessly transparent about his emotions in person. Though he would later insist he was "not at all ANGRY," you could tell he was by his expression. You could tell by the way he thanked the press for being there, calling it a "great honor" to have them (not his usual posture toward the "Fake News"). He knew the reporters from the major national outlets had bailed, catching the last planes out of town before the storm. And he knew as well that the night was not going his way. A little after ten o'clock, when he took the stage to speak for less than five minutes, Trump recited his record of endorsing winners, in the primaries and now in the general. He mused aloud, "Wouldn't that be funny, if we were better on the general election than on the nominations?"

It was already quickly becoming clear that that was not to be. Lake was on track to lose by less than one percentage point, Marchant by two, Michels by three, Finchem by almost five, Karamo by fourteen, Mastriano by fifteen. Perhaps worst of all, as Trump's allies would privately admit, the Republican who came out looking triumphant that night was a different Floridian. The governor, Ron DeSantis, won a twenty-point landslide reelection in a usually competitive state, even flipping populous Miami-Dade County, and he delivered a victory speech to chants of "Two more years!" — urging him to run for president instead of serving out his term.

While confetti rained down on DeSantis, Trump loitered quietly at his banquet table, never taking the podium again to welcome the good news that didn't come. By the time he left the Versailles-inspired ballroom around midnight, only a few stragglers remained to cheer him off. Watching Trump work the room that night, it was possible, if only for a fleeting moment, to see him as just the club owner, the host of a party where no one wanted to be.

THAT NIGHT WAS more than a setback for Trump. It was the closest this country has come to being taken over by a radical far-right mass movement. This book tells the story of where that force came from, how it evolved and spread, and the series of accidents, ironies, and failures that narrowly stopped it from succeeding in 2022 — but did not finish it off. The movement has regrouped for another attempt in this November's presidential election.

The movement now called MAGA has long existed in the American political bloodstream; fittingly, Trump's companion motto, "America First," originated in 1940 among isolationists at the outbreak of World War II.* Across every iteration, this movement's

---

* Trump may not personally have been aware of that coinage, but he was certainly familiar with the slogan's deliberate revival in the 1990s by Pat Buchanan, whom Trump ran against for the Reform Party nomination in 2000.

ideology was and is loosely defined by nationalism and traditional social values, fierce opposition to liberalism as a slippery slope to communism, and a tendency toward paranoia and conspiratorial thinking. For most of the postwar era, this worldview remained on the fringe of American politics — that is, unpersuasive to most Americans, and systematically frozen out by the two major parties. In contrast to the mainstream GOP, the fringe passionately opposed immigration and trade and rejected bipartisan compromise, even tolerating violence.

In spite of, or maybe because of, being so marginalized, a core tenet of this belief system was that its adherents were surely right, and most Americans surely agreed with them, if only their views could be heard — that America was inherently and immovably a right-of-center, conservative country, no matter how many times the voters said otherwise. This faction managed to persist and even grow despite the repeated electoral setbacks that befell its champions, from Barry Goldwater to Pat Buchanan. By the 2010s, with the rise of the Tea Party backlash to Barack Obama's election, the coarser side of the American right was gaining strength but still decidedly an outside force pressuring the Republican Party. The movement lacked someone with the political talent, charisma, fame, or resources to popularize its ideology (as Ronald Reagan did for his sunny small-government conservatism) — until Trump. The America of Trump's first inaugural — "this American carnage" — sounded shockingly dark to anyone not already steeped in the harsh pessimism that had long festered on the outer edge of the American right. To those who were, listening to Trump sounded like finally, for the first time, being recognized and represented.

Trump never missed an opportunity to use his presidential megaphone to elevate these views, from defending white nationalist marchers in Charlottesville to railing against "deep state" enemies. He both welcomed more people from the radical fringe into the Republican fold and at the same time mainstreamed their views to steadily radicalize the existing rank and file. In his final year in office, two genuine crises collided to radicalize millions more Republicans with astonishing speed. First, the pandemic upended all semblance of normalcy, injected politics into daily life, and fueled a spasm of conspiracy theories that presented attractive alternatives to experts asking for major sacrifices; suddenly, as government officials started exercising powers unseen in living memory, many Republicans found it a little less far-fetched, a little more credible, to believe that Democrats wanted to control their lives and take away their freedoms. Then, massive street demonstrations responding to the murder of George Floyd created an atmosphere of social upheaval, racial unrest, and, based on portrayals in right-wing media, rampant lawlessness and destruction. Trump's campaign messaging rolled it all up — the "China virus" and the "thugs" — into a vast voter-fraud conspiracy arrayed against him and his supporters. The widespread misinformation about the virus and the protests primed Trump's supporters to reject the result of the election. The names, dates, and places of the supposed theft, to the extent they were ever specified, were always changing and never really mattered. The essence of the stolen-election myth was the latest, biggest expression of insisting America must tilt right, that, as Trump would repeat at his rallies, "this nation does not belong to *them*, this nation belongs to *you*."

The shape and methods of Trump's attempts to overturn the 2020 election results are now well documented in hundreds of pages of congressional testimony and criminal indictments, leading to trials in Washington and Atlanta. But in the MAGA movement, that same sequence of events has taken on an entirely different significance. In this account, Trump came up short not because he was at odds with the law, the Constitution, basic decency, and empirical reality: the cause of his defeat was being narrowly thwarted at almost every step by *fellow Republicans*. The clerk in Antrim County, Michigan, who said the incorrect vote tallies reported on Election Night were just an honest mistake, quickly fixed, was a Republican. The secretary of state in Georgia who refused Trump's demand to "find 11,780 votes," enough to reverse the outcome, was a Republican. The county supervisors in Maricopa County, Arizona, who screened Trump's calls and certified Biden's win were Republicans. Trump failed to pressure every House Republican to object to the Electoral College votes on January 6, and he got only a handful of senators. Even Trump's own vice president refused to help him block the official certification in Congress. As close as he came to keeping himself in power, he came up short only because of uncooperative members of his own party.

The suggestion that Trump did not already fully dominate the Republican Party is surely confusing to non-Trump supporters. Hadn't Republican politicians spent years contorting themselves to conform to his whims and pretending not to have seen his latest tweet? But from the perspective of the MAGA movement, weak Republicans were the clear culprit for selling out Trump when everything was on the line. His supporters learned from this shortcoming and organized to address it. They decided they had to take over the party apparatus from the ground up, beginning with the smallest, lowliest units of political organizing—the precincts—and building up from there to districts, counties, and states, all the way to the Republican National Committee. This plot, known as the Precinct Strategy, proved effective, in that it forced out Republicans who were anything less than completely faithful to Trump and his election denial. At last, the far-right extreme, no longer fringe, captured the institution that had long excluded it: the Republican Party itself.

This strategy's success almost instantly became its own undoing. The MAGA movement now controlled one of the two major parties, but it remained unpopular with a majority of Americans, and they resoundingly rejected it at the ballot box in the 2022 midterms. Democrats discovered that Trump's MAGA brand was widely disliked and exploited it to portray Republican candidates as extreme and dangerous, a rogue's gallery of election deniers who alienated swing voters and even some Republicans.

In the aftermath of the Trump Ticket's dismal showing, prominent Republicans started openly criticizing Trump, blaming him for the disappointing results, and urging the party to finally move on. Trump fans were not immune to acknowledging that the former president might have an electability problem. But that did little to shake their support for him; and even those who entertained a future with DeSantis or another new standard-bearer were not looking for a departure from Trump's reinvention of the Republican Party. Almost two-thirds of Republican midterm voters identified themselves in exit polls with the MAGA movement. And thanks to the Precinct Strategy, the party organization was now firmly in the control of election deniers. The GOP would not moderate. It would not tack toward the middle in the hopes of winning back the political center. The fully empowered MAGA movement would not give up. The threat it posed to democracy would not pass. The movement resolved to try again this fall, in the 2024 presidential election.

It would be wrong to conclude that the Republicans' face-plant in the midterms and refusal to change course in their aftermath mean that they cannot win this November. In a polarized, roughly evenly divided country, either party always has a real chance of winning. And the fringe ideology whose reach Trump elevated from roughly 15 percent of the electorate to close to 50 percent will not subside so easily. He and his supporters are locked in a feed-back loop pushing one another to become ever more extreme. Together, they are growing more disconnected from the rest of the country, more hostile to reconciliation, more mistrustful of more institutions. Trump is now desperate to avoid criminal penalties, determined to portray his prosecutions as a political persecution; in the process, he is delegitimizing the justice system in the eyes of millions of Americans, just as he did before with the election sys-tem. The lasting effects of eroding public faith in the law, of vilify-ing federal agents and prosecutors and judges, are impossible to predict and chilling to imagine. Whether the rise of authoritarian-ism is to happen in America or merely to *almost* happen in America, the essential question of this era is how so many millions of fellow Americans could come to authentically believe in and passionately desire such an outcome.

In the story of the mass radicalization of the Republican Party, Trump is a singular, indispensable actor. But his perspective is not where the drama and tension unfold. This book turns the camera around from its usual focus on politicians and operatives, focusing instead on the faces in the crowd: what makes them believe, what motivates them, what stirs them to action. This book tells the story of ordinary Americans whose small, daily decisions add up to changing history in ways that were unpredictable and unexpected, even to themselves. The story begins in the immediate aftermath of the January 6 insurrection — the formative moment for the MAGA movement going forward — and the debut of the Precinct Strategy as the chosen method for redeeming that defeat.

FINISH WHAT WE STARTED

CHAPTER 1

True Believers

A SHROUD OF black mesh fence closed around the bright marble colonnades of the U.S. Capitol campus. The twelve-foot barrier, topped with razor wire and guarded by troops in combat fatigues with flak vests and long rifles, had sprung up to secure the seat of government after it was overrun by a mob of Trump's supporters trying to stop the formal certification of his electoral defeat. Whether the fortifications were too much or too little, they were clearly too late. Their effect now was to sever the federal office buildings from the adjacent neighborhood of Capitol Hill, a picturesque historic district of low, colorful row homes. In the basement of one of these townhouses, Steve Bannon was about to take to the airwaves.

Seated in his podcast studio, Bannon looked, as usual, underslept and overcaffeinated, but on this morning, the first Saturday in February 2021, his beady eyes were bright with excitement. He wore chunky black headphones that swept back his long gray mane until the tips grazed the epaulets of an olive-green field jacket. This MAGA Che Guevara look was new for Bannon, a transformation from the preppy layered collars that he used to wear to his West Wing office, which he'd called "the War Room." If White House strategist to podcast host sounded like a fall from grace, for Bannon it was more of a return to form. He was in his natural mode,

3

playing a role that came easily to him: the outside agitator with a huge online following. This same basement, years earlier, had been the headquarters of *Breitbart News*, the rising voice of reactionary right-wing nationalism, rebranded for an online generation as "the alt-right." Official Washington, Democrat or Republican, didn't know what to do with Bannon when he showed up, with his scruffy neck and multiple shirts. Bannon relished that air of foreignness, dubbing this townhouse the "Breitbart Embassy." Fittingly, the upstairs rooms were decorated as if for a state visit, with yellow brocade curtains, crystal chandeliers, filigree mirrors, and white stars dotting a dark-blue rug running up the stairs to a Lincoln-themed bedroom. It was in those rooms, during a book party in November of 2013, that Bannon had once announced, "I'm a Leninist."

"What do you mean?" asked his shocked interlocutor, a historian at a conservative think tank across town. The historian, Ronald Radosh, was all too familiar with Lenin's contributions to the ledger of human suffering. Lenin's most influential and enduring innovation, laid out in his 1902 treatise, *What Is To Be Done?*, was the revolutionary party: an institution for organizing society not according to competition or merit, but rather based on adherence to an ideology.

"Lenin wanted to destroy the state, and that's my goal too," Bannon answered. "I want to bring everything crashing down, and destroy all of today's establishment."

Bannon's Manichean worldview started young. At a Catholic military school in Richmond, Virginia, he learned about the 1492 reconquest of Spain as the turning point in an ongoing clash of civilizations between the Christian West and the Muslim world. As an adult, he devoured books on Attila the Hun and great military campaigns. He was obsessed with history, specifically the concept of historical cycles — the idea that time was not, as Americans usually learned, a linear march of progress, but rather, more like the view of ancient traditions, a recurring pattern of distinct phases. Bannon especially liked the version of this theory in *The Fourth Turning*, a 1997 book by historians Neil Howe and William Strauss, which ordered American history into generation-long periods of highs, awakenings, unravelings, and crises. The book predicted a coming rise of nationalism and authoritarianism, across the world and in America.

Bannon was not merely a student or passive observer of this prophecy; he wanted to be an agent of it, and an architect of the era that came next. So when he watched Donald J. Trump glide down a golden escalator to announce his campaign for president, in 2015, his first thought was, *That's Hitler!* By that he meant someone who intuitively understood the aesthetics of power, as in Nazi propaganda films. He saw in Trump someone who could viscerally connect with the general angst that Bannon was roiling and make himself a vessel for Americans' grievances and desires.

Bannon's thinking on building a mass movement was shaped by Eric Hoffer, "the longshoreman philosopher," so called because he had worked as a stevedore on the San Francisco docks while writing his first book, *The True Believer.* The book caused a sensation when it was published in 1951, becoming a manual for comprehending the age of Hitler, Stalin, and Mao. Hoffer argued that all mass movements — nationalist, communist, or religious — shared common characteristics and followed a discernable path. "The preliminary work of undermining existing institutions, of familiarizing the masses with the idea of change, and of creating a receptivity to a new faith, can be done only by men who are, first and foremost, talkers or writers and are recognized as such by all." (How about a reality TV star?) But such leaders cannot alone create the conditions that give rise to mass movements. "He cannot conjure a movement out of the void," Hoffer wrote. "There has to be an eagerness to follow and obey, and an intense dissatisfaction with things as they are, before the movement and leader can make their appearance."

Rather than focusing on movement leaders, Hoffer's inquiry concerned the followers — how ordinary people became fanatics. Successful, well-adjusted people did not become zealots. Sometimes they glommed onto mass movements to serve their own ambitions, but that came later. The true believers were seeking not self-advancement but rather "self-renunciation" — swapping out their individual identities, with all their personal disappointments, for "a chance to acquire new elements of pride, confidence, hope, a sense of purpose and worth by an identification with a holy cause." The kinds of people who were most susceptible to becoming true believers were, in Hoffer's idiom, poor, struggling artists, misfits, unusually selfish, or just plain bored. "When our individual interests and prospects do not seem worth living for, we are in desperate need of something apart from us to live for," Hoffer wrote. "All forms of dedication, devotion, loyalty, and self-surrender are in essence a desperate clinging to something which might give worth and meaning to our futile, spoiled lives."

For Bannon, as he was building *Breitbart*'s audience, the ready supply of true believers came from disaffected young men. Bannon had first discovered this untapped resource in, of all places, Hong Kong, while working with a company that paid Chinese workers to play the video game *World of Warcraft*, earning virtual commodities that the company could flip to Western gamers for real money. The business collapsed, but not before introducing Bannon to an online subculture of young gamers and meme creators, whose energies he learned to draw out and redirect toward politics.

Breitbart's traffic figures confirmed Bannon's hunch that candidate Trump was catching fire, and Bannon positioned the site as the Trump campaign's unofficial media partner in thrashing the Republican primary field. By the time Bannon officially took over Trump's ragtag campaign, in the wake of a chaotic convention and spiraling Russia scandal, he supplied a closing message that, if not exactly lucid, did have a kind of coherence. The message was that Trump, the "blue-collar billionaire," was here to blow up the established political order that was plainly failing to serve the needs and interests of the common public, and would be a champion for the forgotten and left-behind Americans. Bannon was not alone in seeing Hoffer's influence on what he was doing: Trump's opponent, Hillary Clinton, dusted off *The True Believer* and shared it with her campaign staff, recognizing in those pages the description of a destructive energy that she concluded she was powerless to subdue.

In the White House, as Trump's chief strategist, Bannon heralded the dawn of a "new political order," but he lasted only seven months. Trump threw him out after white supremacists and neo-Nazis marched in Charlottesville, Virginia, against removing a statue of Confederate general Robert E. Lee, and one of them drove a car into a crowd of counterprotesters, killing a young woman. Trump was the one who defended the torch-carrying mob as including "very fine people," but Bannon, as the face of right-wing nationalism inside the White House (and what a face it was), made a fitting scapegoat.* Though the dismissal set Bannon, temporarily, at odds with Trump, it did not shake his commitment to their shared political project. Bannon moved back into the Breitbart Embassy to plot his comeback.

Bannon was constantly testing things out. With so many bombastic schemes in motion, it could be hard to tell when Bannon was onto something or when he was just blowing smoke. He looked overseas, finding common cause with rising right-wing authoritarians around the world, from Hungary to Brazil. He went to court against the Italian government over a medieval monastery near Rome where he unsuccessfully tried to start a training academy for European nationalists. He found a new patron, the fugitive Chinese billionaire Guo Wengui, who cast himself as the shadowboxing action hero in music videos about taking down the Chinese Communist Party. Together, Bannon and Guo landed in the SEC's crosshairs for a cryptocurrency offering, called G-Coins or G-Dollars.† Bannon started a podcast, calling it *War Room*, and playing Guo's music video as the interlude for commercial breaks. And he reunited with some old friends in a bid to crowdsource money for Trump's border wall. More than 250,000 people donated, many saying they could only afford a few bucks but desperately wanted to help fulfill the president's signature campaign promise (never mind that Mexico was originally supposed to foot the bill). Bannon and his buddies dutifully assured the donors, publicly and privately, that they were all volunteers and all the money was for the wall.

By the summer of 2020, it might have been easy to laugh Bannon off as a has-been and a sideshow. There he was, reading a book, having a coffee, relaxing on the deck of Guo's 150-foot superyacht in Long Island Sound, when who showed up but the Coast Guard with federal agents to arrest him. Prosecutors accused Bannon and his friends of misusing the millions they'd raised from Trump

---

* An equal or even greater impetus for Bannon's firing was that he'd given interviews contradicting the boss, appeared on the cover of *Time* magazine, and participated in Bloomberg reporter Joshua Green's book, *Devil's Bargain*, whose cover photo put Bannon and Trump on equal footing.

† Guo was arrested in 2023 and charged with wire fraud, securities fraud, bank fraud, and money laundering amounting to more than $1 billion.

supporters, spending the money on their own salary, travel, hotels, and credit-card debts. Trump shrugged to reporters in the Oval Office, "I haven't been dealing with him for a very long period of time."

In truth, they had started talking again. Trump was by then running for reelection, and though he'd entered 2020 in a formidable position, the COVID-19 pandemic had paralyzed the economy and showcased a president in ineffectual denial, refusing to wear a mask, demanding to suppress case counts by slowing down testing, and musing about injecting bleach. By June, Joe Biden had put up a double-digit lead in national surveys, and Trump was longing to replace his campaign manager (digital strategist Brad Parscale, who was about to have a mental-health crisis) and recapture his 2016 magic. But Bannon turned down the job. Based on how badly the White House was squandering the COVID emergency, leaving the response to Jared Kushner, Mike Pence, and Dr. Fauci, Bannon thought the race was already over. The Trump campaign was beyond saving. Undermining a Biden presidency, however, was something Bannon said he knew how to do, and he could start laying the groundwork in advance.

On his *War Room* podcast and in speeches to Republican groups around the country, Bannon addressed audiences who were feeling sure that Trump would win, because they'd seen massive boat parades of Trump supporters, and they didn't personally know anyone who was voting for Biden. Bannon warned them to stay focused, pay attention. Trump had been saying since the summer that the Democrats would use mail ballots to steal the election, using COVID as an excuse to change the rules. Bannon explained how it would all play out. The Election Day votes would show Trump ahead, and he would declare victory that night. But the Democrats and the media would cry, *No, you have to wait for the mail ballots*. The Electoral College results would be disputed, and it would be up to Congress to settle the outcome when it met to formally certify the results on January 6. At that point, Bannon promised, Congress would either return the election to Republican-controlled state legislatures or decide it in the House of Representatives, where Republicans controlled a majority of state delegations.

Could they really pull it off? Didn't matter. "I had no downside," Bannon would later say. His aim was to use the occasion to stage such a spectacle that it would undermine Biden's legitimacy with millions of Americans — "shred that fucker on national TV," permanently hobble his ability to govern, "kill the Biden presidency in the crib." All that mattered was for Trump supporters to *believe* it was possible for Congress to block the election results that day.

So while Trump was busy calling Republican officials in Georgia, Arizona, and Michigan to pressure them to declare him the winner; and while Trump's lawyers were filing far-fetched lawsuits seeking to invalidate the results, and rounding up Republicans to put themselves forward to the Electoral College, and lobbying Vice President Mike Pence to accept them as the rightful electors; and while Republican activists around the country organized Stop the Steal rallies to protest the results; and while militia groups bought weapons and drew up attack plans for the biggest rally of all, Bannon kept hyping January 6 to his hundreds of thousands of podcast listeners. "This is more important than November 3, this is more important than even Trump's presidency," he'd say on the show. "This is more important than this fight between the nationalists and the globalists. This is more important than the fight between progressives and conservatives. It's more important than this fight between Republicans and Democrats. This gets to the *heart*—you go read Roman history, this is like toward how the republic fell, right, and became a totalitarian or authoritarian empire. We're at that moment."

He didn't say exactly what everyone was supposed to do once they got to Washington on January 6. His point was that his listeners, the *"War Room* posse," needed to show up, they didn't want to miss this. They had to be there. Their success depended on it. "I know people have work, family, kids, school, everything like that — however, these types of days happen very rarely in the history of our country. This is something you can participate in. This is something they're gonna be able to tell their kids and their grandkids about, 'cause this is gonna be history. Living history."

When the day finally dawned, as the crowd he'd conjured took shape, Bannon marveled at how his plan was materializing, like the invisible sound waves of his podcast finding physical, human form. "This is a massive turnout, I think it overwhelms everybody's — every anticipation of what was going to happen," he said on the show that cold morning. "Because of this audience. You have brought this to the cusp. We are right on the cusp of victory." Behind him in the studio, on a white fireplace mantel lined with MAGA hats, a TV was streaming CNN. The chyron read, SOON: TRUMP TO SPEAK TO SUPPORTERS IN DESPERATE COUP ATTEMPT. Bannon was saying, "This is not a day for fantasy. This is the day for maniacal focus. Focus, focus, focus. We're coming in right over the target, OK? Exactly. This is the point of attack we always wanted. OK?... I said from day one, for months and months and months and months—because they're trying to steal it, they're gonna be caught trying to steal it—President Trump's massive victory is going to be affirmed in a contingent election in the House of Representatives...Today, the trigger can get pulled on that. We are on, and when everybody out there, people getting fired up—we are on the cusp of victory because of you. Don't ever forget that."

The show tuned into Trump's speech live at noon. *"We will never give up, we will never concede,"* the rallygoers on the Mall, and the *War Room* posse listening back home, heard the president say. *"You don't concede when there's theft involved."*

"Fight for Trump!" the crowd chanted. "Fight for Trump!"

He recounted how Election Night went down, exactly as Bannon had foretold. *"Our election was over at ten o'clock in the evening. We're leading Pennsylvania, Michigan, Georgia, by hundreds of thousands of votes. And then late in the evening, or early in the morning, boom! These explosions of bullshit. And all of a sudden, all of a sudden, it started to happen."*

"Bullshit!" the crowd responded. "Bullshit!"

"And after this," Trump instructed them, *"we're to going to walk down—and I'll be there with you... We're going walk down to the Capitol, and we're going to cheer on our brave senators and congressmen and -women...Today we will see whether Republicans stand strong for integrity of our elections, but whether or not they stand strong for our country."*

Soon the lawmakers in the Capitol could hear the crowd roaring outside. Trump didn't come (the Secret Service wouldn't let him). The mob broke in and the lawmakers fled. For hours the counting and certification of the electoral votes was stopped. Once police and National Guardsmen secured the Capitol and the lawmakers reconvened, Pence refused to do what Trump demanded, and not enough Republicans objected to the votes to force a contingent election in the House. The massive victory Bannon had promised did not come to pass.

Whose fault was that? Not Bannon's. Not the *War Room* posse's. Bannon knew his listeners were angry, he knew they were disappointed. He wanted them to understand: "These were not Democrats that were thwarting us," he said on the next day's show. "These were *Republicans*."

In the weeks that followed, Bannon's show got booted from YouTube, Trump was banned from Twitter, rioters started getting arrested, Trump got impeached, Biden got inaugurated, and at the last possible minute before Trump left office, he pardoned Bannon. The pardon did more than rescue Bannon from criminal jeopardy (his codefendants in the fraud case, by the way, were still on the hook); it also restored Trump's imprimatur. Whatever their disagreements over the years ("Steve Bannon has nothing to do with me or my presidency," Trump said in 2018, "he lost his mind"), Bannon must have done something worth rewarding or retained some value to Trump. As Trump skulked off to Mar-a-Lago, Bannon kept rising as the essential voice of the MAGA universe. The pro-Trump media ecosystem splintered into alternative platforms and fringe websites such as Rumble, Telegram, and BitChute. MyPillow sponsorships for all. But Bannon stood out from the pack by any measure: he reached more listeners, had the most in-demand guests, churned out more content, set the agenda. He kept distributing through Apple's podcast app, repeatedly topping the charts. He also streamed his episodes as videos, and his *War Room* became like a far-right *Meet the Press*, the go-to interview for Trumpworld celebrities and aspiring candidates.

For three hours every weekday, and two on Saturdays, Bannon and his guests developed a canon of the Stolen Election myth. The fraud was just the first part. The Democrats always tried that; it was a given. The second part, the crucial step, was the stab in the back— the Republican election officials and state legislators who *knew* the election was stolen and *let* the Democrats get away with it. All the tumult of 2020 had, as Hoffer foretold, done the preliminary work of undermining institutions and creating a receptivity to a new faith. Now it was up to Bannon to transform the defeat of January 6 into the galvanizing moment for the next phase of the MAGA movement.

"OK, live from the nation's capital, you're in the *War Room*," your host began today's show. "It's still an occupied capital. The question still needs to be asked, why are seven thousand National Guard, up-armored National Guard, still in the nation's capital?" The answer, according to Bannon, was that the show of force was a "psyop"—a form of psychological warfare meant to cow the MAGA movement, to break Trump supporters' will to resist. That was also the purpose, he would say, of the Democrats' vote to impeach Trump for inciting the insurrection, and the Senate trial that was about to begin.

Bannon announced the date, as he usually did at the top of the show, in a grandiose way: "Saturday, the sixth of February, the year of our Lord 2021. The podcast," he went on, assuring his listeners that they were not alone and that he was not speaking into a void, was "closing in on 34 million downloads."

Bannon wasn't messing around with basement kids anymore. The MAGA movement had matured. His audience now was grayer—people in their fifties, sixties, and beyond, a lot of empty nesters and retirees—but with a similar need for connection, and perhaps even memories of a gentler time. He was speaking to people who didn't look like radicals, and certainly didn't think of themselves as extremists; it was the world around them that had lost its mind. The social critic Christopher Lasch, another Bannon influence, had written about this beginning in the sixties: how liberalism was a failure because people looked at the world that "freedom" got them and decided they didn't want it. It sucked. Modern life was so fragmented, so disembodied, so alienating. Dealing with that alienation was what *War Room* was all about. "Action, action, action," Bannon would say. "This is all about your agency." He was offering his listeners a path to self-empowerment, and in the dark days that followed January 6, Trump supporters were starving for a sense of direction, a suggestion of where to go next, an idea of what to do with their feelings of shock and disaffection.

One idea that was now generating buzz with Trump supporters was starting a third party, a Patriot Party, to fight for Trump in all the ways the Republican Party had so clearly failed. The source of this proposal was Trump himself, who meant it as a threat to the Republican senators about to try his impeachment. But Trump's rank-and-file supporters were getting carried away with the third-party idea, and Bannon needed to put a stop to it. He knew a third party would be a fool's errand, a waste of everyone's time and money. Even Teddy Roosevelt couldn't win back the White House on a third-party ticket. All third parties did was help elect someone from the two major parties. George Wallace helped give you Richard Nixon. Ross Perot got you Bill Clinton. Bannon had a better idea.

The way Bannon saw it, there already was a third party: that was the establishment he hungered to destroy. The neocons, neoliberals, big donors, globalists, Wall Street, corporatists, elites. He sometimes called them "the uniparty," because they were the only ones who ever got power, no matter whether Democrats or Republicans won elections. This formulation was not entirely wrongheaded, to the extent that the structure of having two pluralistic, big-tent parties pushed them both toward the center, producing a measure of stability and continuity. Nor was Bannon baseless in believing that this stasis could produce bad outcomes, particularly in foreign affairs, the domain of the so-called Washington Blob. Outside the uniparty, as Bannon saw it, there was the progressive wing of the Democratic Party, which he considered a relatively small slice of the electorate. And the rest, the vast majority of the country, was MAGA. Bannon believed the MAGA movement, if it could break out of being suppressed and marginalized by the establishment, represented a dominant coalition that could rule for a hundred years.

In his confidence that there were secretly millions of Democrats who were yearning to be MAGA followers and just didn't know it yet, Bannon was again taking inspiration from Hoffer, who observed that true believers were prone to conversion from one cause to another since they were driven more by their need to identify with a mass movement than by any particular ideology. Bannon was not, like a typical political strategist, trying to tinker around the edges of the existing party coalitions in the hope of eking out 50 percent plus one. Bannon already told you: he wanted to bring everything crashing down. He wanted to completely dismantle and redefine the parties. He wanted a showdown between a globalist, elite party, called the Democrats, and a populist, MAGA party, called the Republicans. In that matchup, he was sure, the Republicans would win every time.

How to put the Patriot Party idea in its place, and harness the MAGA movement through the Republican Party where it belonged? Bannon had just the man for the job, someone he'd known for years, someone who used to blog for him back at *Breitbart*. His name was Dan Schultz, and his time had come.

During a break, before bringing Dan Schultz on the air, Bannon asked him, "How should I introduce you?" This was a standard question for any of his guests; usually everyone had a website or a podcast or a book or a PAC or a 501(c)(4) — some hustle to promote. "What organization are you representing?"

But this guest had a different sort of answer. "The Republican Party," Dan Schultz said.

There was a long pause. Then Bannon chuckled.

"The Republican Party."

CHAPTER 2

Extremism No Vice

IN SEVENTH GRADE, Dan Schultz took a course on civics. Dan was more studious than a lot of his classmates, who didn't have too much time or energy for homework between milking cows, baling hay, and working on the river. Dan's parents also grew up on farms, but he was a "city kid," meaning he lived in town. The "city," so to speak, consisted of a railroad track, a Main Street, and a Second Street, bounded by the Mississippi River on one side and a forested bluff on the other. Alma, Wisconsin, population 956. Dan and his brothers used to climb up the bluff and go exploring for caves. He went fishing every day if he wanted to (ice fishing in the winter) and hunted quail, deer, squirrel, and duck. When Dan read about the adventures of Tom Sawyer—stories of looking for treasure in caves, playing pirates, painting a white picket fence—he thought that pretty much summed up his life, and that's how he learned to describe his upbringing to people who weren't from Alma.

At the time Dan started the class, in the fall of 1968, civics was about as standard a part of the American public-school curriculum as reading Mark Twain's classics. For as long as there had been public schools in America, teaching civics had been core to their mission, developed as a way of assimilating immigrants, instilling a common culture, and preparing children to be productive citizens in a democracy. "A government resting upon popular suffrage cannot be successful unless those who elect and who obey their governors are educated," the influential reformer John Dewey wrote in 1916. "But there is a deeper explanation. A democracy is more than a form of government; it is primarily a mode of associated living, of conjoint communicated experience." For the purposes of educating good democratic citizens, Dewey emphasized the importance of instruction in the humanities. But by 1968, the pressure of beating the Russians in the Cold War was shifting the emphasis to math and science, with performance measured as a condition of federal funding, and civics education was often one of the courses that got squeezed out.

A lot more was changing across America in 1968. The nearest newspaper, the *Winona Daily News,* ran wire stories under banner headlines like "Press Search for King's Assassin — Shooting Brings Violence — Dozen Cities Blistered by Riots, Looting"... "Kennedy Said 'Extremely Critical'; Surgery Removes Bullet from Brain — Waves of Shock, Dismay, Sorrow Travel the World"... "Police Fight with Yippies in Chicago — Democrats Go Behind Barbed Wire, Troops." But that was all worlds away from tiny Alma, where the population was 100 percent white and the news centered on an annex to the Buffalo County courthouse, techniques to prevent soil erosion, and the high school's championship basketball team. A Holstein cow in Alma named Prairie Hill Pat Velma set a record for producing 118,911 pounds of milk and 3,795 pounds of butterfat in seven years. People born in Alma, or in the surrounding, similarly sized towns, tended to die there too, and if they ever traveled beyond the Midwest, that was a big deal.

Dan took an early interest in politics. His dad was an elected city council member and county board member, and Dan used to ask him to tag along to those meetings. He wanted to see how it worked. In the civics course, he learned about America's founding documents, the Declaration of Independence and the Constitution. He studied line and block charts with the three branches of government, the separation of powers, and checks and balances. This might have been dry stuff for twelve- and thirteen-year-olds, but what made the class special was the teacher, Mr. Alvord. Dan admired him. Mr. Alvord was *that* teacher whom the boys looked up to and the girls had crushes on. He was twenty-four, six foot two, and lean (under two hundred pounds). Mr. Alvord always wore a shirt and tie, like any of the teachers, but he added cowboy boots. He supervised the school's AV club and, in the summers, was the town lifeguard. He actually ran the whole beach, from stocking and staffing the concessions stand to cleaning the bathrooms.

Mr. Alvord lived within sight of the school, in a trailer by the highway. He was living there with his wife and newborn son while saving up to build their dream house. Some of the other boys from school would often come by to watch Mr. Alvord working on his cars. Mr. Alvord would make a little extra money doing paint jobs and body work for other folks in town, and for fun he'd fix up old Corvettes and Mustangs with parts he found at the junkyard. As the boys watched, he would explain to them what he was doing and how the engine worked.

It wasn't clear where Mr. Alvord picked all this up. He had grown up a few towns over, where there were eight streets. He never had much of a relationship with his father, who died a few years after coming back from World War II, while working on an electric pole. The Buffalo Electric Cooperative offered the family one thousand dollars restitution, and they took it; they weren't the type to sue. Somehow they scraped by, living off fish and turtles from the river. So being handy was partly from necessity, since the family couldn't afford to hire hands, but also out of a cherished spirit of self-reliance. Mr. Alvord's mom and younger brother depended on him, and he learned to approach any task with a can-do self-confidence. Whatever it was, fixing cars or installing a dishwasher or an air conditioner, Mr. Alvord would figure it out. His wife, a farmer's daughter, grew up in a family that shared the same values, and they taught their son, Sammy, "We are going to be as self-reliant as we can, and not depend on anybody."

Mr. Alvord taught English and reading besides civics; he didn't have a special passion for politics. But the civics curriculum took a firm position on encouraging the students to be politically active. After the first semester covered what the government was and how it worked, the second semester covered how to get involved in politics through political parties. For reference, the students used an official government-issued almanac, like a user's manual for citizens of the state. Most states had them back then; theirs was called the *Wisconsin Blue Book*, because of the customary color of its cover. Dan also had a copy at home — his dad always got the latest issue when it came out every two years. The 1968 edition had a whole chapter dedicated to political parties. Dan read how even though political parties were not technically part of the government, they nevertheless played a crucial role in how American democracy functioned. "The decisions made by political parties of today," the *Blue Book* said, "will tomorrow determine the policies of our government, and the course of our lives."

Mr. Alvord told the seventh graders that when they turned twenty-one and became old enough to vote, they could choose to register with a political party. That meant they could vote in that party's primary. But it didn't make them an actual party member. The parties, he explained, were real organizations. They looked like a pyramid. Starting from the top, they had national committees, state committees, and county committees. The base of the pyramid was the precincts. These were the smallest building blocks of politics. Everyone lived in a precinct, Mr. Alvord said. Since this system was so decentralized, it was hard to answer basic questions such as how many precincts there were. Even the *Wisconsin Blue Book* did not say. Every precinct had a polling place where you went to vote, usually in a borrowed space like a school or a church, because there were no official precinct buildings. And every precinct had its own party representatives. These were not political professionals or zealous ideologues, just everyday normal people, volunteering their time, doing their civic duty, and helping people to vote.

Just because these party precinct positions weren't prominent did not mean they were not powerful. To the contrary, the *Blue Book* said, "the *actual* power of each party is found in the voluntary organizations," and the "precinct committeemen" were their "practicing, 'card-carrying' activists." These party officials at the precinct level chose their leaders at the county level; the county officials chose their state officials; and so on, all the way up to the national party chair.

The United States had a two-party system, and the 1968 edition of the *Blue Book* said that was part of what made America's democracy better than her totalitarian enemies abroad. American political parties, the book explained, were not like "the communist parties throughout the world, which are based on Marxist ideology and leave no room for political disagreement within their ranks." Communism fascinated Dan, even at this young age. The principal's husband had come in to speak to his second-grade class about escaping Poland, and how his family was still back there, suffering under communism. Dan became captivated by the idea of this exotic, distant civilization that seemed so at odds with the life he knew in Alma.

Dan read in the *Blue Book* that American political parties did not enforce loyalty, dogma, or conformity like communist parties. Instead, they were broad coalitions of diverse interests. "Depending on what part of the nation we live in, and depending also on what political label at a particular time happens to be in control of the state, federal, or local government, the terms 'Democrat' or 'Republican' can have widely different meanings," the book said. At the decade's outset, the Republican Party was an unhappy marriage of Eastern economic elites and heartland Protestant farmers, while the Democrats counted on Southern segregationists and Northern urban machines. Those internal contradictions, according to the *Blue Book*, were as parties should be: "There is room for 'right wing Republicans' or 'liberal Republicans,' 'left wing Democrats' or 'conservative Democrats.'" Dan's dad told him that he always voted for the person, not the party. The fact that both parties had to constantly hold together a wide-ranging mix of constituencies in the hopes of winning a majority exerted a moderating influence, at least in theory, or from the idealized viewpoint of the 1968 *Blue Book*, pushing both parties' leaders toward the center, promoting bipartisan cooperation, and preventing any extreme faction from ever seizing power.

The most important thing that Dan took away from the civics course came at the end. As Dan would remember, Mr. Alvord told the class that he'd now taught them how American politics really worked. The seventh graders were too young to use this knowledge then; "but some day," Mr. Alvord said, "we may get into a real political crisis. And when that day comes, I've equipped you now with the knowledge that you need to get involved in party politics and save the republic."

A comment like that seemed out of character for Mr. Alvord, who never discussed his personal politics, even with his own wife. Maybe the whirlwind of 1968 somehow got through to him all the way in tiny Alma. Then again, other students would not recall Mr. Alvord ever saying anything like what Dan remembered. But for

Dan, Mr. Alvord's parting words made a lasting impression. It became a moment he would never forget, and a message that would shape his life.

As Dan got older, he did something almost unheard of in Alma: he moved out of state to attend an elite university. Meanwhile, Mr. Alvord started a trucking business, Sam & Son, and moved his family into his dream house, overlooking the Mississippi, with a clear view of the lights on the bridge to Minnesota.

A few nights before Christmas, in 1979, Sam Alvord was driving home after working late at his truck shop. If he had been listening to the radio, he might have heard an update about gas rationing or the American hostages in Tehran, two issues that were already becoming emphases for Ronald Reagan, who'd just announced his White House bid. At the wheel, Mr. Alvord was probably pushing seventy-five. He loved to speed. He liked to go out snowmobiling with his friends, and they'd race across the endless acres of pristine farmland, blowing fresh tracks in the white blanket under a black starry sky. On one of those nights, he'd charged up a steep hill he hadn't tried before and barreled over the edge of a bluff. For a moment he was airborne—weightless. Then he'd crashed back to earth and rolled across the powder. His snowmobile was wrecked, but Mr. Alvord had stood up, laughing it off, unharmed. Not this time.

There was no snow on that night shortly before Christmas. The pavement was dry. A passing driver reported a crash at the bottom of the embankment on Highway 37, six miles north of Alma. Officers determined from the car's tracks that it had veered onto the shoulder, and that the driver must have flipped the wheel and overcorrected, because the car whipped left and careened out of control for seventy-six feet. It rolled over two and a half times, launching Mr. Alvord's big frame through the driver's window, landing nineteen feet away. He was pronounced dead at the scene.

The sheriff and the minister went to notify Mr. Alvord's wife and son. The sheriff told Mrs. Alvord that Sam must have fallen asleep at the wheel, but she didn't believe that—Sam would never. Maybe he saw a deer? "Are they sure it's Dad?" Sammy said. The whole community was devastated. The yearbook editors ran a full-page photo, with a short note saying they'd always remember Mr. Alvord for his service and understanding. Every kid in the school wrote a card for Mrs. Alvord, and she kept them in a box in her basement, never able to bring herself to read them.

The most striking tribute of all arrived decades later, when she received a package in the mail from one of Mr. Alvord's most talented former students, who'd long ago grown up and moved far away from Alma. She opened it to find a slim self-published book, *How to Get Into the Real Ball Game of Politics Where You Live to Help President Donald J. Trump Make America Great Again*, by Daniel J. Schultz. She opened the book and turned to the dedication page, where Dan had written: "To the late Sam Alvord, who taught me basic American Civics in junior high school in the late 1960s in Alma, Wisconsin."

BY DAN'S SENIOR year of high school, he stood out in Alma as a star: class president, prom royalty, baseball champion, National Honor Society. But he also knew he was a nobody kid from nowhere, with no political connections. He wondered, could he get into the United States Military Academy? Dan called it his very own "civics experiment." His experiment might have had a confounding variable. It was 1974 — the draft had just ended, the troops were finally coming home from Vietnam, and most young men Dan's age wanted nothing to do with the military. Dan was different. He got in, boarded a plane to New York City, then rode a bus up the Hudson River to West Point.

Dan and fourteen hundred other young men stepped onto campus on a sunny summer day thinking themselves the best their country had to offer; and now, they were untouchables, less than human — plebes. They could not do anything right. March. Salute. Dress. They could not speak without permission. They could not eat without permission. They'd sit in the mess hall at attention, watching the ice cream melt on their pies, and every bite had to be taken at a ninety-degree angle. Every movement, every waking second was controlled. This was Beast Barracks, the grueling first two months of training, mixed with the less official but no less thorough ritual of hazing.

The point of breaking down the plebes this way was explained by the commandant, whose name was General Feir (pronounced "fear"), during an address in Thayer Hall: to take these young men out of society and prepare them to survive and succeed in combat. The academy would remold the cadets into Cold Warriors. At the end of Beast Barracks, the plebes woke up at 4 a.m., strapped on their rucksacks with all their gear, and hiked fifteen miles through the hills from the training ground back to campus. They paraded past the superintendent's house and lined up on the Plain. In that moment they had left their old selves behind and joined the "long gray line," the image of West Pointers throughout the centuries, ready to save Americans from their enemies.

If the plebes arrayed on that stately lawn had been allowed to turn their heads, they might have looked to their left and right, and one of them would not make it through to graduation. Dan would, but not at the top of his class. There would be no gold star on his uniform collar. He ran for student government and lost. Other cadets focused on memorizing and regurgitating exam-ready factoids, in a process known as "passing the poop," but Dan took seriously the assigned reading on comparative politics: Soviet communism, European social democracies, American capitalism.

After graduation, he went into Army intelligence. His job would be to recruit people for dangerous missions, so secret that if they were caught the government would deny knowing them. The army trained Dan in how to develop a strategy: start with your main objective and work backward. He learned how to hunt the enemies' spies and protect his own forces from recruitment by the other side. The key was understanding what could motivate someone to betray their country. Spy services had a mnemonic for the four basic forms of motivation. *Money* meant enticing people financially; people will do all kinds of things for money. *Ideology* meant taking advantage of or manipulating people's genuine convictions, their political persuasions, or identification with a cause. *Coercion* meant forcing people, by finding out compromising information about them as a means of blackmail, or putting them in impossible situations where they felt like they had no choice but to do what was being asked of them. And *Ego* meant exploiting people's grudges and gripes, flattering them, and making them feel like a powerful person doing something important. Put together, they made a nice acronym, easy to remember: Money, Ideology, Coercion, Ego — MICE.

One day in spy school, the instructors brought in a KGB

defector. For his protection, the instructors wouldn't give his name. The lack of identifying details made the story impossible to corroborate. As Dan would tell it, the guy was a beast, with fingers as big as Dan's entire hand. This was who they were up against, he thought. When Dan got the chance to ask him a question, he wanted to know: before he defected, did he tell his wife and kids? The guy looked at Dan like he was an idiot. *Of course not,* he said. Dan asked why. The defector said, *Because I couldn't trust them.* Dan strained to imagine living in a society like that. It was unrecognizable. He felt the horror of the communists' wanting to take over the world and destroy the American way of life.

While stationed at the Army intelligence center at Fort Huachuca, in the Arizona desert, Dan stopped into a used bookstore near the base and picked up a worn-out copy of *The Conscience of a Conservative*, by Barry Goldwater. When it debuted in 1960, the book became an unlikely bestseller, with half a million copies in print. The book advocated for a more aggressive foreign policy against the threat of Communism, and domestically, for a complete rollback of the social safety net and federal bureaucracy that had expanded under Franklin D. Roosevelt's New Deal. Goldwater's vision of a conservative movement electrified Republicans who had come to resent their party's domination by an Eastern establishment, descended from its Gilded Age alliance with big business and incapable of offering voters any real alternative, just a watered-down version of the Democratic platform. Fans begged Goldwater to sign their copies, calling it their Bible. They urged the Arizona senator to run for president. But Goldwater declined to run, instead falling in line behind the establishment heir apparent, Vice President Richard Nixon. Dan was only four years old then, but he remembered his dad and uncles and aunts and cousins talking about it, and he was "a fly on the wall," absorbing it all.

Nixon went on to lose the 1960 election by a whisker to Democrat John F. Kennedy, and there were droves of disappointed *Conscience of a Conservative* readers who thought Goldwater could have done better and remained tantalized by the possibility of an "honest-to-God conservative" in the White House. In the summer of 1961, a group of Goldwater supporters met in secret to launch an operation to win him the 1964 Republican nomination. There were 1,308 delegates to the Republican National Convention who would pick the nominee; it took 655 to win. At that time, only sixteen states chose their delegates through public primaries, where anyone could vote, amounting to 541 delegates. The other 767 were chosen in caucuses: the proverbial smoke-filled rooms, the domain of party bosses and backroom deals. These pro-Goldwater conspirators devised a strategy. As their ringleader, Clif White, announced, "We're going to take over the Republican Party."

They would begin at the bottom rung of the party structure, in precinct positions that were often vacant because no one was paying attention. They would fill these slots with hard-line conservatives, tapping into grassroots networks of like-minded groups, who thought the Republican Party should be more right-wing. The Goldwater conspirators did not create these groups, but they were eager to find common cause with them. There were the Young Republicans, Young Americans for Freedom, the National Gun Alliance, United Republicans of California. There was also the John Birch Society, a nationwide network of clubs that taught the government was being infiltrated by communist agents (including President Eisenhower), and even members of the Ku Klux Klan, the secret brotherhood that upheld the South's Jim Crow system of segregation and disenfranchisement through violence and terror. From the precinct level, these foot soldiers would in turn elect delegates at the county, district, state, and eventually national level, at every stage elevating radical right-wing true believers.

The Goldwater plotters had figured out that they could short-circuit the party establishment through simple geography and arithmetic. By mastering the arcane rules of delegate math, a few committed zealots could conquer an entire institution. The radicals prevailed in state after state. The party's moderates began denouncing the movement. Pennsylvania's Republican governor, William Scranton, called the activists "extreme reactionaries, who are anything but conservatives, those radicals of the right who would launch a system of dime-store feudalism." But by the time the Republican National Convention arrived, Goldwater's supporters had done their math right. He had the votes.

Dan had a memory from when he was eight, of a kid two doors down whose dad went as a delegate to the 1964 Republican National Convention in San Francisco. The scene was bedlam. Civil rights demonstrators marched with signs reading GOLDWATER

FOR FUHRER. Goldwater supporters arrived chanting, "We want Barry!" The rowdy convention made riveting TV, beginning with the debate over the party platform. New York governor Nelson Rockefeller (grandson of the Standard Oil baron) spoke in support of a resolution to officially repudiate "the efforts of irresponsible extremist groups, such as the Communists, the Ku Klux Klan, the John Birch Society, and others to discredit our Party by their efforts to infiltrate positions of responsibility in the Party," but got drowned out by chants of "We want Barry!" The resolution failed overwhelmingly. The next proposal, another anti-extremism amendment, this one from Michigan governor George Romney, also went down in a thunder of nays.

For Goldwater and his followers, this divisiveness was the point. His campaign's whole strategy was to kick out the GOP's liberals such as Rockefeller and Romney. In their place, Goldwater aimed to convince conservative Southerners to cross over from the Democratic Party, courting them in large part by being one of only six Republican senators who supported the record-long filibuster against the landmark Civil Rights Act of 1964. Alabama's segregationist Democratic governor, George Wallace, performed surprisingly well in a primary challenge to President Lyndon B. Johnson, even in the northern states of Wisconsin, Indiana, and Maryland. Goldwater's play was to turn those Wallace Democrats into Republicans. Senator Strom Thurmond of South Carolina showed the way, switching parties and campaigning for Goldwater by addressing the crowds as "my fellow extremists." By forging this new coalition, Goldwater's campaign aimed to replace the two pluralistic parties with one national conservative party (the Republicans) and one national liberal party (the Democrats). That, in the judgment of an editorial in the *Washington Evening Star,* was "the greatest danger" he posed: "that this reactionary takeover of the Republican machinery will induce a radical new alignment of the parties, splitting them once and for all into organizations of the right and the left." The result, the editorial feared, would be to "render our two-party system inoperable."

Goldwater addressed this controversy head-on in his acceptance speech. "Anyone who joins us in all sincerity, we welcome," he said. "Those who do not care for our cause, we don't expect to enter our ranks in any case." Next came the essential line, the one he had underlined in the copy he was reading, and also in the copies distributed to the press: "I would remind you that extremism in the defense of liberty is no vice." The crowd roared for forty-one seconds before he could finish, "And let me remind you also that moderation in the pursuit of justice is no virtue." He got a standing ovation.

Outside the cavernous convention hall, in the light of day, the public was shocked. Rockefeller called the speech "dangerous, irresponsible, and frightening." The last Republican president, General Eisenhower, called it repugnant to "the whole American system" and privately scolded the nominee for his apparent overture to "right-wing kooks." California governor Edmund Brown said the convention carried "the stench of fascism"; Senator William Fulbright saw in Goldwater's movement an American "equivalent of Russian Stalinism." President Johnson's campaign seized on Goldwater's speech to cast him as extreme, unhinged, and dangerous, so that come November, even though Goldwater drew record crowds, having to deliver one speech twice in order to accommodate everyone who'd shown up, and even though bumper stickers for Goldwater outnumbered those for Johnson ten to one, LBJ won in a historic landslide. The famous columnist Walter Lippmann called the result "indisputable proof that the votes are in the center."

But Goldwater's humiliating defeat did nothing to dim his supporters' enthusiasm for their cause. The campaign attracted 1.5 million donors—a thirtyfold increase over the 1960 Nixon campaign's fifty thousand contributors—and enrolled half a million volunteers. Many of them caught a lifelong bug for politics—not just the ideology but the mechanics of it: licking envelopes, knocking doors, persuading coworkers, talking to reporters, counting delegates, whipping votes—and became the foot soldiers for a generation of Republican campaigns. They nurtured their fledgling movement by founding the American Conservative Union, best known today for its Conservative Political Action Conference (CPAC). Goldwater became "the Moses of the conservative movement," Pat Buchanan later eulogized. "He led us to the promised land but didn't make it himself." More immediately, when Nixon plotted his comeback for the 1968 election, he called on the masterminds of Goldwater's party takeover to run his own delegate strategy. From then on, the path to the Republican presidential nomination ran through the Right.

Nixon, and later Reagan and Bush, found ways to harness the energy of Goldwater's conservative movement in a package that was more palatable to a majority of the American electorate. But they would never be "honest-to-God conservatives" in the White House. Nixon was an internationalist who made nice with Communist China. Reagan was tough on communism but supported immigration, free trade, and gun control, and his characteristic optimism clashed with the hard right's more militant edge. Bush was a blue blood whom conservatives never trusted, and whose "new world order" sounded eerily similar to the "one world government" that the Birchers always warned about. Dan Schultz, for one, was never big on Nixon or Bush. But when he tucked into *The Conscience of a Conservative* on his army post, it was one of those books that could reach out through time and shake you by the shoulders. His hero would be Goldwater.

There was a lot for Dan to like in this little book, including the chapter on the Soviet menace. He was struck by the first few paragraphs. "America is fundamentally a Conservative nation," he read. "We Conservatives are deeply persuaded that our society is ailing, and know that Conservatism holds the key to national salvation— and feel sure the country agrees with us." The question, then, was why the government was run by liberals. "Why have the American people been so unable to translate their views into appropriate political action? Why should the nation's underlying allegiance to Conservative principles have failed to produce corresponding deeds in Washington?"

Dan finished his required active duty, got married, and, following up on an interest he developed from his West Point course reading, went to law school back in Wisconsin. He ended up at a top-tier law firm in Los Angeles. Dan had it made: money, status, an Audi with the vanity plate ESQKIER. But Dan was not content. He tore through books about Communism, Stalin, Lenin…*Gulag Archipelago,* pamphlets from the John Birch Society, *The Great Terror, Stalin: Breaker of Nations…The Making of a Top Soviet Spy, Inside the Soviet Army, The KGB: Masters of the Soviet Union, The Discovery of Freedom: Man's Struggle Against Authority…* When Congress

banned assault rifles in 1994, Dan thought this was how it started —
the government was trying to subdue the people. He couldn't let it
happen. It was like a trip wire for him.

Dan became convinced that the federal government was about
to confiscate everyone's guns, and that every individual gun owner
needed to start taking steps to prepare to resist. He was outraged by
the deadly standoffs with federal agents trying to enforce weapons charges in Ruby Ridge, Idaho, in 1992 and in Waco, Texas, the
following year. His fixation was shared by a growing movement of
far-right citizen militias that started organizing to resist federal
authority, especially where it came to gun control. The movement's
followers included Timothy McVeigh, who killed 168 people with a
truck bomb at a federal building in Oklahoma City in 1995. President Bill Clinton responded by calling the militia groups domestic
terrorists. "There is nothing patriotic about hating your country, or
pretending that you can love your country but hate your government," he said in a commencement speech in Michigan, where the
militia movement was especially potent. "How dare you suggest
that we in the freest nation on earth live in tyranny? How dare
you call yourselves patriots and heroes?" Dan objected to that por-
trayal by Clinton and much of the media. He insisted that militias
were not dangerous and were protected by the Second Amendment.
The idea of an individual's right to bear arms was at that time a
fringe idea, and most Republican politicians (with some notable
exceptions) were keeping militia groups at arm's length. Still, they
accepted the support of militia members, and over the next several
years, opposition to gun control grew into the party's consensus
position.

The militia movement spread over shortwave radio, magazines,
and newsletters like one Dan wrote articles for, circulated by a Second Amendment group he cofounded. The connective power of an
online message board, a site like *Breitbart*, or a podcast like *War
Room* was still far in the future. In 1996, Dan traveled to Washington to speak at a Bill of Rights rally on the National Mall, but it was
sparsely attended, just three hundred instead of the fifteen thousand that organizers had predicted; they blamed traffic and the
stigma of McVeigh for keeping people away. The rally included
warnings that the FBI was kidnapping children to send them overseas and that the media was rigging election outcomes so citizens

should demand paper ballots. Dan spoke about the importance of reading the Constitution and the Declaration of Independence. He quit the American Bar Association to protest the group's support for gun control and volunteered to represent people accused of gun crimes. He encouraged allies to run for office and lobby their elected representatives. But he grew frustrated with the lack of action. He was still searching for something more concrete and specific he could call on people to do, a strategy for fighting the government before it was too late.

DAN'S LAW PRACTICE focused on litigating insurance claims, and he mostly hid his politics from his coworkers, but they could still tell he was very right wing. At home, his marriage fell apart. He got divorced and changed firms. When his new firm got conflicted out of his biggest case, Dan chose to keep the case and strike out on his own. He remarried, had a daughter, and then had triplet boys. He didn't want to raise his kids in LA, and one of his sons was autistic and would need a lot of help for his entire life. The family moved to Arizona to be closer to support from Dan's in-laws, and for a few years Dan commuted back and forth to work in California.

When Dan finally joined the family in Tempe, he didn't become politically active there. He didn't think he needed to. He assumed that here in Goldwater country, the Arizona GOP was getting along fine without him. Then, in 2007, he heard news reports saying illegal immigrants were committing rapes and murders in the city because the southern border was out of control. Dan thought he'd go see for himself what was going on. There were a bunch of border militias that splintered off from the Minuteman Project in 2005, when armed men (including a few neo-Nazis) spent a month guarding the crossings from Mexico — "vigilantes" was what President Bush called them. The largest offshoot, the Minuteman Civil Defense Corps, grew to set up chapters in dozens of states and claimed to have thousands of members. Dan found a meeting. When he got there, a guy stood up. If you asked Dan later to describe the man, he would say he was a young, clean-cut kid in a suit, but Dan never saw him again, and wouldn't recognize him if he did. As the story went, this guy stood up and said going down to help the Border Patrol was fine, but there was another thing they all could do: become Republican precinct committeemen. There were tons of open positions.

Dan remembered what he'd learned in Mr. Alvord's class, and he instantly recognized what this young man was talking about. He walked up to him and said he lived in Maricopa County, what should he do? The young man said to call the county Republican committee. Dan must have called twenty times. It reminded him of what he'd gone through in Beast Barracks; the army had taught him how to navigate a bureaucracy. Sometimes you had to be persistent. Finally, after about a week, someone called Dan back and gave him the time and place for the next meeting. Dan showed up and was surprised to find only about twenty people there. He asked how many precinct committee slots the district had. About a hundred and sixty. And how many were filled? Only forty.

Dan was stunned that the Republican Party was operating at a fraction of full strength. Clearly the precinct operation that Goldwater's supporters had engineered had long since atrophied. Dan's assumption that the party infrastructure here would be stacked, with no need for him, had been wrong. It was just as Ayn Rand had written in *Atlas Shrugged*: "Check your premises." He'd had a bad premise. Now that Dan knew the party was an empty shell, it was little wonder to him that the GOP soon went on to lose the 2008 presidential election—and to a Marxist, a guy named Hussein, someone who Dan believed wanted to destroy the country. "That guy is not one of us," Dan said.

Dan imagined what could happen if people like him snapped up all the empty precinct committee slots. From seventh-grade civics to his Army intelligence training to that border militia meeting to now, it was like his whole life had prepared him to develop this plan: the Precinct Strategy. He started pitching the Precinct Strategy to anybody who would listen.

In the early months of Obama's presidency, conservatives started organizing under the banner of the Tea Party, invoking the spirit of the American Revolution to object to taxes, government regulation of health care, immigration, and, often, Obama's eligibility to be president, based on a conspiracy theory that he was not born in the United States. Dan went to an early Tea Party event in

Tempe, equipped with three-by-five index cards instructing people how to become precinct committeemen. Holding a rally isn't going to do anything, Dan told the speakers — they should tell people to get involved in the Republican Party. He imagined how the politicians inside the Capitol would look outside at the rally and laugh, saying to themselves, "These people still haven't figured out the political process." The real ball game, where politics really happened, was at these mundane monthly precinct meetings.

Even though most states now had public primaries rather than the backroom caucuses of Goldwater's day, the precinct committee members still held the power to elect party leaders, influence the party platform and campaign spending, and choose the delegates who could decide a nominee at a contested convention. And they were the volunteers the party's candidates would count on to register voters, knock doors, phone bank, stuff mailers, get out the vote, and monitor polls. The precinct meetings could be boring, but was that such a high price to pay for real political power? There was an old Plato quote that Dan thought got it just right: "One of the penalties for refusing to participate in politics is that you end up being governed by your inferiors." Dan started using a catchphrase he found in an old brochure by Phyllis Schlafly, calling precinct positions the most powerful political office in the world. As he went around to Tea Party meetings and other groups, Dan would always tell people, "Look, I can't guarantee that if we all take over the Republican Party we're going to save the republic and not slide into socialism. But I can guarantee you this: if we don't do that, we are going to go into socialism."

He knew he sounded like Chicken Little, or a broken record. He did not care. He would not stop. He knew his plan could work. One time, Dan used his party committee seat to support the endorsement of a conservative candidate for county attorney, helping him win the primary, and the candidate even went on to be appointed to the state supreme court. Another time, Dan's friend Frank Schmuck (yes, really) ran for state senate against an incumbent who'd voted to expand Medicaid under Obama's health-care law, after promising not to. Dan agreed to run Frank's campaign by putting the Precinct Strategy into action, assigning all the precinct committee members in the district to call and canvass the voters in their precincts, showing "what a real schmuck the incumbent was and how our Schmuck was better." They turned out people who didn't usually vote in primaries and won. If it could work for a guy named Schmuck...

IN THOSE YEARS, a new militia group started up, picking up where the nineties' militia movement left off, and specifically recruiting people who'd served in law enforcement or the military. The group's premise was that the oath those veterans swore, to protect and defend the Constitution against all enemies foreign and domestic, never expired. They called themselves the Oath Keepers. The Oath Keepers signed up these veterans to swear a new pledge, spelling out ten orders that they would refuse to obey. These orders imagined apocalyptic scenarios such as, "Disarm the American people... invade and subjugate any state that asserts its sovereignty...blockade American cities, thus turning them into giant concentration camps...force American citizens into any form of detention camps under any pretext." The U.S. Department of Homeland Security, formed after the September 11 terrorist attacks to improve the government's monitoring of and response to dangers to public safety, developed a new intelligence assessment warning that right-wing violent extremist groups like the Oath Keepers were exploiting fears about the financial crisis, the election of the first Black president, and gun regulations to recruit and radicalize disaffected military veterans. When the report was leaked, congressional Republicans seized on it to accuse the Obama administration of persecuting conservatives for their views and veterans for their service. Under pressure, the DHS secretary apologized and shut down the team that had written the report. The firestorm inspired T-shirts that Americans proudly wore to embrace the label of domestic terrorist, and it signaled to federal and local law enforcement that investigating far-right extremism was politically radioactive. The government focused resources elsewhere.

When Dan Schultz heard about the Oath Keepers, he loved the concept, if not the organization. It resembled an idea he'd had himself years earlier, asking elected officials to swear an oath he'd written opposing gun control. Dan hated seeing politicians straying from the Constitution as he understood it. He took seriously the oaths he had sworn at West Point, in the army, and as an attorney. Those oaths didn't have expiration dates. Dan considered himself an "oath keeper" — he kept his oaths — though he never became a member of the organization. Dan thought it was fantastic when Oath Keepers showed up to help a Nevada rancher named Cliven Bundy, who was defying the feds in 2014.* But Dan didn't like that the Oath Keepers were skipping straight to preparing for war. Dan dreaded the idea of using his AR-15 in his own neighborhood. He feared that America's cherished tradition of a peaceful transfer of power was on the brink of breaking down, if people like him were left with no other choice; and he thought the last best hope was to take over the Republican Party through the Precinct Strategy.

"Why don't you all join me and the other Oath Keepers who are *inside* the Party already," Dan posted to the group's internal forum in 2014, "so we can join with other conservatives and fill up ALL of the vacant precinct committeeman slots? If we conservatives were to do that, we'd OWN the Party." Dan even tried calling into a radio show with the Oath Keepers founder, Stewart Rhodes, to ask him why he never encouraged people to become precinct committee members. Rhodes said something like, "Of course, we've always talked about that." Not that Dan had ever heard.[†]

Dan wasn't famous, he didn't have a huge following, and he knew he needed someone who did to give him the chance to get his message out. If he could just get himself in front of a big enough microphone, he could finally recruit enough precinct officers to take over the Republican Party. He started a YouTube channel, using his iPad to record himself explaining his plan on handwritten note cards. He blogged on the right-wing website *RedState*, constantly urging readers to go out and join a precinct committee. Even by the standards of the early 2010s right-wing blogosphere, Dan's vitriol was too much for some people. (From one post: *"You think we can't beat the conniving libturds who took advantage of our complacency and goodness and faked out some of us good, decent Americans*

---

* Participants in the standoff were later indicted on assault and weapons offenses, but the charges were ultimately dropped because of prosecutorial misconduct.

† In May 2023, Rhodes was sentenced to eighteen years in prison for seditious conspiracy and other charges in the Capitol riot of January 6, 2021.

into casting our votes for a presidential candidate, who was nothing more than a teleprompter-reading Nancy-boy, because of our collective generational guilt over slavery?") Commenters asked Dan to tone it down. He wasn't sorry. He challenged his critics to name anyone he'd driven away. He didn't want the faint of heart anyway. He wanted fighters. He wrote his blog under the screen name ColdWarrior, since he thought publishing under his real name would get him fired.

Dan swore he didn't even like politics. He was only doing it to save his kids from socialism. They were not going to come to him and say, "Hey, Dad, why didn't you do something when we still had a chance?" He assigned his kids to read his books on Communism and, when they were old enough, signed up three of them to be precinct committee members, all except his autistic son. Dan worried for him the most. "He's going to be exterminated, I guarantee it," Dan once told a few friends. Because in a communist regime, he thought, his son would be viewed as "just a mouth to feed. And they're going to kill all these people, alright? Read about Cambodia. Read about Communist China. Read about the Soviet Union." He saw it starting to happen in America too. He was not going to live in a society like that. He would resist. "I'm going to a camp," Dan said. "I'll be executed. I'll be one of the first."

In 2013, Dan's blog posts caught the eye of Steve Bannon at the time when he was building up his alt-right audience at *Breitbart News.* Bannon asked Dan to start writing for the site. Every article would be a variation on the same theme, trying out any hook that might get people interested in precinct committees, in the clickbaity parlance of the time: "The 'Hobbits' Plan to Take Over the GOP"..."One Weird Trick About How and Where Conservatives Should 'Rally' Against the Iran Nuclear Deal." "Long ago, I was trained to find, recruit, train, and then send people on secret and dangerous missions," Dan wrote in one post. "The mission I am giving you won't be secret or dangerous to you personally, but it also involves our nation's survival...You will be helping to save our republic."

When Trump became president and Bannon became his chief White House strategist, Dan volunteered to serve as Trump's pick to chair the RNC. "I'll grow the party, I'll fill up every vacant precinct committeeman slot with a Trump supporter," he offered. Trump did not pick Dan to chair the RNC. Dan did not fill up every vacant precinct committeeman slot with a Trump supporter. Instead, Dan wrote out his Precinct Strategy in a book, the one he dedicated to Mr. Alvord. He gave it a catchy title and listed it for sale on Amazon for $9.99. He wanted it to be as cheap and short as possible. More than half the volume was taken up by large-type, double-spaced reproductions of the Declaration of Independence and the Constitution, but Dan was not just padding his pages — he wanted people to read them, study them, memorize them on the toilet, learn these texts that the socialists did not want them to know. Dan sent a couple of copies to President Trump and got a form letter back. He imagined the books sitting in an unopened box in a warehouse somewhere. Dan dreaded that Trump was failing to recognize this critical power vacuum in the Republican Party. At the start of 2020, he posted a new video, this time with computer-generated slides, making a direct appeal for Trump to use his bully pulpit to implement the Precinct Strategy. "It's real simple, it's basic American civics," Dan growled. "The message needs to come from President Trump himself."

The message never came, and on Election Day, when Dan checked around different precincts in Tucson as a poll watcher, he noticed the Democrats had more observers in place and the Republicans barely had anyone. Dan figured the Dems were surely bused in from California. That night, just two and a half hours after the polls closed in Arizona, Fox News called the state for Biden. Even the hosts on the air could not believe it. "I think it's too early... What is this happening now, why is Arizona blue?" Bill Hemmer said at the big screen with the map. "Did we just call it? Did we make a call in Arizona?" Later Trump appeared in the East Room, visibly peeved as he walked out. *"We were winning everything and all of a sudden it was just called off,"* Trump said. *"This is a fraud on the American public."*

Dan never doubted the election was stolen — "everybody and their dog knew it," he said. He expected nothing less from the Democrats, but the problem was the Republicans who were letting them get away with it. Dan watched with disdain as the *Republican* county supervisors in Maricopa County summarily rejected all the alleged irregularities and certified the results. Then the *Republican* governor of Arizona signed the certification, stopping momentarily to literally silence a call to his cell phone from Trump himself. And the *Republican* state legislators—what did they do? Dan emailed every single one, telling them to reject this election and appoint their own electors for Trump. Dan argued that the Constitution gave the legislatures the exclusive and unlimited power to regulate elections. In this election, officials all around the country had started making accommodations on account of the pandemic, like drop boxes and drive-thru voting. In Dan's view, those accommodations made without express authorization from the state legislatures had been illegal, so the state legislatures should declare the election was fraudulent and assert their power to decide the outcome as the people's representatives. They didn't even need to give a reason, Dan thought. They could have said it was because they'd had Frosted Flakes instead of Cheerios for breakfast—it was solely up to them under the Constitution.*

Only these *Republican* state legislators were either too scared or too stupid to go through with it. These were the RINOs, the *fake* Republicans that Dan's Precinct Strategy was meant to eliminate. Instead of doing the one thing they could do to change the outcome, Arizona Republicans were wasting time talking about audits and lawsuits or impeaching the governor. Dan heard Mark Finchem, a member of the Arizona House of Representatives (and of the Oath Keepers), give an interview on a podcast he listened to, hosted by Steve Bannon. Finchem was saying he'd bring Vice President Mike Pence an official finding of fraud as a basis for rejecting Arizona's electors when Congress met in Washington on January 6. It sounded like a pointless stunt. Dan messaged Bannon to tell him he wasn't asking the right questions. Bannon told him fine, come on the show and explain it.

"A beloved figure," Bannon smirked as he introduced Dan on the December 29 episode of *War Room*. "Talk about a honey

---

* The Supreme Court, including two of the justices Trump appointed, rejected this theory in 2023. Chief Justice John Roberts, writing for the 6–3 majority, said, "By fulfilling their constitutional duty to craft the rules governing federal elections, state legislatures do not consent, ratify, or elect—they make laws."

badger," Bannon said, alluding to one of his favorite memes, a "badass," "fearless" mammal that takes on snakes and bees and "don't give a shit." "Talk about a guy that grinds." Bannon was projecting chumminess with Dan, as though he knew him well and everyone in the audience must too (even though Bannon kept calling him Daniel instead of Dan). Bannon's show was like that; guests appeared out of nowhere and disappeared just as abruptly. Was this someone legitimately famous, or someone with an obscure cult following, or a total rando? There was no context, no proportionality, just an endless swirl of names and groups and causes and grievances. "He's the head of the Precinct Project," Bannon flubbed, "which is trying to do a hostile takeover of the Republican Party, by precinct men throughout the nation...What's going on? You've got a very different take on the strategy. Just walk through concisely, what is your theory?"

Dan beamed into the show wearing a sky-blue shirt and flag-print tie, his gray hair clumping at the temples, his diplomas cluttering the wall behind him, a pair of skis leaning in the corner next to an overflowing bookcase. "State legislatures have all the power," Dan said, "and the Republicans hold majorities in all five of these key states," meaning the states that flipped from Trump in 2016 to Biden in 2020: Arizona, Georgia, Pennsylvania, Michigan, Wisconsin. "The Constitution says we can do it," Dan said. "The Democrats, they play to win. They play hardball. Republicans, even the so-called conservative ones who say they play hardball? No, no, no. They're playing wiffle ball. Without the balls."

"Do you think, Daniel Schultz," Bannon asked, "that if the Republicans don't step up here and do the right thing in the state legislatures, is that the end of the Republican Party as we know it?"

Dan's eyes lit up. He took a moment, then pounced. "It doesn't have to be," he said. "And it'll only be if the conservatives who have not gotten into the precinct committeeman ranks of our party — you know, our party has about four hundred thousand of these precinct committeeman slots at the precinct level. They elect everybody. They're the most powerful position in the world, in terms of politics. Phyllis Schlafly had a nice pamphlet about that. It's still there on her website. You know, I wrote a book about this..."

Bannon let Dan go on for about a minute. "Daniel," he

interrupted, "we're gonna have you back on, because this is a topic we've got to drill down into..."

NOW THAT TIME had finally come, in February of 2021, on the cusp of the Senate impeachment trial, with Trump accused of inciting the mob that sacked the Capitol. Dan reappeared on *War Room*, having gotten a haircut, and wearing a big white button that said PC.

"Dan," Bannon said on the air, "the floor is yours. Take it, and tell people — you're about to offer a course on personal political empowerment. How do they do it, Dan?"

"It's...it's real simple, and most people learn this, at least I did, back in the late sixties, in seventh-grade social studies, in civics class," Dan began. "Essentially, what we have to do is we conservatives have to take over one of the two major political parties. Our party is, the one we've been using, is the Republican Party. The problem is we're not in control of it. And the reason we're not in control of it is we're not *in* it. You asked me before I came on, 'What group are you promoting?' And the group I'm promoting is the Republican Party. But you're not in the party unless you're one of these — see, I've got my PC button on: precinct committeeman. Precinct committeemen *are* the party."

Dan asked Bannon to put up a slide showing the structure of the party organization. "It's a pyramid," Bannon offered, "and this is the base of the pyramid."

Dan explained all the powers of precinct committee members, and all the open slots that were there for the taking. "The key thing is you elect everybody," he explained. "You're going to get to elect your county chairman directly. You're going to elect the officers of your local committee directly. You're going to elect state committeemen who directly elect the state chairman...You can run for delegate...The delegates elect the national convention delegates directly and then they also elect the national committeemen and committeewomen on the RNC. That's real political power. We can take over the party if we invade it," Dan said. "I've told people this since 2009...I can't guarantee you that we'll save the republic, but I can guarantee you this: we'll lose it if we conservatives don't take over the Republican Party. We're going to lose our republic."

"OK, Dan, hang on one second," Bannon interrupted. "Here's the key: you don't need to talk about third parties. It'll cost a billion dollars, it's never gonna go anywhere. You've got the ability, everybody out there, and it's not going to cost you a dime. Everybody's saying, 'I need to know what to do.' This is an actionable item."

What Dan was offering was so pure, so simple — seventh-grade civics. Bannon knew there was a hunger out there for that. It reminded him of the rare, raw political talent he'd recognized in Alexandria Ocasio-Cortez, the young Democratic congresswoman from New York, when she used to stream herself cooking on Instagram Live and take questions from her followers on the political process, as if explaining mundane, basic civics were like sharing an intimate secret. For a lot of people, it was. Americans were suffering from a breakdown of community bonds — what Bannon had read the political scientist Robert Putnam, in his influential 2000 study *Bowling Alone*, call a decline of social capital. They voted less, attended fewer rallies and speeches, volunteered less, went to church less, didn't attend town meetings, didn't serve as officers or committee members in local clubs or organizations, didn't belong to PTAs or unions anymore, had fewer bridge clubs and card games and picnics and dinner parties. Instead, they spent more time watching TV and on the internet. The Precinct Strategy could help restore that missing connective tissue. Bannon wanted his listeners to get out and go to a meeting. One meeting would lead to another. There was already a structure, an organization, a hierarchy. Bannon didn't have to build this or coordinate it. If he just got people in the door, the existing organization would take over on its own momentum. Someday soon, people would come up to Bannon and thank him for changing their lives. They'd tell him they were so depressed after January 6, and he'd given them hope. All he'd done was sit there and tell them, *You're not alone. We got this. Start meeting some people that are taking action.*

"Here's where I want," Bannon said now. "I want everybody to pound in right now to Dan Schultz's information. This guy has been saying this, it's now time to do it. Stop talking about a third party. Your opportunity to take over the Republican Party is all about your agency. That's what Schultz keeps saying: this is all about you, this is all about *your agency*. If all the unwashed masses in the MAGA movement, the deplorables — we've got many more than four hundred thousand people that listen to this site. We've got thirty, what? Thirty-four million downloads on the podcast, one of the biggest shows in the world. I want people pounding into Dan Schultz today. Right now. This is your call to action."

CHAPTER 3

Nobody, but Somebody

BANNON COULD TELL right away that the Precinct Strategy was going viral. He had a small staff who constantly monitored chat rooms and online forums, getting real-time reaction to how *War Room* segments were playing, and the interview with Dan Schultz immediately started blowing up. The video rocketed across Gab and Telegram, alternative social networks that Trump supporters flocked to after Facebook and Twitter cracked down on election misinformation. Traffic spiked to Dan's blog, clocking almost a hundred thousand hits over a few days.

In Miami, the chairman of the county GOP started hearing from a crush of strangers who suddenly wanted to join his committee. Up in Polk County, between Tampa and Orlando, people were "coming out of the woodwork"; the county chair said he'd never seen anything like it — it was even bigger than the Tea Party. In Fort Worth, people kept calling the Tarrant County Republican Party wanting to become "precinct committeemen," which gave away that something was up, because the term in Texas was "precinct chair." Southwest of Green Bay, the GOP chairman in Outagamie County got slammed with voicemails from people demanding to become precinct committeemen, a position that did not exist in Wisconsin. It's a patchwork system — every state is a little different — and when the chairman tried to explain that the smallest party unit in Wisconsin was the county committee, some of the callers fumed that he was the establishment standing in their way.

In Cobb County, Georgia, twenty miles northwest of Atlanta, the Republican county chair, a clean-cut, khaki-wearing political science lecturer named Jason Shepherd, had friends anxiously asking him what he thought of the surge of new volunteers who were signing up with the county party through something called the Precinct Strategy. Jason looked up the Precinct Strategy's website and checked the materials it recommended for Georgia. They turned out to be a video and a handbook that Jason himself had made. So he thought, "I'm not worried about these people. In fact, I'm excited that they're there." Jason had been around politics a long time. In the College Republicans at UGA in the nineties, he'd crossed paths with Sean Spicer, the future White House press secretary; Chris Carr, the future attorney general of Georgia; and Kevin McCarthy, the future House Republican leader. He didn't get too worked up about stuff like a bunch of new people wanting to take over the county party because they believed the 2020 election was stolen.

For his part, Jason knew it wasn't. He acknowledged the possibility of isolated instances of fraud. No election was perfect. But enough to change the outcome? Jason didn't see it. He thought there was nothing mysterious about the election results — they were even predictable. He'd actually called his old contact Sean Spicer to tell him Trump was running a lousy campaign in Georgia and was going to lose, and Jason was far from the only Georgia political insider who gave the Trump campaign that warning. A good friend who was a pollster had shown Jason his turnout model. Based on how well Trump was doing in early voting, he looked on track to win by one or two points. But the president didn't hit the numbers he needed on Election Day. Not enough people showed up. That made the difference.

The Trump campaign and the state party, though, seemed caught by surprise. The day after the election, Jason got a call from the state party's political director saying they needed volunteers to help "cure" absentee ballots — a process that gave voters a few days to fix mistakes on their mail ballots so that their votes could count. Jason rounded up his volunteers and gave them the guy's contact information. When they didn't get an answer, Jason called the state political director back and was told the whole staff had been reassigned because Donald Trump Jr. was coming for a rally and they needed to pack a crowd to look good for the cameras. "Are you kidding me?" Jason said.

Then Jason got asked to be a named plaintiff in a lawsuit seeking to overturn the presidential election results. The lawsuit was to be filed in Georgia, with counterparts in the other key states, by Sidney Powell, a lawyer working with the Trump campaign. Powell had promised in a Fox News interview that these lawsuits would "release the Kraken," a mythical monster made famous in a 2010 action flick starring Liam Neeson. Jason read the complaint. The first page misspelled DISTRICT COURT in the header. He kept reading. It alleged that the state's voting machines were compromised by Venezuelan dictator Hugo Chávez and manipulated by Chinese and Iranian agents. It asked the judge to impound the voting machines, order the governor to decertify the results, and declare Trump the winner. Jason did not think this lawsuit stood much of a chance, but his county committee voted for him to join in his capacity as party chair, and Jason did think the Trump campaign deserved the opportunity to present its evidence in court. The so-called Kraken lawsuits were widely mocked in the press as legally, factually, and typographically pathetic. Even Trump distanced himself from Powell.*

Moving into 2021, Jason was term-limited as county chair, and in the race to succeed him, he wanted to stay neutral. There were three candidates running. Two of them had been active in the county party for years, which was typical for people who'd run for county chair. Then there was Salleigh Grubbs, a woman who'd been active in the party for less than a year and had been recruiting her friends and Facebook followers to become precinct chairs using a video of Dan Schultz.

Salleigh had voted Republican since Reagan; she watched Fox News and listened to Rush Limbaugh, and she could tell you all about the scandals with Benghazi, Seth Rich and Jeffrey Epstein, Hillary Clinton's phones, and Hunter Biden's laptop. But politics had always been a side interest for her. She first learned to pay

---

* In October 2023, Powell pleaded guilty to illegally conspiring with Trump to overturn the 2020 election in Georgia, in a case brought by Fulton County district attorney Fani Willis charging Powell, Trump, and seventeen others.

attention to politics from her dad, who was a prominent attorney in the county. Before Salleigh was born, her dad ran for Congress (finishing last in a four-way race) and served on the Marietta city council. As a trial lawyer, Salleigh's dad liked to represent the underdog: he won a malpractice suit against a local hospital and stopped a country club from building a road that neighbors opposed. The case that stuck with Salleigh the most was when the court appointed her father to represent a notorious serial killer, a member of the Dixie Mafia. She remembered how her mom, who founded a charm and modeling school in town, didn't like the idea of her father representing an accused murderer, but he insisted that the man had a right to a fair trial.*

Salleigh was what you'd call "old Marietta," meaning her family had been in Cobb County long before new housing developments started creeping up from Atlanta. Growing up, she used to help out in her dad's law office and trained as a paralegal. She bounced around manufacturing jobs and then for a decade worked as a real estate agent (sometimes scoping out bear-inhabited woodlands with a shotgun slung over her shoulder). In 2016, she became the general manager of a company that sold liquid and powder coating equipment. It was a good job but not exactly a calling. Her two boys were grown and moved out; one had gotten married. She had no partner (twice divorced) and no grandkids yet. She took care of her ninety-two-year-old mother, and she had three rescue dogs and a pet tortoise named Henri. Like many people of her generation, she started spending more time on Facebook.

Salleigh called herself a "keyboard warrior." She became increasingly outspoken. In late 2019, the Democrats held an early primary debate in the race to challenge President Trump. Fox News came to Marietta to record a segment about the reaction of "regular voters" in the town diner. Salleigh showed up in a MAGA cap and said she wished the candidates had spent more time talking about impeachment, because "the more they talk about impeachment, the more I'm sure that Trump is the man to do the job, and he represents the American people." Congressional Democrats were

* In the end, though, Salleigh's dad did not see the case through to trial. According to news reports from the time, he got himself removed from the case by antagonizing the judge.

plowing ahead with impeaching Trump for withholding foreign aid to Ukraine unless the country's president agreed to investigate one of his potential rivals, former vice president Joe Biden. Salleigh watched the impeachment hearings live and cheered for Trump's acquittal. On the eve of the Senate vote, Trump delivered a triumphant State of the Union address, and at the end House Speaker Nancy Pelosi tore up her copy of his speech. Salleigh mailed Pelosi a fresh copy.

The next month, March 2020, the pandemic hit. Salleigh took it seriously at first. She wiped down her groceries and prayed for doctors and nurses. She watched the daily White House briefings with President Trump and Dr. Anthony Fauci. She found their candor reassuring. It sounded like they were doing everything they could. She was grateful that month when Congress funded relief programs to help people with small businesses and student loans. She even supported stronger social distancing restrictions to stop the spread in Cobb County.

But as the "two weeks to stop the spread" turned into four, and March turned into April, Trump started saying we had to get on with our lives. New infections were just barely leveling off, hospitalizations and deaths were still climbing. But Trump wanted to reopen the country in time for Easter. He didn't wear a mask, even though the CDC said you were supposed to in public settings, so Salleigh figured, if you wanted to wear a mask, fine. If not, don't. If you wanted to stay home, fine — but let other people open their businesses or go to work. She read a column by the Fox News legal analyst Andrew Napolitano that asked readers like Salleigh to imagine how they would have reacted six months earlier to the idea that the government could tell them when to leave home, go to work, go for a jog, go to the store, or attend church. "Why do Americans accept this?" Napolitano asked. "We have fought wars against tyrants who wanted to tell us how to live." People like Napolitano had been talking for ages about Democrats wanting to control people's lives, but now that government officials were wielding emergency powers like no one alive had ever experienced, these warnings suddenly started to look more like reality.

In April, the Democrats consolidated around Biden as their best hope to beat Trump, and just about every poll was showing Biden ahead. Trump had looked like a strong incumbent before the pandemic, but now his handling of the crisis was driving down his ratings. Around the country, local-level officials were responding to the emergency by expanding mail ballots, drive-thru voting, large voting centers, or other options to help people feel comfortable voting in a pandemic — accommodations that were popular with most Americans. These methods were already in use in most states and had been for years, but now all the sudden changes struck Salleigh as strange. She cherished her memories of Election Days with her dad, when he used to come to the polling place at her school during lunchtime so he could eat with her, and then would take her into the little booth with a curtain. She thought taking that away was un-American. She didn't understand why Georgia officials said it was safe enough for people to go to Home Depot or Walmart but not to their regular polling station. Trump was telling his supporters not to trust mail ballots, that they were "RIPE for FRAUD," and that all these sudden changes to voting procedures were a plot by the Democrats to steal the election.

Starting in late May, masses of protesters started filling the streets — the largest outpouring of demonstrations in American history. In cities across the country, people were demanding change after the murder of George Floyd, a Black man killed by a police officer who kneeled on his neck for more than eight minutes. All eight-plus minutes were captured in an agonizing cell-phone video. For many Americans, Floyd's death became a symbol of the tragic toll of the discriminatory treatment of Black people by law enforcement. Salleigh did not watch the video. The protests made her feel confused. For months, government officials had been telling everyone to stay home because of the pandemic, but now suddenly it was OK to gather in large crowds? The protesters called themselves peaceful, but Salleigh saw them on the news clashing with police. In Atlanta that June, a Black man named Rayshard Brooks fell asleep in his car at a Wendy's drive-thru. The police came to wake him up, and Brooks struggled with them and tried to run. They shot him dead. Two nights later, demonstrators came and burned down the Wendy's. The flaming restaurant was broadcast all over the news. Salleigh was not alone in thinking the protesters were out there trying to incite violence or destroy property: 42 percent of Americans thought so, and 59 percent of Republicans. Now the pandemic-related changes to voting procedures looked even more suspicious to her. She saw Trump post, "IF YOU CAN PROTEST IN PERSON, YOU CAN VOTE IN PERSON!" To Salleigh, it felt like everything was out of control. On Facebook she posted an upside-down flag, widely recognized in right-wing online circles as a distress signal.

That summer, Salleigh's son Nick came to her in a crisis. He'd gotten married two years earlier to a woman Salleigh adored. Now he told her that they were not planning to have children. He didn't think he could give his kids as good a life as Salleigh had given him. She was stunned. That's not what God wants, she told him. "It's not in God's plan to not have children." But she needed a plan too. She could not merely be a keyboard warrior anymore. Voting was not enough either. This election was too important. She got in touch with the county GOP to become a volunteer.

There were a lot of volunteers coming out because they were fed up with shutdowns and masks and attacks on police. There were a lot of Democrats, too, who were stirred up by the pandemic and the protests, with the opposite view. It was a divisive time. Cobb County was the largest source of Republican votes in the state (only two or three counties were more populous, and they were overwhelmingly Democratic), and for decades it had formed the bedrock of the modern Georgia GOP. Cobb County had launched the careers of Newt Gingrich, the nineties House speaker; Johnny Isakson, the recently retired senator; and Tom Price, Trump's first health secretary. Hillary Clinton narrowly carried the county in 2016 — a minor political earthquake. It was unfamiliar to Salleigh to see Cobb County as contested terrain. It was one of the places where political scientists started using the term "status shock" to describe the reaction of white voters seeing their majority shrink. The population was growing fastest south of Marietta, around the Braves stadium and the highway into Atlanta, where clumps of apartment buildings were springing up. The Republicans did not even bother to campaign there.

Salleigh's main concern wasn't actually the campaign — it was the election itself. She kept seeing red flags. Her son sent her an article about how voters in Pennsylvania would be consolidated into huge voting centers instead of using their neighborhood precincts. The stated reason was social distancing, but it didn't add up to Salleigh. She thought all these improvised "emergency" changes to voting procedures were part of the plan to steal the election. When Fulton County (Atlanta) announced a consolidated voting center of its own, Salleigh emailed and called the secretary of state's office until she finally got through to the state's director of elections. He told her it wasn't his decision; it was up to Fulton County. Which was true — every jurisdiction is responsible for running its own elections, and the state didn't tell counties where to put their polls any more than the federal government did. But it didn't sound right to Salleigh. This was the state's director of elections, and he couldn't do anything about it, or didn't care? He basically admitted as much to her.

As Election Day approached, Salleigh asked all her friends what they were doing to make a difference. Her friends liked all her Facebook posts and told her she was so brave and patriotic, she was beautiful inside and out, it was an inspiration just to know her, they'd vote for her when she ran for office. She updated her Facebook profile picture with a QAnon slogan; a lot of people were doing it. Salleigh stopped coloring her hair to her younger self's natural brunette and started growing out her roots: a shock of white around her crown and temples.

Salleigh saw an article online, on a site affiliated with Bannon's *War Room*, laying out how the Democrats were going to steal the election: "WARNING: Democrat Data Firm Admits 'Incredible' Trump Landslide Will Be Flipped by Mail-In Votes Emerging a Week After Election Day." The article quoted a Democratic analyst interviewed on an HBO news show saying, "When every legitimate vote is tallied and we get to that final day, which will be someday after Election Day, it will in fact show that what happened on Election Night was exactly that, a mirage. It looked like Donald Trump was in the lead and he fundamentally was not when every ballot gets counted." He was explaining that the in-person votes would favor Trump, because the president had discouraged his supporters from voting by mail, and those would get reported first, while the mail ballots that would lean Biden would get counted later. But if you didn't trust the mail ballots, then the mirage was the reality, and the eventual count was the fantasy.

Even though Salleigh was preparing for the steal, the results still stunned her on Election Night. In her own Cobb County, Republicans lost up and down the ballot, including the county commission chair, district attorney, and sheriff. Salleigh thought these were all races the GOP should not have lost. That Saturday, November 7, the major networks called the election for Biden. But Trump was still contesting the key states, filing lawsuits, and pressing for recounts, including in Georgia, where Biden was winning by just over eleven thousand votes.

Salleigh thought about traveling to Washington the next weekend to protest, and she asked around for a ride, but she didn't end up going. Instead, she was at a doctor's appointment with her son when a friend sent her a video from inside Jim Miller Park, an event center where the Cobb County government was conducting a hand recount of the ballots in the presidential election. The recount had been ordered by the secretary of state, a Republican, under pressure from Trump and his allies, who insisted he hadn't really lost the state. The county's election director gave a local news interview to spell out how the recount would work. It was conducted by full-time county employees and, because there weren't enough of them, temporary poll workers, sometimes through staffing agencies. They were randomly assigned to teams of two, and reassigned again every day. Each team got a batch of ballots. Both people looked at each ballot and confirmed which candidate the voter chose, then sorted the ballot into bins for Trump or Biden. At the end of each batch, the pairs would count up the stacks and record the results on a tally sheet. Then they'd seal the ballots back in their original box and turn over the tally sheets to be entered into the database. Any ballots that were damaged or unclear would go to a review panel for further inspection, composed of one person picked by the Democratic Party, one person picked by the Republican Party, and one nonpartisan election worker. The elections director cautioned that the final numbers would probably be a little different from the original results, because there are usually human errors in hand counts — not to mention, they were working long shifts, day after day, and it was stressful, especially with concerns around catching the virus. But she affirmed she hadn't seen any anomalies or reasons to doubt the outcome.

The video Salleigh saw was taken on a cell phone inside the event center. It showed someone trying to observe the recount while being ordered to stand back. Salleigh thought she had to see this for herself. She recalled a memory from her childhood. On

Saturday mornings, her grandmother used to take her to lunch at the local drugstore. It was an old-fashioned lunch counter with stools and tiny booths. One time Salleigh was eating her toast and chitchatting with her grandmother having her sausage biscuit. At the counter, there was another older woman with a girl who looked like she had an intellectual disability. The girl spilled her milkshake and the woman raised her hand, preparing to slap her, but Salleigh's grandmother grabbed that woman's arm mid-strike and said, "Don't you ever hit that child again." The woman grabbed the girl and stormed out of the luncheonette.

Now, channeling her grandmother's spirit, Salleigh showed up to the recount at Jim Miller Park on November 13, 2020, and she became, as she would say, half-joking, "a total Karen." She barged in like, *"I want to speak to your manager. Who's in charge here?"* Inside a big exhibit hall, with beige walls and concrete floors, about forty folding tables were set up where workers wearing gloves and masks were sorting ballots into bins. Only official monitors who had party credentials were allowed to walk the floor. Public "observers" had to stay behind a line of caution tape strung between orange traffic cones. This setup was standard in polling places and counting facilities — to let observers watch while blocking them from interfering with voters or election workers. But Salleigh, cordoned off behind the yellow tape, struggled to understand how the "observers" were supposed to "observe" anything from such a distance. They would have needed binoculars to see what was actually on the ballots. Despite that, Salleigh thought she could see for herself that some ballots had a slightly different color or paper weight and were suspiciously all Biden votes. There was a stack of ballots that the election workers said totaled 454, but it looked more like seven hundred or a thousand. She wanted to know what was going on in Exhibit Hall B and the elections director told her there's nothing to see there, stay in Exhibit Hall C. It all seemed like a joke. But how was this funny?

Salleigh met another woman, named Susan Knox, who wore taupe and black stilettos, thick mascara, gold hoop earrings, and chunky gold bangles. They quickly became sisters in arms. At one point Susan got fed up with having to observe from afar and walked right up to one of the workers and looked over his shoulder, trying to watch what he was doing. One of the supervisors, seeing this, told Susan with obvious exasperation that she needed to follow the rules.

"There's no need to be rude to her," Salleigh said.

"I'm not being rude," the supervisor replied. "I'm simply asking her to give these people some space." Then she walked over to one of her colleagues and sighed, "I'm gonna call the police."

"She needs to be able to see whether it's Biden or Trump, though," someone else said.

"That is not six feet," the supervisor said.

"Give me a break," Susan said, as her paper surgical mask slipped off her nose.

"This is getting ugly!" another observer said. Salleigh wondered why the workers were acting so defensive if they had nothing to hide.

Susan recorded videos on her phone to post online so the public could see how bad it was. "This is a fraud," Susan drawled in one of her videos, "and ridiculous, and we're just going through the motions." Susan was used to seeing election workers who were little old white ladies with white hair whom you'd see at the church or the library — "Q-tips," they were called, after the cotton swabs. But now she said she felt like she had woken up "in the middle of Nigeria." She said she could tell these election workers were not from Cobb County because she noticed a lot of out-of-state license plates in the parking lot, and some of the workers spoke with an accent. "I'm not being judgmental or ugly," she said, "but they just...their pants were halfway down, they absolutely were not professional, they weren't dressed nice." In case her meaning wasn't already clear enough, Susan elaborated: "They were Black as spades."

The next Friday, November 20, the recount was still going, so Susan came back to Jim Miller Park. She pulled her car around the back, thinking she would take a video of the license plates in the parking lot, when she saw a huge box truck. The name on the side, in green and blue, was A1 Shredding & Recycling. SECURE ON-SITE DESTRUCTION SERVICES.

"Oh. My. God," Susan said.

A guy in khakis and a blue shirt was wheeling forty-eight-gallon trash bins out from the loading dock and over to the truck. He put the bins under a big chute on the side of the truck, and then Susan could hear the sound of the machine whirring like a giant fan, sucking everything out and ripping it to shreds.

"Un-buh-lievable."

Susan felt a surge of adrenaline. She was scared and furious, but also thrilled—she'd kept hearing that the Democrats would steal the election, and now *she* was catching them in the act. She had to see what was in those bins. She got out of her car and walked over to the loading dock. The bins were stuffed with envelopes that read: OFFICIAL ABSENTEE BALLOT. There was a cardboard box with a crudely drawn diagram saying SHRED, right next to all the neatly stacked and labeled boxes of ballots from different precincts. Susan hid before the truck driver could see her and called 911.

"There is a shredding machine outside of the area where we had an election," she said, "and I need a policeman, please, here ASAP."

"I'm sorry," the operator said, "you said there's a shredding machine outside of *what*?"

"The area where all the ballots were counted for this election. They're shredding ballots! I see them shredding ballots as I speak to you right now."

"All right," the operator replied. "I need to get the people's descriptions. Are they male or female?"

"Male," Susan said. "Black guy." She got impatient. "Ma'am, I need to go video this, will you send a cop now please?"

SALLEIGH WAS IN her office when she got a phone call from a friend who knew Susan. *Susan's at Jim Miller Park—they're shredding ballots!* the friend said. Salleigh grabbed her keys and bolted out of work so fast, people thought someone in her family had died. Salleigh got in her silver Toyota Venza and practically flew the fifteen miles to the counting site at Jim Miller Park. She rolled up and parked her car sideways to block in the shredding truck, like she'd seen them do on *Starsky and Hutch*. Then she met up with Susan.

Salleigh stepped out of her car wearing flip-flops, black leggings, a navy-blue NRA T-shirt with an American flag made up of rifles on the back, and frameless oval eyeglasses, and she was carrying a white and green Michael Kors bag. Together she and Susan started photographing the truck. Salleigh tried talking to the driver—"*Who called you? What's the deal here?*"—and he held up a piece of paper in the cab window to cover his face. Salleigh thought that was suspicious — what was he hiding? She thought it was like watching a kid with chocolate smeared on his face while swearing he didn't touch the cookies. Fifteen minutes had passed. No officers had arrived. Susan dialed 911 again.

"It's an emergency and we need them here *now!*"

"OK," the operator said, a different woman this time, "so I do see the call in for service. Our officers are aware. It looks like they're busy in that area. Now, you said, it's going to be referenced, a Black male with a white shredding machine?"

"Yep," Susan confirmed.

"OK. Does anybody have any weapons?"

"I don't know. I'm not close enough. All I can tell you is there's a shredding machine outside of an election office in Cobb County, Jim Miller Park. So would you please send an officer ASAP — "

"Ma'am, ma'am, hang on one second," the operator said. "We're gonna send our first available unit. The sergeant is already aware of the call. The units are busy in that area."

"I would think that the presidential election would be pretty much as important as anything in our country for a policeman in Cobb County to get over to Jim Miller Park," Susan said.

Before the operator could begin to try to deal with that, the truck started to move, and Susan cried, "It's pulling off. The truck is pulling off!"

The driver managed to maneuver around Salleigh's car. So Salleigh jumped back in and took off after him. Susan followed.

Salleigh tailed the truck for eleven miles, until she ran out of gas. She ditched her car at a RaceTrac station and hopped into Susan's Mercedes.

"Get in, girl," Susan said. "I've got a full tank of gas and I just had the car washed."

They were back in pursuit of the shredding truck. Susan had a TRUMP sign in the backseat. The SoulTown channel was playing on her XM radio. Salleigh thought they were like Thelma and Louise, or maybe Lucy and Ethel from *I Love Lucy*. The truck driver must have known they were tailing him because he cut through parking lots and shopping centers. It was like a Hollywood car chase. The truck made a right turn from the left lane, and ran a red light.

Salleigh knew her way around, but Susan wasn't as familiar with this part of town, and she started to worry. What if the driver called someone? They were just two women chasing a shredding truck. The driver stopped in the middle of a four-lane road and put his flashers on. Susan and Salleigh were hiding behind a dumpy tire store, unsure of what to do next. That's when Susan said, "We might not need to keep going." Salleigh agreed. They decided to go back to Jim Miller Park to collect more evidence.

At the park, Salleigh and Susan met up with a lawyer from the local GOP. Party lawyers were used to responding to complaints at polls and counting facilities, and the county party was working on a lawsuit to demand more access for observers. The two women decided to gather more evidence of shenanigans at the counting site. They started recording videos of the election workers. There were similar videos posted online from all around the country, from Trump supporters filming election workers, pointing out any move they didn't understand or thought looked suspicious. Salleigh was committed. She'd camp out all night if she had to — she was not going to let them shred more ballots. Now the police did show up. Salleigh figured the staff must have called them. The 911 call log identified Salleigh as a white female in her fifties with multicolored hair. The cops told the two women that they were not allowed to be there, the area was closed to the public. They could go down to the police station to file a report.

At the station, the staff told them no one there would take a report and instead directed them to a wall-mounted phone. Salleigh picked it up, and the operator on the phone told her the police weren't taking any election-related complaints; she could call the secretary of state, who was the state official in charge of elections. Salleigh squinted as she listened, darted her eyes from side to side. "Do you know who made that determination?" she asked. "Do you have any idea who that was?"

Salleigh listened to the operator's answer and repeated it back so Susan could hear. "You were just told that about ten minutes ago? Wow. OK. And what's your name, please? Operator 3442," Salleigh repeated, rolling her eyes. "OK, perfect. Thank you so much. We appreciate what you guys do. Uh huh, buh bye."

Salleigh twirled around to untangle herself from the phone cord and hung up the handset. She shot Susan a look: eyes wide with disbelief, jaw dropped. Just ten minutes earlier—what a coincidence! Salleigh kept thinking the FBI would show up in their blue-and-yellow jackets to impound the shredding truck and seize the evidence. (She didn't know the FBI actually would investigate; the allegation would go all the way up to the U.S. attorney in Atlanta, and after doing their due diligence, the officials would determine there was no evidence of any wrongdoing.) At the police station, Salleigh struggled to understand why the officers didn't seem to care about this crime in progress. They hadn't showed up when Susan called about the shredding truck, but they'd showed up when election workers called them about Salleigh and Susan taking videos. Now Salleigh wondered, how far did the corruption go?

Salleigh and Susan posted some of their photos and videos from Jim Miller Park, and they quickly went viral. President Trump's own lawyer, Lin Wood, retweeted them to his hundreds of thousands of followers. "Looks to me like they may be destroying election documents in Cobb County, GA," Wood wrote. "What do you think? #FightBack Against Election Crimes." It was just one in a torrent of rumors that Wood and other Trump allies were feverishly amplifying. Another, promoted by Trump lawyer Rudy Giuliani, was that two Black election workers in Fulton County's State Farm Arena were "passing around USB ports as if they are vials of heroin or cocaine." The workers, a mother-daughter duo named Ruby Freeman and Shaye Moss, were actually handing each other a ginger mint. But the wild and well-publicized accusations against them inspired three people from the Chicago area to call Freeman, show up at her house, and threaten her to confess to election crimes she did not commit.*

Back in Cobb County, people were calling the police to report the shredded ballots they'd seen on the internet, even a guy from Tennessee who referenced the president's lawyer. The shredding truck company was getting slammed with hundreds of calls. People started showing up at the company's office. The manager was scared

---

* Giuliani and the three people accused of harassing Freeman were indicted in August 2023 by the Fulton County district attorney as part of the conspiracy and racketeering case involving Trump. Giuliani's false accusation was also quoted in special counsel Jack Smith's indictment of Trump, which described Giuliani as a coconspirator. In December 2023, Freeman and Moss won a $148 million judgment in a defamation lawsuit against Giuliani, and he filed for bankruptcy.

for his drivers. There was so much commotion that the county government, through its election director, put out an official statement. The election director said the document shredding was "routine" disposal of "non-relevant materials." The envelopes that said OFFICIAL ABSENTEE BALLOT were just empty envelopes. All the actual ballots had been saved and stored, as required by state law. But Salleigh thought she would never know for sure, now that the evidence had been destroyed. To her, it was proof of what she already thought: there was no way Republicans could have lost that election.

A FEW WEEKS went by. At the end of December 2020, Salleigh and Susan decided to go to the State Capitol, in Atlanta, for a hearing on election irregularities. They hoped their eyewitness accounts would help persuade the state legislature to call a special session, where they could reject the election results and award Georgia's Electoral College votes to Trump.

They waited in line for a chance to speak. Susan went first. She passed out printouts of the photos she'd taken of the trash bins at Jim Miller Park. One of the senators, Bill Heath, asked, "Do you have any photographs of actual ballots being shredded?"

"What do you think were in that can that he was shredding?" Susan said. "It says an official ballot."

"That appears to be the envelopes," Senator Heath replied, "that are the inner envelopes from — "

"If you look closely some of them look like they've never even been unsealed," Susan said.

"I was just, I was trying to find ballots in the picture, and I don't see ballots." Susan played him her video recording.

"Look," Senator Heath went on, "I'm not trying to discredit your testimony, I just don't see ballots. I just see envelopes here."

"Do you not see where it says B-A-L-L-O..."

Salleigh could not believe what she was hearing. Senator Heath was a Republican! How could he not see what they clearly saw in the video? When it was Salleigh's turn at the podium, everyone in the room got to see her in the outfit she chose for the occasion: a sharp red blazer and black shirt. Her hair was now fully white. She started to calmly explain what she'd seen, but then interrupted herself to pull out her phone and read a Facebook post by the secretary of state's chief of staff (another "Republican"). He had posted about an FBI warning that Iranian actors were targeting U.S. election officials, trying to undermine public faith in the election. "Those continuing to claim the election was stolen are supporting the tactical actions of Iran," he'd written. Salleigh started pounding on the podium. "I want him to come in here and explain to me how I'm like someone from I-*ran*," she said, her voice getting louder and higher. "We have seen the fraud. We have been lied to, we have been distracted, we've been held up, and we're tired of it." She was almost shouting now. Her voice started to quiver. "I am tired of people that we vote to put in office stabbing us in the back."

All she wanted was for the lawmakers to call a special session, to look into the fraud. "I don't know what it's going to take, I honest to God don't know," she said. "We are the citizens of this state, we deserve to be heard! Are you hearing us yet? Is anyone hearing us yet? What do you need to know? Would you like to see my phone," she asked, holding it up again, "that I've backed up in five different places because I'm afraid someone's gonna steal it and steal the evidence?" She sounded panicked. She said there was fraud happening again right at that moment, in the runoffs for both of Georgia's Senate seats that would decide control of the chamber. "That election needs to be stopped until we have a better way to vote."

She paused then to collect herself. "I'm passionate," she said. "I'm not going to apologize for being passionate. And I'm not going to apologize for being a patriot either."

Someone in the gallery whooped and clapped. Salleigh gave a big phony smile. "Any questions?" she asked, though she could sense that the lawmakers were not interested. She felt like she could have showed up at the State Capitol with a dump truckload of ballots filled in with crayon and nobody would care.

The committee chairman who was running the hearing laughed nervously. "No, ma'am," he said sheepishly. "I think what you said is something that's felt by many people across this state, hundreds of thousands of people." He spoke gently, carefully, trying to ease the tension. "So thank you for doing what you've done and for being willing to stand up and tell about what you've seen."

Soon it was time to hear from Rudy Giuliani, appearing on

behalf of the president of the United States. "America's mayor" had been through a rough couple months. There was the time he held a press conference at a Four Seasons that turned out to be a landscaping business in a ragged corner of Philadelphia instead of the luxury hotel downtown. At another appearance, hair dye streamed down his sweaty temples. He'd been scorned for presenting baseless claims at unofficial "hearings" with Republican state legislators in Pennsylvania and Michigan, as Trump tried to pressure lawmakers to reject the results in all the pivotal states. But that day, in Atlanta, Giuliani looked and sounded more like the former prosecutor famous for cleaning up New York. His suit was crisp and so was his speech. "I sat and listened to a good deal of the testimony before I stood here, and I can't imagine that people are ignoring it," Giuliani said. "The recount in Cobb County is a joke. It's an insult."

Rudy gets it! Salleigh thought. He was right on point, saying exactly what needed to be said. Salleigh went up and talked to him after the break. He was so happy to meet her. He offered to connect her and her friends with John Eastman, a constitutional lawyer who was advising the president and would help Salleigh put together her documentation.*

Trump had tweeted for people to watch the hearing as it was being live-streamed online, and Salleigh got so many texts and calls from people all across the country who loved her testimony, strangers she didn't even know. When people asked her who she was, she'd say she was just a regular person, a mom of two wonderful sons who had worked her whole life to provide for them. "I'm just nobody, really," Salleigh told them, "but I'm somebody who loves my country." In certain circles, she was becoming something of a legend: the woman who chased a shredding truck.

---

* Salleigh never connected with Eastman, and she never had another conversation with Giuliani. In August 2023, Giuliani and Eastman were indicted by the Fulton County district attorney in the racketeering case involving Trump and sixteen other defendants. The indictment specified Giuliani's testimony at the December 30, 2020, hearing as one of the acts in the conspiracy. Giuliani and Eastman were also described as coconspirators in special counsel Jack Smith's indictment charging Trump with working to overturn the election.

* * *

UNBEKNOWNST TO SALLEIGH, the legend made it all the way to the president of the United States. An official in the Justice Department heard there was a woman who'd testified in Georgia about seeing a shredding truck at an election site in Cobb County, and he wanted the department to use this and other allegations to make a formal finding of fraud. The official, Jeffrey Clark, got the president's attention,* and on January 2, 2021, Trump called Georgia's secretary of state, Brad Raffensperger, asking him to "find 11,780 votes," enough to change the outcome.

"What about the ballots, the shredding of the ballots? Have they been shredding ballots?" Trump demanded on the call.

"They have not been shredding any ballots," Raffensperger's lawyer, Ryan Germany, answered. "There was an issue in Cobb County where they were doing normal office shredding, getting rid of old stuff, and we investigated that."

Trump groaned. *"It doesn't pass the smell test,"* he said. *"Because we hear they're shredding thousands and thousands of ballots, and now what they're saying, 'Oh, we're just cleaning up the office.'"* He laughed.

That was exactly how Salleigh had felt about the official explanation, too. Her testimony did not convince the state legislature to call a special session to throw Georgia's electoral votes to Trump. She was disappointed, but still thrilled by the whole experience. She had never in her life made so many friends so quickly. She met all these amazing, reliable, prayerful, capable women — like Susan: Salleigh had met her only a few weeks earlier, but it felt like they'd known each other their whole lives.

Salleigh and the other women made a plan to go to a Trump rally an hour away in Dalton, Georgia, on the eve of the Senate runoff, on January 5. But then a friend of hers snagged a VIP pass to a rally in Washington the next day, on January 6, where Trump supporters from all over the country were coming to protest the formal certification of the election results in Congress. Trump tweeted, "Be there, will be wild!" Bannon said it would be "living history."

---

* Jeffrey Clark was later described as a coconspirator in special counsel Jack Smith's indictment charging Trump with trying to overturn the election. In August 2023, he was indicted in the Fulton County racketeering case. A spokeswoman said Clark "was simply doing his job."

Salleigh jumped at the chance. She would stay at the Trump International Hotel and sit in the first section for the Save America March in front of the White House. It was the opportunity of a lifetime.

Salleigh hadn't been to Washington since she was a kid. Maybe it was the weather (cold and gray), but as soon as she got off the plane, Salleigh felt like she was in a book or on TV: there was a cloud hanging over the land. She'd packed her bag with protein bars, not sure where her next meal would be coming from or what else to expect. The D.C. mayor had shut everything down. She had to follow these ridiculous social-distancing rules, like you had to wear a mask while walking through the hotel lobby, but you could take it off once you sat down at the bar. Salleigh believed COVID was real, but this stuff was silly. Still, nothing could stifle the amazing energy inside the Trump hotel. Everyone there loved the president.

Salleigh and her friends got up the next morning teeming with excitement. It was almost freezing and they'd be outside all day, so they each put on two pairs of pants and two pairs of socks. They walked a couple blocks to the rally site, on the Ellipse, between the White House and the Washington Monument, and went through the Secret Service security screening. Salleigh strung a VIP pass around her neck and got to meet famous people she admired, like Patrick Byrne, the Overstock.com founder, and Diamond and Silk, two Black vloggers who had gained a huge following as Trump fans. She saw CJ Pearson, a college student with a huge audience on his pro-Trump podcast. Mike Lindell, the MyPillow guy, and Ginni Thomas, the wife of Supreme Court justice Clarence Thomas, were there too. Two rows behind her was a group of nuns, and every so often she glanced back at them, seeing their hands clasped in prayer. Her seat was right up front, not far from Alex Jones, the *InfoWars* host, and Ali Alexander, the organizer of Stop the Steal rallies, and about a dozen rows from the stage where President Trump himself would soon speak. The crowd behind her stretched all the way back to the Washington Monument. The Mall was full of patriots just like her. Salleigh had always known that Trump was fighting for her, but now she was fighting too. She understood all these people were there because no one else was going to change things for them. They were the ones they had been waiting for. She was the one she had been waiting for.

"Just remember this," Trump told them from the stage. *"You're*

stronger, you're smarter, you've got more going than anybody. And they try and demean everybody having to do with us. And you're the real people, you're the people that built this nation. You're not the people that tore down our nation."

"Fight for Trump!" the crowd chanted. "Fight for Trump!"

"We fight like hell," they heard Trump say. "And if you don't fight like hell, you're not going to have a country anymore... So we're going to walk down Pennsylvania Avenue... and we're going to the Capitol, and... we're going to try and give our Republicans — the weak ones, because the strong ones don't need any of our help — we're going to try and give them the kind of pride and boldness that they need to take back our country. So let's walk down Pennsylvania Avenue."

By the time he finished, it was already after one o'clock, and it took Salleigh and her group a while to leave the fenced-in VIP area. They joined the river of people heading east on Constitution Avenue, past street vendors selling scarves, hats, T-shirts, and flags. For a block or two, the Capitol and the Trump hotel were in the same direction. Would they all follow Trump's directive? Some of Salleigh's friends wanted to march to the Capitol. She wasn't sure. They'd been standing out in the cold for hours. Her feet and back hurt. She wanted to go back to her hotel, warm up, get something to eat, maybe even take a nap. If she was being honest, the real reason was that her son did not want her to go. He thought something might happen, and he was afraid she might get hurt. She didn't want her son to worry. She knew he wouldn't be happy until she was safely back in her hotel room. She got in bed, ordered a cheeseburger, and switched on Fox News. She was there, curled up in the plush hotel sheets, watching on TV like millions of others around the world, close to the action but not there herself, when everything changed.

At 2:19 p.m., the news flashed across her TV: US CAPITOL ON LOCKDOWN AS PROTESTS ERUPT. She knew this would be one of those historic moments, like the Kennedy assassination or the *Challenger* explosion, when everyone would remember exactly where they were. She took a picture of the screen to memorialize the moment. If anybody ever asked, she was not at the Capitol, she was in the hotel, and she had a time-stamped, geo-tagged photo to prove it.

Salleigh texted the photo to someone she knew who had gone down to the Capitol. "There's something going on," she said on the phone. Her friend said, *No, we're singing "Amazing Grace,"* it was all fine. "Well," Salleigh said, "I think you better head back to wherever you're staying, because it looks like it's getting dicey."

The TV screen was split between images of the mob outside, climbing up the walls of the building, and a feed from inside the House chamber. "It's not like it's a siege," Bret Baier was saying on the TV. "It seems like they are protesting."

"It looks like the House has maybe decided to take a break," Fox's Dana Perino said. "It's interesting to think they are debating this while all of this is happening."

Then the feed from inside the House chamber cut out. Now the whole screen was filled with the crowds outside, dark figures flowing across the terrace, flags streaming in unison.

"One Capitol Hill police officer was being carried away from the scene," Martha MacCallum, another Fox host, said. "It looks like he got one of those flash-bangs in the eyes. There are safety concerns." Then she quickly added, "At this point, it remains peaceful."

Salleigh knew this crowd, and they were not violent people. It didn't make sense to her that Trump supporters would break the law; they were all about the rule of law. They were upset for good reason, she thought, because they were fed up with all the Democratic politicians' crimes that had gone on for years, and the riots of the past summer. No one was ever held accountable. They were there to hold people accountable. That's why they had come: not to break the law, but to enforce it. And it was working.

The chyrons got scarier.

REPORT: ARMED STANDOFF AT DOOR OF HOUSE CHAMBER.

REPORTS OF SHOTS FIRED IN CAPITOL.

GUNS DRAWN ON HOUSE FLOOR.

SHOOTING VICTIM TRANSPORTED FROM U.S. CAPITOL.

She was glued to the TV, alone but sharing this moment with millions of others around the country and around the world. Depending what station they were watching and what they'd already believed going into that day, some were shocked, disgusted, speechless, or energized, thinking this was the time when everything Trump had called for was coming true. That was in fact what was happening, whether you thought that was a good thing or bad. The peaceful transfer of power, a sacred hallmark of American democracy, what Reagan once called "nothing less than a miracle," was broken, as the riot sent members of Congress and even the vice president fleeing for their lives.

Salleigh's viewing was finally interrupted when her friends burst through her hotel room door in a whirlwind of excitement. They showed her photos and told her everyone they'd met had been so nice and happy. Salleigh was relieved. Their stories confirmed what she'd thought, despite what she'd seen on TV (even Fox could be "fake news"). Relying on what her friends told her, Salleigh would never believe the footage that surfaced later of cops beaten with flagpoles or crushed in doors; of rioters shouting that Trump had sent them, that they were there to punish the traitors. She pulled up the Facebook group that she'd started, "Angry Patriots of Georgia," around when she testified to the state legislature. Since then, it had grown to hundreds, even thousands, of followers.

"All," she posted. "DO NOT BELIEVE THE NEWS. Trump people are not violent. The Capitol protest was fine until Antifa coopted and committed violence."

WHEN SALLEIGH GOT home, she laid low for a few days, wondering what to do next. It wasn't clear how things would turn out. Some people who'd gone to Washington for January 6 were getting arrested. Trump got impeached again (on January 13, one week after the riot and one week before his term ended, on one count of "incitement of insurrection.") It was a confusing time. She found comfort listening to Bannon's *War Room*, and she heard Bannon interview Dan Schultz about the Precinct Strategy.

Salleigh had heard people talking about a third party, but that hadn't sounded right to her. The infrastructure was already there, in the Republican Party — why not use it? Susan encouraged Salleigh to run for a party position, and Salleigh set her aim higher than the precinct level. She decided to run for county chair. She would mobilize her friends and Facebook followers, who would flood the county's precinct caucus, becoming qualified to vote for her. She proudly passed around the video of her testimony at the state senate hearing. "I'm a dedicated woman," she described herself at a forum with the other county chair candidates. "I chased the shredding truck." The audience laughed and cheered.

The party meetings to elect a new county chair were often not the most exhilarating, but this year, the party headquarters, in a Marietta strip mall, wasn't big enough. The gathering, held in April 2021, moved to the church across the street. When Salleigh saw all the new members show up, it reminded her of the scene in the movie *Network* when everyone shouts, "I'm as mad as hell, and I'm not going to take this anymore!" She looked at all these people who'd heard about the Precinct Strategy and decided this was what they had to do. Even though it was a three-way race, Salleigh won on the first ballot, with nearly a supermajority. Jason Shepherd, the outgoing chair, handed her the gavel as the audience cheered.

"It's a great day in Georgia. Patriots are at work already," Salleigh told the rowdy hall. "So y'all be happy. You go home, you sleep tonight, because tomorrow, we get to work...Let's turn Cobb red again."

The crowd clapped and whooped as Jason reclaimed the podium to officially adjourn the meeting. "I disagree with you, Salleigh," he said. A moment of tension hung in the air. But just as instantly, it vanished when he said: "We start *today*."

Salleigh gave a few radio interviews, where the hosts held her up as a poster child for the Precinct Strategy in action, which was how the MAGA movement was going to take over the Republican Party, exactly as Dan Schultz said they should. She got an email from a guy in Florida who was recruiting precinct chairs in Broward County and connected her with Dan Schultz directly, starting a group thread to coordinate efforts across the country.

A few days after her election, in April 2021, Salleigh was sitting in her first committee meeting at the party headquarters when she got a call from a blocked number. She had a feeling who it might be.

"*Hello, Salleigh,*" a familiar voice said over the phone. "*This is your favorite president.*"

Salleigh was speechless. The meeting screeched to a halt. Salleigh pointed to her phone and mouthed, "It's President Trump!" She stepped outside so she could focus. The party secretary came out to see what was going on, and Salleigh put the phone on speaker for a second so she could hear. "Oh my gosh," the secretary cried, "it's really President Trump!"

Trump called a lot of people, usually rich friends and Republican politicians. His aides sometimes liked him to surprise unsuspecting supporters, but it was not every day he called a lowly county chair. He'd gotten Salleigh's number from the Georgia state chair, who'd wanted Trump to know her story, how he'd inspired regular people to join the party, so many of them becoming sentries of the cause like Salleigh. It was happening in Cobb County and all over Georgia. It was happening in North and South Carolina, in Florida and Texas, Michigan and Wisconsin. Trump told Salleigh she was a real winner. He said he was proud of her for her big victory, and it was great that she ran as an America First candidate. He was so polite and kind, Salleigh thought if everyone could have a minute with him as she had, it might change a lot of his critics' minds. She said it was, as Trump himself might say, "a perfect phone call."

CHAPTER 4

A Hundred and Thirty-Two Coffees

IN THE WEEKS and months after Dan Schultz debuted the Precinct Strategy on Bannon's *War Room*, Kathy Petsas, the Republican Party chair for a legislative district in Maricopa County, Arizona, started getting deluged with applications to become precinct committee members. They came in like a haboob—one of those fits of rain, wind, and dust that sweep across the desert in the summer monsoon season, causing everyone's phone to buzz with an emergency alert warning them to get off the roads. The influx didn't seem accidental; it had to be coordinated, since the volume was staggering and most people had never heard of precinct committee members. It was an obscure role, and Kathy was used to getting two or three people a month who might express interest in becoming a PC. Now she was getting as many as forty or fifty applications a week—what was going on?

Strangest of all, this wave of applications came from people Kathy did not recognize. Usually, the people who'd sign up as PCs were friends of friends, people who were already widely known for being active volunteers in the party at the grassroots level. Kathy would surely recognize people like that, being one herself—and then some. She literally grew up in the local GOP. As a young teenager, she used to spend her Saturdays stuffing mailers at the party headquarters, a storefront in a downtown strip mall. Her uncle was the state party chairman during the Reagan years, and that made Kathy, as she would put it, the "child labor." He used to reward her afterward with a burger from the iconic Bob's Big Boy next door.

Kathy's family arrived in Arizona before it became a state, in 1912. Her grandfather immigrated from Greece and opened the first diner in Phoenix, the Busy Bee Cafe, on West Washington Street. He saved what he could and used it to buy land. One of the properties, a patch of orange and grapefruit orchards, went to Kathy's dad when he married her mom, whose family was also Greek. Since Kathy was descended on both sides from the birthplace of democracy, she joked that her commitment to that most precious form of government was written in her DNA. Her passion for politics came from her uncle. He didn't have children of his own and she was his oldest niece or nephew in town, so they became close. The highlight of her year was the Trunk 'n' Tusk dinner, an annual fundraising gala for the state GOP that would draw big names like Bob Dole or Jim Baker. Kathy's uncle would always bring her as his date, because that was the only way he could avoid provoking the jealousies of any of the women who were always crushing on him. Her uncle, together with his friends — the party attorney, fundraiser, and executive director — pooled their money to build a cabin two hours away in Prescott. They called it the Reliable Cabin. This humble getaway was the kind of place that could somehow sleep thirty, even though it had only three bedrooms. It was where deals were struck, strategies were hashed out, candidates were lined up who could win. For Kathy, her uncle always remained the model of effective party leadership. He was just forty-nine when he died, of a massive heart attack, at a Thanksgiving dance he'd organized for his high school alumni.

Now the Reliable Cabin was a weekend retreat for Kathy and her sisters. Her mom still lived in the house Kathy grew up in, though the orchard was now a cul-de-sac. Kathy and her husband (also of Greek heritage) lived nearby, in Paradise Valley. It was an area of thirsty golf courses and red-tile-roofed mansions. The signature landmark was a cactus-tall statue of Barry Goldwater. The legislative district she chaired, LD 28, spanning Phoenix, Scottsdale, and Paradise Valley, was trending Democratic but was still competitive, like the state as a whole. Kathy was proud to note that the district was home to past and present Republican icons including Supreme Court Justice Sandra Day O'Connor, Senator John McCain, and several current state and county officials. They were the type of Republicans Kathy knew, respected, and identified with.

As Kathy sifted through the PC applications, she invited the applicants to meet for coffee. The meetings weren't exactly job interviews, but if these strangers were asking to represent her party in her district, and if she was going to exercise her discretion as chair to appoint them, then Kathy wanted to get to know them a little first. She had 132 coffees. She kept track. At each one, she'd ask: Why do you want to be a precinct committee member? Where did you hear about this? Where do you get your news?

The answers disturbed her. Many of the new recruits said they watched the right-wing networks OANN and Newsmax and read a propaganda blog called the *Gateway Pundit*. They believed a vast conspiracy had denied Trump a second term. Some hinted that Trump was secretly fighting a global cabal of Satan-worshipping child sex traffickers. And many said they wanted to become precinct committee members because of something they'd heard on Steve Bannon's podcast.

Kathy looked up the video they were talking about. There was Bannon: scraggly beard, baggy eyes, wearing a military-style field jacket, ranting into a microphone, introducing a guest named Dan Schultz. Kathy recognized Dan from county party functions here in Maricopa County. He was the guy who'd helped his friend Frank Schmuck pick off a Republican incumbent in the primary and then lose in the general, meaning all he'd accomplished was to elect a Democrat. What else did anyone think would happen with people who'd been radicalized, who believed in conspiracy theories? Kathy couldn't imagine how this Bannon interview would look or sound appealing to anyone. It was extreme, she thought. It was garbage. She couldn't even finish watching the video, so she did not hear Bannon and Dan say that it would be people like her they were determined to get rid of.

Kathy called Dan Schultz to discuss her concerns about the would-be PCs he was recruiting. The call went to voicemail. She left him a message. He never called her back. Kathy and Dan had always been respectful to each other; this was the first time he wouldn't engage with her.

Kathy recognized a while ago that the Arizona GOP was not her uncle's party anymore. She had already spent years fending off extremists and ideologues who were trying to hijack the party. In 2008, when Kathy's hero John McCain was running against Barack Obama, and rumors were swirling online about Obama being a Muslim or having a fake birth certificate, McCain wouldn't tolerate it. A woman at a campaign rally in Minnesota told McCain, "I can't trust Obama...he's an Arab." But McCain shook his head and took the microphone away from her. "No, ma'am," he corrected her. "He's a decent family-man citizen that I just happened to have disagreements with on fundamental issues, and that's what this campaign is all about." But when McCain lost and Obama became president, the conspiracy theories about him only grew more widespread and intense. By 2012, as many as 39 percent of Americans said they believed them, and the leading voice promoting them was Donald Trump.

That year, in Arizona, a new wave of Republican candidates ran on the birtherism nonsense, and the GOP-controlled state legislature passed a law requiring proof of citizenship to get on the ballot. Kathy and some of her friends decided she had to restore sanity to the party, which meant she had to start at the bottom rung: the precincts. She set out recruiting pragmatic, mainstream Republicans to fill vacant precinct committee slots, with the goal of gaining enough votes to reclaim the party leadership and demand better from their lawmakers—her own version of the strategy that Dan Schultz would later promote in that Bannon interview. An *Arizona Republic* columnist who interviewed Kathy about the plan dubbed it Operation DeKookification. In response, the state party's spokesman wrote a blog post calling Kathy's interview a "bitch session." Kathy took offense, but he had proved her point.

It was clear to Kathy from the start that Donald Trump was many things, but he was not a conservative. In the 2016 primary, she supported Ohio governor John Kasich, the only moderate in the field. As Trump started dominating in primary after primary, Republicans who objected to him and his brand of politics started organizing to keep him away from securing the party nomination.

They became known as Never Trumpers, and they worked out a plan to exploit the rules and delegate math at the Republican National Convention to deny him the prize and force a brokered convention. Kathy briefly entertained the idea, but by the time she arrived at the convention as a delegate, she had decided to vote for Trump on the first ballot. Despite all her reservations about him, she feared surrendering to the Democrats more. "I'd rather have a Trump tourniquet than a Hillary hemorrhage," she told CBS News in an interview from the arena in Cleveland, "and that's the difference here."

Kathy couldn't argue with some of Trump's policies, to the extent they were consistent with mainstream conservative positions (tax cuts and business-friendly deregulation). She didn't care for how he talked about women or immigrants or Muslims or Putin. She'd side with John McCain every time. The summer McCain died, in 2018, Kathy ran for a State House seat. She knocked so many thousands of doors in the desert heat that she lost fifteen pounds. But what chance did she, a McCain-style conservative, stand in an election that was all about Trump? That November, Republicans lost the U.S. House and one of Arizona's Senate seats. Kathy lost her race by a few thousand votes. Never mind how she personally felt about Trump, he was not delivering for the party.

It wasn't just that Trump was rude, he brought out the rudeness in his followers; they were not winning anybody over by standing on street corners with Trump signs and guns. Kathy believed that elected officials were supposed to represent everyone, not only the people who voted for them. But everything Trump did was for his base. And everything they did was for him. His cult of personality was probably the thing that bothered her most, as a big-R Republican and a small-d democrat. He didn't stand for anything but himself. There was nothing he would not do for his own aggrandizement, fame, and money, and now, for his own power, either.

She knew she wasn't alone in these views because she heard her neighbors sigh and groan about Trump. Every weekend she went out collecting signatures to get candidates on the ballot or encouraging voters to turn out for Republicans. She always wore a wide-brimmed sun hat, a star-spangled top with red letters reading VOTE that she laundered every night, and a pair of Ilse Jacobsen cushioned walking shoes, which she owned in five colors. She carried her phone on a leather bandolier (people were always asking her where she got it), and she had an app through the party telling her which houses to visit to find likely Republican voters, with a place to record notes about the interaction. On the multiple-choice list of issues that voters said were important to them, Kathy kept telling state party officials they needed to add an option for "Donald Trump," because he was the issue she kept hearing voters raise — as in, they didn't like him. By 2020, Kathy was tirelessly going door to door for the Republican Senate candidate, but she wasn't out there to defend Donald Trump. She couldn't vote for him again. She wouldn't vote for a Democrat either. Being a Republican was core to who Kathy was, and that didn't change just because she couldn't support this Republican nominee.

Since Kathy knew what America was getting with Trump, she was not surprised to hear him start lying about fraud and theft. But what she did find surprising was that *people believed him.* Even worse, in her view, were the Republican elected officials who went along with it despite knowing better — they'd just been elected themselves on the exact same ballots. The Maricopa County supervisors, whom she counted among her friends and neighbors, stood up and told the truth, did the right thing, and certified the election. Yet the party's official response was to condemn them, and they started getting harassed with violent threats.

In December 2020, right after the presidential election, Kathy faced a challenge for her party chairmanship in LD 28. This was before Bannon popularized Dan's Precinct Strategy, but already here was a woman named Nicole Garcia who had never been to a district meeting and recently moved to the state, running against Kathy for district chair. The only thing Kathy knew about Nicole Garcia was the inflammatory posts she made on social media. "Mess with my rights and my Republic and you get what you deserve. 1776," she'd posted in one. The next day, she added, "The people will overthrow this type of government and start new." Kathy trounced her, with something like 80 percent of the vote. She both kept her position and boosted her confidence that the extremism she kept seeing from Trump supporters on Twitter was not representative of her party.

Now, a few months into her new term as chair, in 2021, Kathy kept that faith through coffee after coffee where people would tell

her how she needed to watch this or read that, how they'd personally seen boatloads of ballots being delivered, or gone to a rally outside the building where county officials were counting the votes.
They told Kathy she clearly didn't know anything about how elections worked if she didn't see how the 2020 election had been
stolen.

After each coffee, Kathy would get home and look up the person's voting record. Who you vote for is secret, but whether or not
you voted is public information. Kathy found that a lot of these
people had just recently registered to vote—they'd never even
voted before! Or at least they didn't bother to vote as Republicans
in primaries. And they were lecturing her about how *she* didn't
understand the process? They'd personally seen all this fraud, and
somehow, someone who had lived and breathed politics her whole
life would fail to notice? Kathy was all for people wanting to learn
more about the process and get involved, but this was not the type of
person she thought would make a good precinct committee member.

When Kathy recruited PCs, she looked for "four-four" voters,
meaning people who voted in each of the last four elections (primaries and generals) because that's who she considered reliable
Republicans, people she'd trust to go door to door asking other
Republicans to vote. People who would be knowledgeable about
the Republican platform—trustworthy, good neighbors. People
who would protect the Republican brand. Not single-issue voters
who'd only spout conspiracy theories about election fraud. Some of
the people she had coffee with she frankly wouldn't want going
door to door for other reasons—because they'd give people the
creeps. The four-four standard was an objective criterion she could
use to say to some of these applicants, "Pleasure to meet you, good-
bye." Other times, Kathy rejected people because she found out
they'd signed petitions to recall the governor or the county supervisors. The impetus for the recall was that the officials had done their
jobs by certifying the election. That was a deal-breaker for Kathy—
PCs' job was to elect Republicans, not unelect them.

Other district chairs had a range of views on what to make of
the surge of new PCs. Kathy had a friend named Derrick Rochwalik
who was the district chair in neighboring LD 15, and he was also
getting swamped with new PCs. Derrick was young (in his late

twenties) and smart and full of energy. He was the first openly gay district chair in the Arizona GOP, and he and Kathy worked together to defeat party resolutions opposing same-sex marriage. Kathy thought Derrick could be a future party leader. She became a mentor to him, and they developed a cool aunt / little nephew dynamic of their own. That spring, Derrick sent a message to all the district chairs to ask if they too were getting crushed with new PCs. The other chairs said they were glad to see fresh faces, the party needed new blood, they didn't care what people believed, they weren't screening the applicants at all. Derrick wasn't nearly so sanguine. He was convinced the new PCs were gunning for him and Kathy.

Many of the applicants whom Kathy and Derrick rejected became PCs anyway: the county chair, a Trump loyalist, appointed them over Kathy's and Derrick's heads. Kathy and Derrick disagreed over whether this maneuver was legitimate. Every county in every state had slightly different rules. Under the party bylaws in Maricopa County, the county chair had the power to appoint replacements for *vacant* seats, meaning ones where an existing PC had left. But the county chair was now using this procedure to fill *open* seats, which had no serving PC to begin with. Kathy didn't think the bylaws allowed that, and she knew a thing or two about the bylaws, having served in the past as chairman of the county party's bylaws committee. Derrick thought the chair probably did have the authority to make the appointments. It didn't really matter — there was nothing they could do to stop it.

By May of 2021, to Kathy's disbelief, she was now going to district meetings with QAnon believers on her own committee. Many of the newcomers were fired up about a hand recount of the county's ballots commissioned by the Republican-controlled state senate. This "forensic audit," as it was called, was funded by Trump-supporting Overstock.com founder Patrick Byrne and conducted by a contractor with no experience in election audits but an openly stated conviction for election conspiracy theories. For months, the recount was live-streamed from a Phoenix arena. Contractors and volunteers examined ballots for bamboo fibers, a supposed giveaway for fake ballots from Asia. The county's Republican board of supervisors refused to cooperate with the review, calling it an "adventure in never-never land." That made them heroes in Kathy's eyes. But to her dismay, other party leaders called for throwing the supervisors in jail. In the end, even this partisan review concluded that Biden had won Arizona. To its promoters, though, that was fake news: the "audit" "proved" there were fifty-four thousand "illegal" ballots, five times Biden's margin of victory. Trump supporters in other states began demanding their own "audits" modeled after Arizona's.

In Kathy's own district, the new PCs started making mayhem like shutting down a school board meeting by refusing to wear face masks, and demonstrating outside a hotel where the government was temporarily housing legal asylum seekers. After the asylum protest, Kathy's LD lost its meeting space; the building manager told her he was sorry, but he didn't want these people in his building. "I thought we had a normal group." Kathy thought it was worse than embarrassing; it was unhealthy for the party and for American democracy. She'd always publicly announced the information for her district meetings, but now Kathy started requiring RSVPs, because all the venues she approached about holding the meeting wanted to know exactly who was coming.

In June, Derrick asked Kathy out to drinks and dinner. She knew something was up because Derrick was never the one to ask. This time he even paid. Sure enough, he had an agenda. Derrick had come up with a plan that he wanted to bring Kathy in on. Derrick was aware that the new PCs in his district wanted to recall him, and that they now had the votes. He wanted to beat them to the punch. Derrick figured out that if he and all the other party officers in LD 15 resigned together, there was no means of succession to reconstitute the district's board. The new PCs would be paralyzed.

Derrick went ahead with the plan, and it did succeed in immobilizing the committee for months. But it only emboldened the new PCs, and once they got around to reorganizing the board under new leadership, they counted the takeover as a victory for the Precinct Strategy. Kathy thought it was self-destructive for the party to be antagonizing rather than elevating young leaders such as Derrick, and she hated to see him lose his position. But she did the math in her own district, which had had fewer open slots for newcomers to seize, and she concluded her seat was safe. She knew her neighbors, she knew her district, she knew her party, and she believed they still sided with her.

ONE OF THE applicants to become a PC in Kathy's district was a woman named Merissa Hamilton. Merissa did not even get a coffee with Kathy, because Kathy looked up her voting record and saw that she hadn't voted in the 2018 Republican primary. She wasn't even a registered Republican from 2016 to 2020. Kathy knew of some more consistent voters in Merissa's precinct, so she went out and signed them up instead.

Bannon had warned the *War Room* posse that taking over the party wouldn't be easy; the establishment wouldn't give up power without a fight. Merissa felt like she was being silenced by the people in power, and she was tired of feeling that way. She especially didn't like how Kathy Petsas treated people like her who were working hard to demand answers about the 2020 election results — calling them names such as *conspiracy theorists*.

Merissa did not consider herself a Stop the Stealer; the rallies weren't for her. But she believed in a project she had launched after the 2020 election to prove the folklore that dead people had voted. Her volunteers looked up voters over age ninety and ran them through a popular credit-check database to see if they had died. They reviewed almost four thousand voters and found about 10 percent of them were identified as deceased. Yet about 10 percent of those ballots had been returned — that was forty dead voters! The group provided its findings to the state attorney general (a Republican), whose office eventually reviewed the data and concluded that only one person was in fact dead. The woman who cast that ballot, which belonged to her late mother, was later sentenced to two years of probation and a $1,730 fine. Merissa considered that a success. But her activism took a toll: in the 2022 primary, she would receive a mail ballot at her home that was addressed to an abusive ex who hadn't lived there for years. Merissa thought the county official in charge of voter registration had done that as retaliation against her dead-voter research, as opposed to an innocent mistake that happens all the time when people move without updating their voter registration. "It was just weaponized against me," she told friends.

When Merissa heard what had happened next door in LD 15, where super MAGA Trump-supporting PCs overthrew the entire establishment board, she wondered what it would take to do the same in LD 28. She approached Dan Farley, a real estate broker in LD 28 who'd been recruiting PCs across the county.

"Did you see what they did?" Merissa asked him.

"Yeah," he said.

"So what do you wanna do?"

"We're firing Petsas."

CHAPTER 5

The Virginia Model

THROUGHOUT THE SUMMER of 2021, Bannon made Dan Schultz a *War Room* regular. Bannon presented Dan as an American original, an everyman who had an idea, worked tirelessly at it, and inspired a movement. But Dan was a little *too* authentic. He would come on the air with his hand-written slides and say things like, "Conservatives suffer from CPPPDS: conservative political party participation deficit syndrome." "He's a little dry," Bannon would say. "Also, behind the scenes, Dan's got a real edge to him."

Bannon tried to raise Dan's game. Professional designers took over Dan's WordPress blog and turned it into a slick new website. Two former Hollywood guys made him a snappy one-minute promo: *"Democrats are pushing a radical Marxist agenda, while weak Republicans let it happen,"* a deep voice said over scary movie music. *"Do you feel helpless? Want to know how to fight back? Well, here's the answer."* Bannon connected Dan with a wealthy Trump donor who could help fund his cause, and Dan asked the guy if he was a precinct committeeman. He wasn't. Dan said that was the problem: "Your wealth isn't going to save you," he told the donor. Dan went back to his warning about what he believed the communists would do with people like them once they took over. "You're gonna end up in a camp unless you do this."

Bannon and Dan's alliance started to fray. Dan was always

harping on the hundreds of thousands of precinct slots that remained unfilled, whereas Bannon thought people needed to feel some wins. Dan would bug him at three in the morning, asking why Bannon wasn't having him on the show more, and finally Bannon snapped, *Because you SUCK as a salesman.* He was putting the audience into a coma. Dan went off to other shows, even fringier than Bannon's. He talked with hosts who were hawking cryptocurrencies, who said the September 11 terrorist attacks were an inside job, even the original QAnon influencer, a woman in South Carolina named Tracy Diaz, who went by the screen name Beanz. Dan thought QAnon was ridiculous, some guys in a basement making stuff up, but that did not stop him from doing interviews on QAnon shows; maybe he could convert QAnon followers into Republican precinct committee members. After talking with Dan, Beanz and her supporters showed up at their local GOP meeting in Myrtle Beach and elected her to the state party executive committee.

Bannon would assure Dan he was already a legend — people knew his name, they'd mention his book, they'd call it Dan Schultz's Precinct Strategy. But, Bannon told him, he needed a marketing guy. "You're not the marketing guy." In Broward County, Florida, Bannon found a born salesman named Steve Stern. Bannon called Stern the most ambitious eighty-year-old he'd ever met. Bannon actually liked getting texts from him at four thirty in the morning. He was like the exact opposite of Dan; he was "Mr. Happy Clappy... Mr. Glass Half Full." He appeared on *War Room* modeling the patriotic apparel he sold online: a billowing American flag across the torso, like a sash, and wedges of the Declaration of Independence on the shoulders.

Bannon's other partner in promoting the Precinct Strategy was John Fredericks, a talk radio host whose show aired daily in Georgia and Virginia. Fredericks lacked the national profile of the late Rush Limbaugh, his successor Dan Bongino, or young stars like Charlie Kirk and Ben Shapiro. But he was an influential regional voice who mattered in races for county offices, state legislatures, congressional seats, and statewide offices like attorney general and governor. Talk radio reached more than 15 million Americans, overwhelmingly right wing, and every red state had a handful of talk radio hosts who could be kingmakers in local Republican politics. When Trump was in office, his political team had recognized the importance of hosts like Fredericks and invited them into the White House briefing room or showered them with access to the president and his advisers and family members.

Bannon considered Fredericks a genius. They shared a heterodox political orientation that didn't fit neatly into either party, and they both despised the establishment GOP. The throughline of their worldview was to pit the left-behind working man against the profiteering global elite. Fredericks was not averse to praising Democrats (he enjoyed watching Massachusetts Senator Elizabeth Warren beat up on bank executives), and he self-identified not as a Republican but as a Trump supporter. There was no Trump offense he wouldn't defend: "grab them by the pussy" was "gross bad-boy banter — nothing more"; "shithole countries" was "not about race... it's about economics." Fredericks took his cues from the listeners who called into his show, a resource that led him to predict on the air, long before Trump became the Republican nominee — before he even officially announced he was running — that Trump would win the White House.

Fredericks grew up in Madison, New Jersey, west of Newark, with a stutter so strong he couldn't answer the phone. He worked his way through college as a horse trainer because the job didn't require talking. Then he decided he would never overcome his stutter unless he confronted it, so he set out to become a teacher. He got laughed out of one interview. Finally he found a job at a for-profit business school. Schools like that catered to low-income people trying to improve their lot, and were often accused of being scams; Trump had one once. Fredericks's class had about thirty students — Black and Latino, single mothers, former inmates. "Maybe we can get through this together," Fredericks told them. They didn't judge him. They rooted for him. It changed his life.

As his stutter abated, Fredericks left teaching to become an advertising executive with the McClatchy newspaper chain, the parent company of big-city dailies including the *Miami Herald* and the *Sacramento Bee*, along with papers in Kansas, Kentucky, and Idaho. For decades these properties had been cash cows, but their business model collapsed as the internet sapped paid subscriptions and local classified ads. Fredericks noticed a different trend: that the papers' editorial pages tended to be more liberal than their core suburban readers, and were alienating those subscribers. He saw a business opportunity. He and his wife put their life's savings into founding *The Beacon*, a new right-leaning weekly newspaper in Atlanta's north suburbs, to compete with the *Atlanta Journal-Constitution*. It was 2007, just as the Great Recession was about to gut commercial advertising and plunge the newspaper industry into a full-blown crisis. Fredericks lost a million dollars, shut down the paper, and declared bankruptcy. In 2011, he landed at the local newspaper in Newport News, Virginia, and tried moving their editorial page to the right, but he didn't get along with management and lasted only six months. Fredericks lost his home and moved his family into a day-rate motel outside Atlanta. He worked odd jobs to scrape by: cutting grass, parking cars, mopping floors.

In those years, Fredericks watched his family suffer while the Democrat-run government bailed out the banks, and his personal politics moved further right. At the same time, the economic and technological changes that put his newspaper out of business were devastating local news across America, leaving behind a vacuum of professional, nonpartisan political coverage and scrutiny of local government. But there remained a place for radio, catching people in their cars, kitchens, and break rooms. Regional talk radio was a blue-collar medium, a way to reach people who were too busy with work and family to watch the Fox News prime-time lineup. Fredericks had been onto something with his political bent; he'd just been in the wrong medium at the wrong time. He and his wife put together another business plan, and in 2012 he started broadcasting in an afternoon slot on an AM station in the Hampton Roads area of Virginia. At last, Fredericks struck commercial success, and in becoming a radio host, reached the final stage of beating his stutter.

Fredericks woke up every day at three-thirty, put on a suit and tie, and went into his studio to prepare to take to the air at six. He blamed this grueling routine for putting on thirty pounds, but he made light of his weight gain by dubbing himself the Godzilla of Truth. He got connected with Bannon through Trump's 2016 campaign, for which Fredericks was the Virginia state chairman and a delegate to the RNC. After the election, Bannon gave an interview attributing Trump's surprise victory to the nation's uneven recovery from the 2008 financial crisis, which Bannon said had fractured the country into haves and have-nots. When Fredericks first read it, he thought, *Oh my God, Stephen K. Bannon is talking about me. That was me. I went through that. I experienced that. He got it! He got why we're "deplorables." He got why the working class got screwed. And he got why Trump won.* He kept a copy of the article in his office and reread it every morning, to remind himself what he was doing and why.

In 2019, Fredericks had been following this routine for seven years and was watching Sunday football on his day off. His wife, who ran the business side, came in and said she'd spoken with Bannon and he wanted to start a radio show. At halftime, Fredericks called Bannon back, like, "What the hell?" and Bannon said, "Dude, I wanna start a radio show: *War Room: Impeachment.* I want to start it Tuesday." It was Sunday afternoon! But Fredericks's wife said they could do it. Somehow they cobbled together some microphones and got them up to D.C. to set up in the basement of the Breitbart Embassy. Fredericks gave Bannon some airtime on his radio network, and that was the start of Bannon's *War Room.*

As 2019 turned into 2020, *War Room: Impeachment* became *War Room: Pandemic,* and Bannon and Fredericks frequently appeared as guests on each other's shows. The cross-promotion continued even as Bannon's reach far outgrew Fredericks's. After the 2020 election, Fredericks spent eight weeks camped out in Georgia, covering the two U.S. Senate runoffs. He told the White House what his callers were telling him: Trump supporters weren't going to turn out to vote for the incumbent Republican Senate candidates, David Perdue and Kelly Loeffler, unless Perdue and Loeffler fought for President Trump to keep him in the White House.

The runoffs caught the two incumbents in a bind. With control of the Senate hanging in the balance, the obvious move was for them to run on checks and balances, to present themselves as the last line of defense against unified Democratic control of Washington. But saying that would acknowledge that Trump had lost, that he was leaving office. Trump wouldn't like that, and the senators needed him to come campaign for them. Many congressional Republicans and campaign professionals would blame Trump for losing those two pivotal Senate seats by telling his supporters their votes didn't count and thus suppressing their turnout.

The lesson John Fredericks learned from the Georgia runoffs was that Trump supporters had lost faith in the system, and if that meant 5 to 10 percent of them stayed home, Republicans would keep losing. Fredericks's solution for people who didn't trust the system was to bring them inside the system. If they didn't believe in the party, they had to *become* the party. Once Dan Schultz supplied the blueprint, Fredericks became the leading cheerleader for the Precinct Strategy throughout Georgia's party reorganization process in the spring of 2021. He brought Salleigh Grubbs on his show to celebrate her victory in Cobb County. "Talk about action, action, action," Fredericks said. "Salleigh Grubbs is like a superhero in Trumpworld, in the deplorables' world of getting things done."

Now Fredericks turned his attention to the other state on his home turf, Virginia, which had an off-year governor's race coming up in November 2021. Fredericks had in the past supported the Democratic nominee, Terry McAuliffe; he even called him "Terry McGenius" during his previous term as governor, for bringing jobs to the state and expanding Medicaid. But now Fredericks was all-in for the Republican, Glenn Youngkin. Youngkin, a former private equity executive, was not Bannon's type: "total globalist, in business with the CCP" (Chinese Communist Party). And Virginia was increasingly looking like a blue state; Biden had won it by ten points. But sometime over the spring and summer, Virginia captured Bannon's interest. Angry parents were showing up to school board meetings, demanding to end mask mandates and restrict classroom materials about race and sexuality. Inflation was beginning to creep up from higher gas prices and pandemic supply-chain bottlenecks. Biden's legislative ambitions stalled because of Democratic infighting in Congress. And then thirteen American service members died in the chaotic U.S. withdrawal from Afghanistan, as the Taliban swiftly retook the country after twenty years of American investment. Biden's approval rating sank into negative territory and never recovered. With this much backlash to Democratic rule, even Virginia looked winnable, and Bannon knew the message an upset there would send.

Fredericks warned him Republicans had a problem. He said Virginia would be another Georgia. "Unless people are convinced that their vote is going to count and not be cheated, they won't turn out," Fredericks told Bannon privately. "We're going to lose in Virginia because of this." What were they gonna say? *Just kidding, we lied, elections aren't rigged, you have to vote?*

Bannon and Fredericks were not alone in coming to this realization. A parallel conversation was occurring at the top level of the party structure, the Republican National Committee. The RNC hired Kellyanne Conway, the Republican pollster and Trump adviser, to survey GOP voters on how many believed the election had been stolen. The result was 70 percent. The party's national chair, Ronna McDaniel, began telling associates that she'd have to make "election integrity" a top priority. She impaneled a special committee to review the party's "election integrity" efforts. Her stated goal, to "restore confidence in America's elections," could sound a bit rich, considering it was Trump and the Republicans who'd just torched that confidence. But it was actually sincere in the sense that the party leaders recognized they had a problem if people concluded their votes didn't count and stayed home; the party had to find a way to assure voters who believed the 2020 election had been stolen that they could trust the next election enough to participate. The committee concluded that the RNC should dispatch full-time "election integrity directors" to all the key swing states.

They got started in the Virginia governor's race, where there was already a groundswell of grassroots activity focused on monitoring the polls. Those efforts reflected how the Precinct Strategy was working exactly as Bannon had hoped: once he got people in the door at their local party meetings, the local party would take it from there, providing its own structure and momentum. County GOPs were chartering their own "election integrity subcommittees" to pore over voter rolls, scrutinize their county registrars' practices, and sign people up as poll watchers and poll workers. As the grassroots infrastructure joined forces with the Youngkin campaign and the RNC, Virginia became the test case for the ground war that Bannon and Fredericks were fielding. This off-year election would be their first chance to prove that the MAGA movement could be a winning electoral banner.

In October 2021, a few weeks before the Virginia gubernatorial election, Fredericks hosted an election integrity–themed rally for Youngkin in a packed suburban Richmond restaurant. Bannon would be there too, and the even bigger draw would be a call-in from Trump. The rally began with a Pledge of Allegiance to an American flag that, the emcee said, "was carried at the peaceful rally with Donald J. Trump on January 6." The crowd cheered and clapped and whistled before rising for the solemn pledge.

Youngkin wasn't at the rally, though he'd called into Fredericks's show two days earlier, thanking him for organizing the event. Soon after, on the campaign trail, he confronted reporters asking him about the insurrection flag. "I wasn't involved and so I don't know," he demurred. "But if that is the case, then we shouldn't pledge allegiance to *that* flag." The campaign followed up with a statement calling the pledge to the January 6 flag "weird and wrong."

Fredericks and Bannon understood what Youngkin was doing. He'd been walking this tightrope the whole campaign. To win a state that Trump had just lost by ten points, Youngkin had to both mobilize Trump's rural base and make himself more acceptable to suburban moderates. He avoided saying either that Biden had stolen the election or that he'd legitimately won. He dodged a question on how he would have voted had he been in Congress on January 6. He campaigned with a state senator who'd been censured by her colleagues for calling the rioters patriots, and joined her calls for election audits. When a woman outside his campaign office asked Youngkin about the conspiracy theory that Trump could somehow be reinstated as president that fall, Youngkin seemed to entertain the fantasy. "Ma'am, I don't know the particulars about how that can happen, because what's happening in the court system is moving slowly and it's unclear," he said. His campaign tried to clean it up as "politely" correcting the supporter.

"Here's what Glenn Youngkin has done, which is brilliant," Fredericks reassured his listeners in a segment with Bannon right after the flag controversy. "When they say, 'Well, Glenn Youngkin doesn't talk about voter integrity,' obviously Glenn Youngkin believes that the election in 2020 got stolen. Because he's pouring millions and millions of dollars into Virginia to set up a voter integrity infrastructure that will stand the test of time. That is the brilliance of his campaign. If he didn't think there was voting fraud, he wouldn't be setting up this model, which now the RNC has embraced, in order to take national."

"He's speaking with his actions," Bannon agreed. "He knows they stole it and that they'll steal it again. That's what every Republican out there should understand: even if Glenn Youngkin's not your cup of tea, you don't think he's embraced President Trump enough, they're doing the things that have to be done right now, to make sure we're serious about not having another stolen election."

It didn't take long on that Election Night, November 2, 2021, to find out if Youngkin's high-wire act had worked. He outperformed Trump's 2020 tallies in rural counties *and* suburban counties. There was a counting problem in Fairfax County, the state's biggest and bluest; a technical glitch forced officials to rescan some twenty thousand early ballots, delaying the results. Republicans started murmuring, *The Steal was happening again!* "All eyes are on Fairfax, why the delay?" Trump demanded in a statement. But soon McAuliffe conceded, Youngkin declared victory, and no one cared about the Fairfax glitch anymore (which had been fixed quickly anyway).

There was something exciting but also threatening about Youngkin's victory. He showed the possibility of a Republican future without Trump. What if any old Republican could adapt the MAGA playbook and make it work for them? Just like the Precinct Strategy was getting away from Dan, many Republicans were wondering if the MAGA movement was getting away from Trump. The movement was becoming more institutional, which made it more durable. But where did that leave Trump, still in political hibernation, hidden from the headlines he used to dominate? Could figures like Bannon and Fredericks become power centers independent of him?

"This is the shout-out to the entire *War Room* posse, whether it's the Precinct Committeeman Strategy, whether it was being an election official," Bannon spun the win on his show the next morning. "This is the coalition that works...Youngkin came toward our policies, these policies that were the backbone of this."

"It shows you, MAGA voters control the party," Fredericks agreed. "They control everything if they get out and they vote."

"Let me tell you the other thing we learned. Be a poll watcher, be an election official, get trained," Fredericks said. "There was an infrastructure of 'stop the cheat' in place. As soon as Fairfax County was going down, lawyers were on it. We Stopped that Steal. There were simply too many eyes on it for them to cheat. And that's a big thing. That's the model, Steve, going forward."

CHAPTER 6

Red Wave

DAN SCHULTZ DEVELOPED barometers to forecast America's chances of stopping socialism: his website traffic, his book orders, and sign-ups for precinct committeeman positions. He watched these indexes rise throughout 2021, but he still thought the levels were not nearly high enough. He could go on these shows and keep saying, "This works, it's seventh-grade civics and it's very easy to do," and people would think, "Who the hell is Dan Schultz?" He realized he needed a platform bigger than Bannon's. He needed a messenger better than himself. He needed Donald Trump.

Trump had, throughout 2021, started taking more deliberate steps toward a rematch with Biden. He survived the Senate impeachment trial and received conciliatory visits to Mar-a-Lago from the leader of the House Republicans, Kevin McCarthy, and the head of the Senate Republicans' campaign arm, Rick Scott. Then Trump gathered strength from the disastrous Afghanistan withdrawal and from Youngkin's triumph in the Virginia governor's race that November. Trump still lacked his megaphone on mainstream social media, and he maintained only a skeleton crew of political advisers huddled around him at Mar-a-Lago. But he was sitting on a hundred million dollars in his political action committee, much of it raised by promising his supporters to fight the "stolen" 2020 election. And he resumed holding his signature mega-rallies, bringing those crowds in on his plans for revenge. They'd start with ousting the ten House Republicans who'd voted to impeach him after the January 6 riot.

Trump's instrument for reasserting his primacy in Republican politics would be making endorsements in the 2022 primaries. Candidates fell over themselves to play along. As early as March 2021, contenders for an Ohio Senate seat flew to Trump's golf club to stage a private debate for an audience of one, like a scene out of *The Apprentice* or even *The Hunger Games*. Later on in the year, two rivals for Senate in Pennsylvania, both fueling their campaigns with their own personal wealth, launched an arms race for hiring former Trump advisers in the hopes of securing the former president's support. The going rate for a campaign to hire a Trump associate to lobby him for an endorsement was ten thousand dollars a month; one consultant pulled in two hundred thousand (and didn't deliver).

Campaigns could hire all the Trump White House alumni money could buy, but the candidates knew what they had to do: they had to talk about the Rigged and Stolen Election. As a result, Trump ended up backing a lot of first-time candidates with unorthodox backgrounds. To challenge Senator Mark Kelly of Arizona, Trump endorsed Blake Masters (a former aide to iconoclastic tech billionaire Peter Thiel), who made a campaign video of himself shooting guns in the desert and called the Unabomber an "underrated" thinker. To challenge Democratic attorney general Josh Shapiro for governor of Pennsylvania, Trump endorsed Doug Mastriano, a state senator who had become a *War Room* fixture while trying to override the state's electors in 2020. To challenge Michigan governor Gretchen Whitmer: Tudor Dixon, who hosted a show on Real America's Voice, the same right-wing streaming channel that aired Bannon's *War Room*. In North Carolina: a congressional candidate who attended the rally on January 6 and had been accused of domestic violence.

These were not the candidates who gave experienced Republican campaign professionals a ton of confidence. But Trump would fete them with rallies, heralding them as the Trump Ticket. And looking ahead to the midterms, 2022 was a year that seemed to offer Republicans every historic advantage: an unpopular Democratic president, inflation at a forty-year high, freshly gerrymandered

House districts in GOP-controlled states, leads in voter registration, and polling advantages on voter enthusiasm and the generic ballot. In such an environment, Republicans could reasonably expect to withstand some relatively weak individual campaigners and still win handily.

Dan imagined what would happen if Trump got up at one of his rallies and asked for a show of hands for who in the crowd was a precinct committeeman. He was sure if he could just get twenty minutes with the former president—ten minutes, four minutes—he could convince him to endorse the Precinct Strategy. He asked the Arizona GOP to see if someone could help him get in touch with Trump. He asked around about raising money to place an ad in *The Wall Street Journal*, whose coverage Trump was known to pay attention to. He thought about staking out Trump on the golf course, or chartering a plane to fly a banner up and down the beach at Mar-a-Lago, saying "PrecinctStrategy.com for DJT."

Steve Stern, the flag-shirt salesman Bannon had found in Florida, came through with a different tack. His son-in-law's neighbor was friends with a woman who worked for Trump (got it?), so she invited Steve over to Mar-a-Lago to have lunch, in December 2021. They were lingering at the table for a couple hours when guess who strode into the dining room, fresh off the golf course? He came over because he seemed to recognize someone in the group, maybe the woman carrying a blue and white bedazzled purse reading JE✡IT. She worked with an organization called Jexit (consisting mainly of her and a few friends) that encouraged Jewish Americans to leave the Democratic Party and join the GOP. Trump chatted with her for a bit about what she was doing on the Jewish vote, and how she was going to give Trump an award. Then Steve Stern got a word in and asked Trump if he knew about the Precinct Strategy. Trump said he did not, and invited Steve to set up an appointment to come back and talk about it.

Trump's invitation did not immediately turn into an actual appointment. Trumpworld was like that: there were official channels (his staff) and unofficial channels (everyone he called on the phone or ran into at his club), and one side often didn't know what the other was doing. Steve and Dan went back to working their connections. They did an hour-long interview on Mike Lindell's online talk show, after which Lindell sent Steve a pile of pillows and towels, and promised to talk to Trump directly about the Precinct Strategy.

Finally Bannon arranged a conference call between them and Liz Harrington, a former editor for his *War Room* website who'd gone on to join Trump's small proto-campaign. She functioned as a liaison to the *War Room* posse and fringier corners of the MAGA-verse. Even within Trump's small circle of political advisers at that time, many of them had never heard about the Precinct Strategy or the lobbying for Trump to endorse it. After the call, Dan drafted a statement. He kept it short. He wrote it in Trump's voice, to go out in Trump's name. But Steve and Dan never got to go in for an appointment, or to hear Trump say he understood the Precinct Strategy and wanted his supporters to follow it. They could not even be sure if he ever read the statement before his political operation blasted it out to his millions of followers.

"Just heard about an incredible effort underway that will strengthen the Republican Party," it said. "If members of our Great movement start getting involved (that means YOU becoming a precinct committeeman for your voting precinct), we can take back our great Country from the ground up...Make America Great Again!"

LEADING UP TO the first anniversary of the January 6 attack on the Capitol, Trump planned to mark the occasion with a press conference at Mar-a-Lago. The House of Representatives had chartered a special committee to investigate the attack, and the panel was hauling in Trump's aides to testify or threatening them with criminal contempt. Federal prosecutors had arrested hundreds of rioters, already the largest criminal investigation in U.S. history, and at that point it remained unclear whether they would ever push the probe beyond the people in the mob to examine the actions of Trump and his advisers who had pointed them at the Capitol. Trump's response to the prosecutions of his supporters for breaking into the Capitol and assaulting police officers was to portray them as patriots being persecuted for their political views. "Political prisoners" was the term. *"There are people that are being held prisoner very unfairly, and that should not be allowed to happen,"* Trump said in September 2021 at a rally in Perry, Georgia, where he'd gone to promote primary challengers to the sitting governor and secretary of state, who'd resisted his pressure to overturn the 2020 election. *"There was no reason to kill Ashli Babbitt,"* he added, of the rioter who was shot by police while trying to break into the House chamber. *"No reason whatsoever. Our hearts are with that group."*

Cheering from the VIP section (next to Angela Deem, the Trump-supporting star of *90 Day Fiancé*) was Salleigh Grubbs. She wore a name tag on her Trump T-shirt identifying her as the chairwoman of the Cobb County Republican Party. Now, as Trump's January 6 press conference approached, some of her committee members wanted to hold a livestream, followed by some speeches and a prayer. Salleigh agreed to put out an announcement: "Cobb GOP Commemorates January 6 2021 Anniversary with Candlelight Vigil for J6 Prisoners."

The *Atlanta Journal-Constitution* got hold of the announcement and ran with the headline "Cobb 'Homage to Treason' planned for Jan. 6," quoting a Democratic state representative. The article began: "A group of far-right activists will hold a two-hour long program Thursday to lionize the insurrectionists who stampeded into the Capitol to prevent Congress from certifying Joe Biden's victory…"

Salleigh hated being called far-right. She wondered, when did beliefs such as limited government, personal accountability, God, and country become "far-right"? But she knew she'd messed up. "Commemorates" wasn't the right word. "Remembers" would have been better. She tried to explain that the intention was "to acknowledge Americans who lost their lives and pray for those who have been denied justice." By the former, Salleigh meant people like Ashli Babbitt and Rosanne Boyland, a young woman from nearby Kennesaw who also died on January 6, crushed under a heap of bodies on the Capitol steps. Boyland's family went on TV, saying she had been "radicalized" by QAnon. Salleigh didn't think so. She thought it was unfortunate that people could get too wrapped up in out-there stuff online. But she understood people being concerned for their country.

By "those who have been denied justice," Salleigh meant people being held in jail without charges. In fact there were no such people. Some were being held in pretrial detention, at the order of a judge, following the same procedure as for any other criminal defendant. But on *War Room* and the other websites and podcasts where Salleigh got her news, the plight of these inmates had become a cause célèbre. Salleigh tried clarifying the intention of the vigil.

She told the press, "Under no uncertain terms are we condoning any form of violence nor the glorification of what happened at the United States Capitol on January 6, 2021. This miscarriage of justice should concern ALL AMERICANS." But it wasn't salvageable. Seeing how the planned event was being characterized, Salleigh encouraged her members to pray on their own. The vigil was canceled. (Trump ended up canceling his event, too, providing a similar explanation: "the Fake News Media.")

Salleigh got that politics is rough; everyone's a critic. She wasn't surprised to catch some blowback from Jason Shepherd, her predecessor as county chair, who'd recently resigned from the committee to protest a resolution censuring Governor Brian Kemp. But she didn't expect such a huge reaction—the newspaper saying she supported treason, people calling her from as far away as New York saying, *How could you do that?* She even talked to the assistant police chief about keeping a watch on her house. Her sons were worried for her safety.

Salleigh was out at political meetings almost every night, sometimes till eleven or midnight. Her ninety-four-year-old mother would call demanding to know when she'd be home, saying she's a woman driving a nice car and there were people out there who'd want to hurt her. She was so busy she missed meals. Her psoriasis was flaring up, but she didn't want to take the doctor-prescribed treatments. (Salleigh caught COVID shortly after becoming chair, after refusing to take the vaccine. A year earlier, she'd been appreciatively watching Dr. Fauci's briefings. Now she treated her infection with hydroxychloroquine and ivermectin, remedies that Trump promoted despite research showing no benefit.) She didn't need this stress. She could have been home watching *Yellowstone*. She wouldn't be doing this if she thought she had a choice. But then Salleigh thought about her grandson...At last, she had a grandson. Her son had decided to have a child after all. He'd come in December, a Christmas miracle, and it broke her heart that she couldn't be there to watch him be born, to be with her own son on the best day of his life, because the hospital was still restricting visitors—almost a year after the vaccine that was supposed to end the pandemic. That's why she couldn't stop. She was doing this for her grandson.

After the commemoration fiasco, the thing that finally cheered Salleigh up was a surprise phone call from someone she admired. Marjorie Taylor Greene was a freshman congresswoman from

Georgia who'd been stripped of her committee assignments for her history of offensive social media posts, but she was a rising star in MAGA world. In redistricting just completed after the 2020 census, Greene's district had been redrawn to include part of Cobb County, and she called Salleigh to ask if she could meet her new constituents at the next party breakfast. As Salleigh introduced Greene, the crowd shouted, "We love you!" and "You go, girl!"

Greene started speaking about how she'd just returned from Washington, where most House Republicans had skipped Speaker Pelosi's memorial for January 6, and Greene instead held her own press conference suggesting that the riot was an FBI setup. "We're asking the hard questions that the Democrats and two sorry Republicans, Liz Cheney and Adam Kinzinger, will not ask," Greene said at the breakfast, referring to the Republican members of the House committee investigating the attack. "They need January 6, they need the lie to continue, so that they can try their best to try to hold onto the House this coming year in this election."

Before long, Greene's comments at Salleigh's meeting became the official position of the Republican Party. In February, the Republican National Committee approved a formal resolution censuring Cheney and Kinzinger. "Representatives Cheney and Kinzinger have engaged in actions in their positions as members of the January 6th Select Committee not befitting Republican members of Congress, which seem intent on advancing a political agenda to buoy the Democrat Party's bleak prospects in the upcoming midterm elections," the resolution read. It accused the two of "participating in a Democrat-led persecution of ordinary citizens engaged in legitimate political discourse."

In Washington, the backlash was swift. Cheney tweeted a video of the riot, a montage of violent combat with police, saying, "This is not 'legitimate political discourse.'" Senators Mitch McConnell, Mitt Romney, and Susan Collins all criticized the censure resolution. But they were never supposed to be the constituency that the resolution was speaking for. The top of the pyramid was responding to the base of the pyramid. The resolution was for Salleigh Grubbs and Dan Schultz and Steve Stern and the Precinct Strategy activists who were now filling up the party ranks around the country. "Outside of the D.C. bubble," an RNC spokeswoman said, "our grassroots are very supportive of the decision."

*   *   *

THE VIRGINIA GOVERNOR'S election was a wake-up call for Navin Nayak. As the president and executive director of the CAP Action Fund, the advocacy and political arm of the Center for American Progress, a prominent liberal think tank, Navin had a major role in conducting public opinion research to help Democrats shape their campaign messages, and he'd already become concerned that the way Democrats were talking about Republicans wasn't working. Glenn Youngkin's win, along with the closer-than-expected reelection of Democratic New Jersey governor Phil Murphy on the same day, portended disaster for the Democrats in the 2022 midterms, on top of the well-established historical pattern of the president's party usually losing seats in Congress. The Democrats had none to spare, hanging onto the slimmest majorities in both chambers — too slim even to advance most of the president's agenda while they still technically had unified control. Biden's signature infrastructure and social spending package was stalled, and federal legislation to counter state-level Republican voting restrictions was dead, unable to break a Senate filibuster. Progressive activists were deflated: even though the Democrats had won the 2020 election, it felt like they'd lost.

As bleak as the Democrats' prospects in the midterms looked, the stakes were even more distressing. There was an understanding — more of a dread, really — among the party's top leaders and donors that the 2024 presidential election would be won or lost in the 2022 midterms: that the widely anticipated "red wave" would sweep into power election deniers determined to block Democrats from winning future elections, including in the pivotal swing states that would decide the Electoral College. Of special concern were candidates for secretary of state, the statewide officers who oversaw administrative functions such as corporate registrations and elections. These races were not usually high profile, but now Republicans were chasing them with Trump-backed candidates who vowed they would not have certified the 2020 election results, and, if they held those positions in 2024, could use them to remove voting machines, purge voter rolls, relocate polling locations, and, if a Democrat still managed to win, withhold the formal certification needed to award electoral votes.

Yet in the face of this mortal danger to the party and democracy itself, Democrats seemed at a loss for how to talk about voting rights or January 6 or protecting democracy. The consensus at the time among Democratic operatives was that January 6 was an inside-the-Beltway concern, too distant or abstract for real, regular voters to care about.

There was no agreement about what the Democrats' message against Republicans should be instead. In Navin's analysis, they were all over the map—there was no consistency. With Trump not on the ballot, not on Twitter, and not in the news nearly as much as he'd been for the previous five years, trying to make the 2022 election about him was not going to work. McAuliffe had tried tying Youngkin to Trump, but it didn't stick. Glenn Youngkin didn't look like Trump, he didn't talk like Trump or act like Trump, and he had mostly managed to avoid engaging with the whole idea of Trump. "If we were going to defy history, in terms of the president's party losing a significant number of seats," Navin would later say, "then we had to find a way to turn the election into a choice and be clear about what the threat was on the other side."

When Navin started working in Washington two decades earlier, twenty-eight senators represented states that had voted for the opposing party's presidential nominee; by 2021 it was down to six. "People increasingly vote for one jersey up and down the ticket," he observed, and Republicans showed admirable discipline in how they attacked Democrats, historically, as tax-and-spend, big-government liberals or, more recently, as radical socialists. The Republicans had succeeded in making the Democratic brand a liability for politicians in many parts of the country, and Navin wanted to turn that around—to damage the Republicans' brand. He started commissioning polls, focus groups, and "large-scale qualitative" research (using machine learning to analyze written responses from thousands of voters) to assess voters' attitudes toward the Republican Party.

Navin embarked on this project with several veteran Democratic pollsters—Geoff Garin of Hart Research, and Jefrey Pollock and Matt Canter of the firm Global Strategy Group—as well as Oren Shur of left-leaning public affairs firm SKDK and Anita Dunn, a top Democratic strategist who was in and out of the Biden White House. To Matt, their regular conference calls were fun as a huddle for a small group of people who'd worked closely together for a long time, but they were also frustrating to the extent that their work ran the risk of being an intellectual exercise that might never lead to actionable ideas or, even more dimly, real electoral success. Matt shared Navin's conviction that what the Democrats had been saying wasn't working, and he felt strongly that as Republicans increasingly painted Democrats as radical and extreme, they couldn't let that go unanswered. If one party consistently called the other extreme and the other party responded by saying nothing, what would voters be left to conclude? Yet it was not as though portraying your opponent as extreme was easy or even necessarily effective; almost a decade earlier, when congressional Republicans were holding the federal debt ceiling hostage to insist on government spending cuts, Matt's own firm had conducted research suggesting that labeling Republicans as "radical" or "extreme" did not work, and Democrats should not try it.

But now, the group's research quickly started producing some early yet clear findings. People believed the Republican Party had changed in recent years, and the overwhelming majority of them thought the change had been for the worse—including independents, by a fifty-four-point margin. The rap on Republicans being the party of the wealthy was still there, but there were new themes emerging: that Republicans were power-hungry and willing to break the rules to gain or keep power.

That presented an opportunity, Navin thought, to reframe the election around how the Republican Party had changed for the worse. Democrats would need to drive that point home to voters and strengthen their perceptions of Republicans as power-hungry and ruthless. They would need to find the right words to capture those concerns—that Republicans were different, extreme and dangerous. On a conference call that winter, Navin had an idea. He asked the team, had anyone ever tested "MAGA"?

CHAPTER 7

Karizona

KATHY PETSAS HAD a feeling that something was off as soon as she walked into the meeting of Republican legislative district chairs from across Maricopa County in February of 2022. The district chairs were the rung of the party ladder between the precincts and the county; these were the people who'd shrugged off Derrick's concerns about the new PCs, right up until the moment the newcomers had ousted him.

Usually, the county party met downtown at the state party headquarters, which Kathy's uncle had built. But the state party had recently decided to sell the building (the stated reason was that the building was falling apart, but Kathy viewed it as a political statement). Now the meetings bounced around other locations. At each one, the county chair, Mickie Niland, presided and assigned the seating. Since Mickie was no fan of Kathy's, she usually sat her off to one side of the room or the other. But today Kathy was seated dead center. She had to wonder what that was about.

The meeting went on with the usual party business, nothing terribly eventful, until the end. Then Mickie announced there were two complaints against committee members. Some of the members groaned. These formal reprimands had become a preoccupation for new party members since 2021. The Hillsdale County, Michigan, Republican Party censured the state's Republican senate majority leader for calling armed protesters who'd stormed the State Capitol "a bunch of jackasses." The Wyoming Republican Party censured Liz Cheney for voting to impeach Trump on incitement of insurrection, and the Piscataquis County, Maine, Republican Committee censured Senator Susan Collins for voting to convict. The Washington County, Pennsylvania, GOP censured Senator Pat Toomey for the same; the county chair explained, "We did not send him there to 'do the right thing' or whatever." The Nevada Republican Party censured their secretary of state for "irresponsible public statements regarding the fairness of the 2020 election" (meaning she'd said the election was fair). The Dorchester County, South Carolina, Republican Party censured Senator Lindsey Graham for supporting the Biden administration's bipartisan infrastructure bill that would bring six billion dollars to the state. The Medina County Republican Party and the Pecos County Republican Party in Texas censured Congressman Tony Gonzales for supporting gay marriage. The Republican Party of Jessamine County, Kentucky, censured Senate Minority Leader Mitch McConnell for supporting a bipartisan bill, after the May 2022 massacre at an elementary school in Uvalde, Texas, to strengthen background checks on gun buyers and expand funding for school security and mental health.

The effect of these official rebukes, depending on the local party rules, could be to strip party members of their ability to participate in party meetings or to withhold campaign funds from politicians running for reelection. Mostly the resolutions were a black eye, and in politics, appearances are everything. Kathy and her allies on the Maricopa County committee thought the party had better ways to spend its time nine months before an election than arguing over whether to chastise fellow Republicans. But there were other members, newer members, who were eager to hear the complaint resolutions.

The first motion was against a Republican PC who, in his day job, was head of a firefighters union that had voted to endorse a local candidate who was not a Republican. The complaint alleged that he'd broken a party bylaw prohibiting PCs from making endorsements opposing Republicans. The second complaint that Mickie Niland announced alleged a violation of this same provision. The second complaint was against Kathy Petsas.

"What the heck?" Kathy blurted out. "What are you talking about?"

Mickie started to explain that the complaint had to do with Nicole Garcia, the woman who'd run against Kathy for district chair in December 2020 — the one who'd posted online about overthrowing the government. Right after losing the chairman's race to Kathy, in December 2020, Garcia tried to win a seat on the Phoenix city council. The city council race was technically nonpartisan, as local elections in Arizona always were. Still, the incumbent, a woman named Debra Stark, was a registered Democrat. A local news reporter called to ask Kathy about the race, and Kathy had said something complimentary about Stark. "This is what you want out of your leaders," she'd said. "You want them to find ways they are going to collaborate and figure out what's best for the communities that they serve." As for Garcia, Kathy said she knew her only by her tweets, and based on that: "She's combative and she doesn't listen to facts when presented to her."

Now, a year later, these members of the county Republican committee were saying Kathy's quote had amounted to endorsing a Democrat, in violation of the county party's bylaws. It was an ambush. The committee voted to hold an "executive session" to adjudicate the complaint.

Kathy spent the whole twenty-minute drive home taking calls from her friends in the party telling her how ridiculous and outrageous this all was. Kathy was disgusted that she, who'd put in more time knocking doors, licking envelopes, and doing other electoral grunt work than any of the people accusing her, was not a "real Republican" in their eyes, just because she would not accept a former president's lie. Now they would be the ones to sit in judgment of her: her credentials as a conservative, her value as a party volunteer.

She couldn't imagine a bigger waste of time for the county committee in an election year. Maybe instead of persecuting their own dedicated volunteers, tearing each other down and fighting over who was MAGA enough, they could have been trying to grow the party and appeal to persuadable voters. All they were doing, she thought, was making sure the Republicans would lose in November. But she understood exactly what her detractors were trying to do. Another election for district chair was coming up, and they were clearly hoping to damage her and force her out. The new PCs who'd taken over the party were following their instructions from Dan Schultz and Steve Bannon and Donald Trump: purge the RINOs.

The executive session to adjudicate the complaint against Kathy was not a real court proceeding, though it mimicked one. It happened on March 16, 2022. How fitting, she thought: one day after the Ides of March. The executive committee sat at a long table at the front of the room, like a tribunal. If the committee found Kathy guilty, she would lose her voting rights as a PC and wouldn't be able to vote in the next election for district chair.

Mickie began by reading out the charge against Kathy: "Lending an endorsement to a non-Republican candidate in an election that had a Republican candidate on the ballot," she said. Then she instructed, "She has to say whether she pleads guilty or not guilty."

"Not! Guilty!" Kathy enunciated.

Mickie called on Kevin Beamon, a bald, bespectacled, and goateed financial adviser by day, who in this proceeding would be playing the role of prosecutor.

"Ms. *Pestas*," he began, "how long have you been a PC and how long have you been a member of the MCRC [Maricopa County Republican Committee]?"

"Excuse me," Kathy replied, "could you please pronounce my name properly?"

"I would love to," Kevin said. "I don't know how to."

"How long have *you* been a precinct committee member?" Kathy asked him. Someone cackled.

"About seven months," Kevin said.

"OK," Kathy said. "I've been one for forty years."

"Congratulations," Kevin snapped.

"Point of order," someone else cut in, "please answer the question."

"Please pronounce my name correctly," Kathy said.

"Please tell me how to pronounce your name."

"It's spelled P-E-T-S-A-S. And it's pronounced *Pet*sas."

"That is exactly what I said."

"You said '*Pes*tas.'"

"OK," Mickie sighed, "go ahead."

"And I'm *Chairman* Petsas," Kathy said.

Kevin started over. "Have you ever read the MCRC bylaws in their entirety?"

"Yes," said Kathy, the former chairman of the county bylaws committee.

"Are you aware of this very clear prohibition against supporting non-Republican candidates?"

"Mmm," Kathy pondered for a moment, "no."

"But you did read them in their entirety?"

"Yes."

"Then how did you not know about this?"

"As it relates to partisan elections, it is completely understandable."

"Excellent point," Kevin said. "Does it say anything about partisan elections?"

"So this trial is you questioning me?"

"Answer my questions, please," Kevin said, louder. "Does it say anything about whether this applies to partisan or nonpartisan elections?"

"Yes, because it implies Republican — "

"Not implies. Does it say?"

"It does say. It says either Republican or non-Republican, which implies and states that it would be that way on the ballot, that that is the type of election that you are looking to, to harass and circular-fire at your fellow precinct committee members that you've known for seven months."

Kevin sighed. "Ma'am," he asked Mickie, "can I have a minute or so?"

They decided this Q and A format wasn't working, and instead Kevin would just present his case. "The definition of an endorsement per *Merriam-Webster's Dictionary* is 'a sanction or approval,'" he said. "The example is that 'they went ahead without the endorsement of his boss' — that the endorsement is a 'sanction or approval.' This article appeared in the *Arizona Republic*. It's also currently available online, I just googled it up. I have the entire article. I will not read the entire article, because only a portion of it applies to Ms. *Pet*sas. Correct?"

"Chairman Petsas," she said.

"This is the section that applies," Kevin said. He read out Kathy's quote from the article. "Yes," he went on, "it is in a nonpartisan election. But it is quite clear that Debra Stark is indeed a Democrat.

And Ms. Garcia ran against Chairman Petsas for chairmanship in the previous year, so clearly, Ms. Petsas knew that Ms. Garcia was a Republican PC, and a PC in her own district."

Now it was Kathy's turn to present her defense. "Are you open to facts or have you already made your decision?" she began. She argued that a polite quote in a newspaper article was not an endorsement. She provided a letter from Stark's campaign saying they never had Kathy's endorsement. Kathy pointed out that she does not live in Phoenix and can't vote in its city elections. She said municipal elections in Arizona are always nonpartisan. And she put up a tweet from Nicole Garcia saying, after she lost the district chair race to Kathy, that she was quitting the Republican Party. How was Kathy to know whether Nicole Garcia had even been a Republican?

Now Kevin made his rebuttal. "It is entirely immaterial that this was a nonpartisan race, and it was quite well known to you that Ms. Stark was a Democrat and that Ms. Garcia was Republican," he said. "As to Ms. Garcia's tweet, maybe it's true. Maybe it's not. It doesn't matter. Ms. Garcia is not on trial here."

When Kevin finished, the executive committee members wrote down their questions and passed them to Mickie to read out loud. The first was clearly from one of Kathy's allies. "If Ms. Lake wins her race for governor, will you condemn her for voting for and contributing to the Obama campaign?"

Kari Lake was one of the Republican candidates running in the Arizona gubernatorial primary. She used to be the news anchor on the local Fox affiliate, so she was a famous name and face across the state. She was telegenic, naturally, and she recorded campaign videos speaking directly to the camera with soft focus, like an Old Hollywood heroine. On the campaign trail, she wore a microphone at all times. And just as often, she talked about the stolen election. Even Trump would joke about it: "If they say, 'How is your family?' she says, 'The election was rigged and stolen.'" Lake's emergence as a MAGA superstar was mystifying for people who'd known her for a long time, who remembered when she'd supported Barack Obama and gone out to gay bars; now she swore allegiance to Donald Trump and railed against drag queens. What happened? Was it something in the hushed scandal around her ouster from the network, or the isolation from the pandemic? Did she really believe it? Those were questions Kathy was asking about a lot of Republicans lately.

Mickie set that question aside. "I don't know what this has to do with anything," she said.

Kathy jumped in. "I think that means, is this similar kangaroo court going to happen to Ms. Lake?" she said. "Since this is a year later and you're bringing something up like this, are you going to do the same thing to Ms. Lake if she's governor?"

"I'm not authorized to do anything to anyone," Kevin replied. "I am given instruction by the chairman and I have to follow those instructions."*

The questioning went on for almost another half an hour. Then it was time to vote. Kathy wanted a roll call, so everyone could see how everyone else voted, but the committee decided on a private ballot. She left the room so they could deliberate.

About fifteen minutes passed. They brought her back inside. Kathy watched them count the votes. The total didn't add up. They counted again. "Wouldn't it be easier if everyone stood or sat down?" Kathy suggested.

More people came over and they counted again. Seventeen in favor of the resolution. Six votes against. Two abstentions. Kathy spotted a no in the yes pile. (And these were the people who wanted hand-counted paper ballots instead of voting machines.) The count was sixteen to seven. "Guilty." Kathy packed up her bag and left.

THE GUILTY VERDICT stripped Kathy of her right as a PC to vote for a new chair later that month. Kathy attended the meeting anyway. The candidates for district chair took turns speaking.

First up was Dan Farley, the guy whom Merissa Hamilton had gone to when Kathy had rejected her PC application, and who'd told Merissa, "We're firing Petsas." He was a real estate broker with a license about to expire and a Twitter profile blanketed with conspiracy theories about the billionaire and well-known Democratic donor George Soros.

"I started in the Tea Party in 2009," Farley told the assembly. "I took leadership of the Tea Party in 2016. I was asked to get engaged in the AZ GOP thirty months ago. Since then, I've given forty to

* Beamon quit the county committee a few months later. He declined to be interviewed.

eighty hours a week to the party. I have self-funded everything that I've done. I've given selflessly." He was shouting into the microphone, getting louder as he went on. "I've helped recruit between five and six hundred PCs last year alone. I've traveled all over the state and almost every county...Merissa Hamilton and I have worked very closely together."

He closed by addressing the other candidate for chair, a moderate named Cory Mishkin. Kathy supported him and expected him to win that night. "I come from an all-red district," Farley said. "Under *his* leadership," he spat, indicating Mishkin, "*his* district turned blue. We're a fifty-fifty district. Do you want to be *red* at the end of November or *blue*?"

Kathy was stunned by this display of rage. She thought he sounded like a lunatic. But the audience whooped and clapped and cheered.

Mishkin seemed astonished too as he began his speech. "I always love personal attacks, that's fun," he said sarcastically. "I will point out that Dan Farley's own precinct went blue in '18 and '20, but mine was still red. That aside—"

"What are you talking about?" Farley shouted back from the audience.

"It was red," Mishkin corrected him. "Yeah, you're welcome."

He tried to get back on track. "I'm running for chairman to help unite our district," he said. "The job of the LD chairman is to work towards a common goal of getting Republicans elected up and down the ballot. It's our job as PCs to unite the party rather than focus on intraparty warfare. It's our job to expand the tent rather than place barriers to entry. The question for all of us is, are we going to openly oppose one another, calling each other names, while playing into the Left's identity politics, or are we going to unite and face the challenge of the day? We need to return to our big-tent ideals and once again put a light on the hill that calls people into our party."

Kathy thought surely sensible people could see the difference. Did they want a chairman who could accomplish something, or a screamer like Dan Farley? It turned out they wanted a screamer. The vote wasn't even close.

Dan Farley might have succeeded in his plot with Merissa Hamilton to oust Kathy as chair, but she thought the joke was on them:

Kathy hadn't wanted to run for legislative chair this term anyway. It was only an eight-month term — a quirk of the calendar because of the once-a-decade redistricting. Kathy's old LD 28 was now LD 4, and the new district chair elected in March would serve only through November. Kathy wasn't interested in being chair for those months because party officials were supposed to stay neutral in primaries, and Kathy didn't want to be neutral about Kari Lake. (Not that the tradition of official party neutrality was stopping Dan Farley and the other MAGA party leaders from making clear whom *they* supported.)

For Kathy and her allies to win back the party leadership, they had to start now. PCs would appear on the primary ballot in August, and the winners would be eligible to vote for district, county, and state party leadership in 2023. She went around recruiting neighbors to join the party — people who she thought would represent the party well, who didn't believe the election was stolen, who were knowledgeable about issues voters cared about and shared genuine commitments to conservative values. But it was a tough sell. People told Kathy they didn't want to associate themselves with a party that behaved this way.

It took ten signatures to get on the primary ballot as a PC. Kathy always gathered more than ten for her own petition, just in case. But for some of her recruits, the petitions she'd circulated were challenged in court. Signature challenges happen sometimes in major races. Usually the opposing party tries to disqualify a candidate by invalidating enough signatures to put the candidate under the threshold needed to make the ballot. It happened that year in Michigan, where several of the leading Republican candidates for governor used paid signature gatherers who did a faulty job, and the candidates didn't make the primary ballot. But at the PC level? Republicans suing other Republicans? Unheard of. Kathy thought it was a stunning waste of resources, and a form of bullying. The lawsuits hinged on petty penmanship issues — literally whether someone wrote down their address as 6332 or 6322. The challenges that went to court got dismissed. She attended the hearings; she would not be intimidated. But some of the PCs she was backing withdrew rather than deal with a lawsuit. It seemed like too much trouble for a volunteer position at the lowest rung of the party organization.

*   *   *

IT WAS THE Sunday before the Arizona primary on August 2, 2022, under a scorching midsummer desert sun. The temperature was above a hundred, and not even a dry heat: more humid than usual for Arizona. Kathy was not afraid to sweat. She thought knocking doors was the best way to turn people out, unlike the rallies and obnoxious sign-waving that the new PCs liked to waste their time on. Today Kathy went out canvassing for Karrin Taylor Robson, the mainstream conservative alternative to Kari Lake in the gubernatorial primary. Taylor Robson lived in Kathy's district, in the old LD 28. They knew each other going back to their Teenage Republican days. Now Taylor Robson was a wealthy lawyer and real estate developer, one of the GOP's largest donors in Arizona. She pumped more than eighteen million dollars of her own money into her campaign, and gained the backing of establishment figures including the outgoing governor, Doug Ducey, as well as Mike Pence, Trump's vice president, who'd stood up to him on January 6 and was now preparing to run against him for the Republican nomination in 2024.

As Kathy went out knocking that Sunday before the primary, there was no answer at the first house. She could hear a TV or a radio on loud, so she reluctantly rang the doorbell a second time. Still no answer. She left some Taylor Robson campaign literature on the doorstep along with her name and number.

On her way to the next house, Kathy got distracted by an estate sale. She loved estate sales. An inlay end table caught her eye. There was a cute cup with a duck design for only a buck fifty. "That's beautiful, if that's something you collect," she said. (Kathy collected decorative roosters, a Greek symbol of vigilance.) Before leaving, Kathy asked the woman running the estate sale if she'd voted yet, but she said she was a Democrat.

A few houses later, Kathy met up with Beau Lane, a candidate for secretary of state. Kathy and Beau went way back to when they were cochairs of the Teenage Republican Club at Central High School, and worked as pages on the floor of the 1980 Republican National Convention, when Ronald Reagan won the nomination. Beau was a tall, beefy man with neatly parted gray hair. His opponent in the Republican primary was Mark Finchem, a state rep who was running with Trump's endorsement. Finchem campaigned wearing a cowboy hat, a bolo tie, and a gun, and he belonged to the

Oath Keepers militia. He'd been in the mob outside the Capitol on January 6, saying he was there to deliver a letter to Mike Pence urging him not to accept Arizona's electoral votes for Biden. If elected secretary of state, Finchem promised to get rid of electronic voting machines and send investigators door to door to root out fraudulent voter registrations. Kathy viewed Finchem as extreme and dangerous, and she hoped voters would choose Beau, a normal person, to do the job the normal way: professionally, administratively, fairly.

Kathy and Beau walked up the driveway to a low-slung Mediterranean-style house and knocked on the door. "Hello?" a woman in her seventies called back, over the yelping of what sounded like multiple small dogs.

"Hi!" Kathy greeted the woman as she came to the door. "Mrs. Cochran?" she asked, using the name provided in her app. "How are you?"

"I'm wonderful," Mrs. Cochran said cheerfully.

"I'm Kathy and I am going door to door with my friend Beau Lane, who's running for secretary of state."

"Hi there," Mrs. Cochran said to Beau.

"Have you voted yet in the primary?" Kathy asked, meaning early or by mail.

"No."

"Well, I'm here to help inspire you to."

"No," Mrs. Cochran said again, this time in response to Kathy's outstretched hand full of material about Karrin Taylor Robson's gubernatorial campaign. "You know what?" Mrs. Cochran explained. "I was considering her, but she did two things that I found unacceptable. One is actually putting Pence up with her. I'm sorry, I barely have any respect for that man. And — God, I can't even remember the other one right now. But she did two things, and that was one of them."

"Huh," Beau said.

"If she's bringing in people that I have no respect for..." Mrs. Cochran said. Then she seemed to remember the other reason she'd forgotten. "And I've also done some research," she said. "She's getting a lot of out-of-state money. I'd much rather see in-state money."

"Well, so is Kari Lake, by the way," Kathy said.

"I don't care about that," Mrs. Cochran said.

"Well, would you consider voting for me for secretary of state?" Beau asked.

"I would consider voting for you," she said. "You have not yet offended me."

"Thank you," Beau said.

"So what offends you about Pence with Karrin?" Kathy asked.

"I've been offended by Pence ever since he was a backtracker," Mrs. Cochran said. "I always got the feeling he was playing a game, trying to benefit himself as opposed to what the people wanted. Actually, I feel that way about a lot of politicians." (Beau chuckled nervously.) "I no longer feel that either side, either party—they're both in it for power, money. And it is just, nope, not interested, thank you."

"OK," Kathy said.

"And my dogs aren't interested either," Mrs. Cochran added, as the yapping kept going in the background.

"And so do you think you're gonna vote for Kari Lake then?" Kathy asked.

"I'm not certain."

"Please think about Karrin again. Beau and I and Karrin are native Arizonans, and we were—"

"Judging by your age, I've been here longer than you have."

"Well, my uncle was chairman of the Republican Party, and we've been active and we've been lifelong Republicans and conservatives—"

"I used to be a Democrat!" Mrs. Cochran said.

"But we would appreciate your consideration of her because we know her personally. We know that she would be a great executive. She has the right skills. She has executive leadership—"

"She's a lawyer!" Mrs. Cochran burst out.

"Well, Kari Lake read content on the news," Kathy smoldered.

"Yes, she did," Mrs. Cochran affirmed. "Which—I don't admire any media, but I do admire somebody who says, 'Enough is enough, I'm not gonna do it anymore.'"

"But you know what?" Kathy said. "She lived in the district that Karrin and I have lived in and been active and been helping elect Republicans. And she lived there for twenty years, and she only came out and talked about this when Trump lost. She was never in the trenches. She's somebody who, when we were trying to get Republicans elected for president—"

"She voted for Obama or whatever—and I don't care," Mrs.

Cochran said. "People get to change their mind. They get to smarten up. I did. At least *I* think I did."

"OK," Kathy sighed. "Well, good luck. And thank you very much."

"Thanks for being a Republican," Beau said.

As Kathy walked back down the driveway in the steaming heat, she heard a faint but unmistakable *"Fuck you."*

Once they were safely out of earshot, Beau asked Kathy, "What was she saying about Pence?"

"That he ought to be hung or something?" Kathy said.

"That he was a backtracker," Beau said. "I don't know what that means."

"Because he wouldn't decertify it," Kathy said, meaning the 2020 election. "What are people thinking?"

Back in the safety of her air-conditioned car, Kathy thought she was living in a bad movie. "How in the world did everything turn on its head?"

ON PRIMARY NIGHT, August 2, 2022, the Taylor Robson campaign held its watch party at the Arizona Biltmore, the oldest and most famous resort in the Phoenix area. Kathy's wedding reception had been held there, after a ceremony at the Greek Orthodox church down the street. Tonight the ballroom was packed with men in navy blazers and women in heels, snacking on canapés such as miniature Gruyère cheese caramelized leek tarts and tiny pieces of beef tenderloin with red onion jam on marble rye. The mood was electric: early returns showed Taylor Robson in the lead. The crowd was milling around, waiting for the candidate to speak.

Kathy arrived late from a victory party for her friend Thomas Galvin, who was on track to win a race for the county board of supervisors. She was one of the only people at the party wearing a T-shirt, since she'd never had time to change after spending all day electioneering outside a polling location. She showed up like a conquering hero, greeting friends with warm hugs. She noticed two men who she knew used to be bitter rivals, but now they were embracing; that was the spirit of respectful disagreements. The setting reminded her of the Trunk 'n' Tusk dinners she used to go to with her uncle: everyone excited by a common goal.

"Old LD 28, we're just gonna call it the Establishment," Kathy said to her friends of her and Taylor Robson's home district, using the number from before the redistricting, when she used to be chair. "We're alive and well. But you know what? Guess what? They work hard, they give money, and they get people elected. And if that's 'the Establishment,' we'll take it. All. Day. Long."

"We can rest at night," said a friend, whom Kathy had just convinced to become a PC, and who had been elected to the position that day.

Kathy quoted a tweet she'd seen that day: "For Arizona, it's just another election. For America, it's an IQ test."

"It's sad but true," the friend said.

Kathy said the problem was people now could look online and find whatever information they wanted, unlike when she grew up watching Walter Cronkite, the authoritative CBS anchorman trusted by millions of Americans to deliver the news every night.

"LD 28 still rules!" another friend came up to her to say.

"From the grave, baby!" Kathy said. "From the grave."

It was getting late. The pace of precincts reporting results slowed down, and the ballroom started clearing out. Kathy spotted Derrick Rochwalik, her young friend who'd chaired the neighboring district until resigning last summer to avoid getting deposed by the new PCs. Derrick had just returned from a trip to Paris to celebrate his thirtieth birthday. He and Kathy decided to get a drink.

They walked over to the bar in the lobby, a long opulent hall built in the style of Frank Lloyd Wright. Kathy said she didn't like the new floors. "I'll let Frank know," Derrick said.

They took a cushy spot near a group of friends who were discussing legislative strategy based on the night's State House winners. Kathy bought Derrick a vodka soda and herself a glass of pinot grigio. At first she was still glowing. A friend sent her a photo where you could spot her in a TV shot from the watch party. She and Derrick debated whether Trump would run for president again (Derrick thought he wouldn't go through with it) and who would be the next State House speaker now that the incumbent, Rusty Bowers, had just lost his primary to an election denier. Derrick slipped off a shoe and put a bare foot on the couch, leading Kathy to feign disgust and inch away.

But as the night went on, Kathy started to let on some more

concern about Taylor Robson's dwindling lead. She found out that several of her PC candidates had lost, meaning she'd failed to reclaim enough seats to oust Dan Farley. Kathy feared he'd be emboldened to run for state chair when that position would become open in January 2023. She took responsibility for the failure, blaming herself for not campaigning earlier and knocking on more doors.

"Oh my God!" she gasped suddenly, and jumped to her feet. She dashed off to sit by herself at another sofa, her face buried in her phone. Derrick waited a few minutes before tiptoeing over. "Politics or family?" he asked gently.

Kathy had just gotten a text from a friend who worked on the Taylor Robson campaign. She'd texted him earlier to see how he was doing, and he'd finally replied, saying they'd left it all on the field. At that moment Kathy realized that Taylor Robson's lead was not going to hold. There was a clear pattern in the election returns. The reason was that Trump had been telling his supporters not to trust mail ballots and to vote only in person on Election Day. In 2020, that meant Trump led initially based on the Election Day votes that were counted first, but then Biden caught up and overtook him with mail ballots. This time, in the Arizona primary, early votes and precounted mail ballots were posted first, and those leaned toward Taylor Robson. But as the Election Day votes poured in, they heavily favored Kari Lake.

Kathy began thinking aloud through the possible outcomes. Taylor Robson shouldn't concede, she said; Lake wouldn't concede if the roles were reversed. They should wait until every vote was counted. There were still 125,000 unopened mail ballots that had been dropped off on Election Day. Derrick wasn't buying it; he'd already concluded that Taylor Robson's initial lead in early votes and mail ballots wouldn't be big enough to withstand the Election Day vote for Lake. "Don't be right right now," Kathy told him.

One of their friends from the other group came over, a young man named Matt, who was wearing a suit. He said the MAGA candidates had swept all the primary races. Mark Finchem had trounced Beau Lane for secretary of state. Another Trump-endorsed election denier won the primary for attorney general. There was no reason to hold out hope that the governor's race would be any different. It was the same story in every Republican primary that year.

With the sole exception of Georgia, where Republicans stuck with their incumbent governor and secretary of state, the GOP primary electorate consistently followed Trump's endorsements, picking the most MAGA candidates to face the Democrats in November, with every expectation that the red wave would carry them into power.

"The party is hopeless," Derrick declared.

"The worst thing we could do now is give up and leave," Matt pushed back.

Kathy was tearing up and staring off blankly. "I'm gonna be sick," she said. "This can't be happening." She muttered that Lindsey Graham, the South Carolina senator, had been spot on when he'd said in 2016 that Trump was an affront to Republican values, and now she hoped that the ghost of John McCain visited Graham every night in his dreams, to torture his former sidekick for becoming another shameless Trump sycophant. "Trump is such a cancer," she said. *I hate Trump*, she mouthed. She thought about what it would be like going to meetings with the new PCs talking about campaigning for Kari Lake in November. "She's gonna be insufferable. All these people in the party are insufferable…I can't be a PC in this."

CHAPTER 8

Suspicious Minds

"LIVE FROM CPAC, it is the *War Room*."

Two days after the Arizona primary, Steve Bannon was in a pan-Asian-themed Dallas convention center, hosting the first-ever on-location edition of his podcast. The occasion was the Conservative Political Action Conference, the storied institution that traced its roots to the aftermath of Barry Goldwater's defeat, and had lately evolved into a MAGA *carnaval*. Republican activists like Kathy Petsas would not go anywhere near CPAC now, and Republican candidates like Beau Lane or Karrin Taylor Robson would never be invited to speak at one. This latest, Texas production was a three-day pageant all building toward the final speaker: Donald Trump.

On this opening day, people streamed in wearing hats that said TRUMP 2020 and TRUMP 2024, GOD GUNS & TRUMP, and SAVE AMERICA, ULTRA MAGA, and LET'S GO BRANDON (code for "Fuck Joe Biden"). For sale in the exhibition hall were bedazzled purses shaped like handguns, a children's book called *The Plot Against the King*, about the investigation into Russian interference in the 2016 election, and a board game called Stop the Steal (tagline: "Relax, it's just a board game"). There were exhibition booths from sponsors offering a whole alternative economy for people who felt shut out by "woke" corporations. Patriot Mobile, America's only Christian conservative wireless provider, pledged to donate an unspecified portion of every dollar to organizations advocating for religious liberty and gun rights. Sovereign Data Solutions ("Independence is everything") offered cloud storage with no dependence on Big Tech. Revere Payments ("Are you next?") offered payment processing for people and organizations banned from GoFundMe, PayPal, and Stripe. A web browser called Tusk and a social network called Parler promised to be "censorship-free." There were shirts showing Biden with a Hitler mustache, and a *Lord of the Rings* parody that read RETURN OF THE MAGA KING, and SEXIEST MAN ALIVE with a picture of a grinning Donald Trump, and ENRIQUE TARRIO DID NOTHING WRONG.* A group of women wore matching red glittery PROUD AMERICAN jackets. Bannon wore three shirts—a black button-down over a black polo over a black T—with three black click pens clipped under the front placket.

"It is Thursday, 4 August 2022," Bannon said into his microphone. It had been two weeks since he was convicted on two counts of contempt of Congress, for blowing off a subpoena from the House committee investigating January 6. He was yet to be sentenced, but each count carried a penalty of between thirty days and one year in jail; and when Bannon talked with Trump about the case, Trump had told him, "Steve, that jail thing is making you a star." Sure enough, a crowd of fans now clumped behind his broadcast set, forming an impromptu live studio audience—so many onlookers that they were blocking traffic to the conference's main stage, which was supposed to be the bigger draw.

"Let's meet some of the posse, Jayne," Bannon said, calling on one of his sidekicks, a young woman in a red, white, and blue cowgirl getup who went by the name Calamity Jayne Zirkle, and was stationed with a microphone amid the gathered crowd.

"Well," Calamity Jayne said, "I am joined by Melissa now. Melissa, tell us why you were compelled to come to CPAC."

"I think it's important to be around people that we all think alike, and we want to save our country," said Melissa, wearing a floral blouse. "And also, I'm Hispanic, so I want to put to rest that idea that we're white nationalists." (The marquee speaker that day was Viktor Orbán, the Hungarian prime minister who'd amassed

---

* Tarrio was the Proud Boys leader charged with seditious conspiracy in the January 6 attack on the Capitol. He was convicted in May 2023.

autocratic power and recently given a speech saying Europeans should not "become peoples of mixed race.")

"Amen," Bannon said, leading a faint round of applause.

"Very good," Calamity Jayne said, moving on to the next fan. "Dorothy, why did you come to CPAC?"

"Because knowledge is power. And I think that I just love what this young man has done, Steve Bannon."

"Jayne, get her name and number," said Bannon, who was sixty-eight, hamming it up.

Next was a woman from Trinity County, Texas, wearing a red TRUMP cap and red GOP shirt, who said she became a precinct chairman and a deputy poll registrar after learning about Dan Schultz's Precinct Strategy on *War Room*. "Well, the 2020 election, and Steve Bannon, being part of the *War Room* posse, I can't help but be involved in the 2022 midterms and the '24 election," she said. "I am going in and this is going to be the next three years of my life."

"Wow," Bannon said. "Amen."

Every time Bannon put one of these fans on the air, he knew there were listeners back home thinking, "I'm not alone, I'm not a nutcase. There are a lot of people who look like me who are there." When they heard these people say they'd become a precinct committeeman or an election official, it reinforced that that was the right thing to do. Bannon instructed his crew to spend more of the show turning the cameras around to the audience.

When his two hours were up and the cameras were off, Bannon worked the rope line. His security detail wanted to whisk him out, but Bannon said no: he wanted to sign every autograph and take every photo. He didn't care if it took three hours. Because this was their vacation. They weren't taking another vacation this summer. This was how they had decided to spend their money. (CPAC tickets started at three hundred dollars, not counting travel and accommodations.) And he was going to make sure to treat them with respect and acknowledge that it was a big deal for them to be there. It was something they *did*, like joining the Precinct Strategy. He realized the getting-out and doing was the most important part. "As people get older, your world gets smaller," Bannon would say. "Your family grows up. Your kids got stuff to do. You lose your friends. Your life gets narrower and narrower. You watch more TV. You're more by yourself. The power of the Precinct Strategy is the camaraderie — it's an opportunity to have your life get bigger. On something that's like a moral cause. It's not like being an Amway salesman. You're actually doing something that you think, particularly if you're a certain age, you think you're going to have a shot to leave your mark in history, that your existence and your purpose — your life will have some meaning to it." It was a movement of lowly "hobbits," he said. "But there's a shit-ton of hobbits, right?"

Bannon was convinced that, if not for this surge of engagement, if not for the Precinct Strategy, Kari Lake would not exist — her victory in the Arizona primary earlier that week would not have been possible. Bannon saw her the next night, at the CPAC gala. Bannon and his entourage strode into the ballroom after everyone else had already been seated, and he took his place at the head table with Lake. She was glowing in a figure-fitting silver gown. Bannon added a black blazer over his black shirts to deliver the gala's keynote. "Kari Lake, you are not only a hero, you're the future of this movement," he said, from the podium, to a standing ovation.

The applause went on for twenty seconds before he could continue. "We're at war," Bannon said matter-of-factly. "We're in a political and ideological war. You can say anything else you want about it, but we're at war...On the twentieth of January, 2021, an illegitimate imposter took over 1600 Pennsylvania Avenue...This is not about Donald J. Trump. This is far deeper than President Trump." The ballroom thundered with applause. He was bringing down the house.

"In the next twenty-four months," he said, "starting on November 8," the day of the midterms, "through the '24 elections, we have the opportunity that will never come again. Ever. Ever. We have the ability to shatter, shatter the Democratic Party as a national political institution. And how we gonna do it? We're gonna do it at school boards. We're gonna do it at election boards. We're gonna do it at medical boards. We're gonna do it at canvassing boards. We're gonna do it at state legislatures, county supervisors, the House, the Senate, all of it...The people out there, the people that come here, the people that worked so hard for Kari Lake, who made that victory possible...we can't mess around this time."

Bannon never missed an opportunity on the podcast to highlight cable news and newspaper coverage calling the MAGA movement a "threat to democracy." Now he said: "All they talk about on

MSNBC is 'democracy, democracy, democracy.' We're gonna give them a democracy suppository on November 8!" (By that he meant, "We're gonna shove it up their ass!")

THE NEXT AND final day of the CPAC conference, Kari Lake spoke as a warm-up act for Trump. She walked out to a techno-rock theme, heavy on drums and electric guitar, a piece of stock music that was available online to license without expensive royalties and marketed as sounding "hopeful." "*Whoaaaa*," she marveled at her reception by the roaring crowd, which broke into a chant of "KA-RI! KA-RI!"

"This fight before us proves to us that God is with us," she said. "He has chosen me, and He has chosen you...He has placed each and every one of us here at this point in history because He knows our strength. He's placed us here because He knows that we will be the ones to save this great republic.

"This is our moment right now to prove to our ancestors that their struggles and losses were not done in vain," she said. "We may have won this battle, and I won an *epic* battle in Arizona. We drove a stake through the heart of the McCain machine," she said. She raised one fist and mimed a stabbing motion, as if to gut the legacy of the legendary Arizona senator, whose death in 2018 weakened, practically and symbolically, the institutional Republican resistance to Trump. Now the audience cheered her for a full twenty seconds. "Who is ready to rise up and go out there and win this war to save America?" Lake finished, raising one arm. "Let me hear you!"

Before Trump came onstage, the giant screens around the convention hall played a new video his team had produced. It began with the patter of rain and a clap of thunder, then Trump's voice whispering, "*We are a nation in decline. We are a failing nation.*" More thunder. Trump's voice continued recounting the miseries of the Biden administration: soaring inflation, falling stock prices, rising energy costs, a deadly withdrawal from Afghanistan, war in Ukraine, "fake news." Two minutes in, the music started. It was another piece of royalty-free stock music — piano, strings, and bells. In an online marketplace, the piece was marketed as "uplifting," "dramatic," and "epic." When Trump's team played him the demo, he'd liked its spooky, gloomy mood, and thought it fit with his words' dark tone. *"We will not bend, we will not break, we will not yield,"* he concluded in the video. *"We will never give in, we will never give up, and we will never, ever back down...Because we are Americans, and Americans kneel to God and God alone. And it is time to start talking about greatness for our country again."*

Trump liked the music so much that he decided he wanted to use it to close his speech at a rally a few weeks later, over Labor Day weekend, to stump for the Republican candidates running in the midterms in Pennsylvania. As the song played, he read out a similar script, like a live reenactment of the video. But when he repeated the performance a couple of weeks later, at the next rally, in Ohio, something unexpected happened. People started raising their arms and pointing their index fingers. Trump's team was at a loss to understand the meaning of the gesture as it swept the crowd.

No one knew exactly who started it. But it came from the front section near the stage, occupied by a group of rallygoers who'd been camping out to get front-row seats to every Trump rally all year long. The group's members were identifiable by the commemorative buttons they collected and wore from each rally. These were not the "Front Row Joes," the groupies who'd flocked to Trump rally after Trump rally, ever since 2015, in matching baseball-style jerseys, with no agenda besides being Donald Trump superfans. This new group was something different.

They called themselves Negative 48. The name meant "opposite of evil," because the letters in the word evil had a numerical value of forty-eight. (A equals one, B equals two, Z equals twenty-six.) They believed this form of numerology, derived from the ancient Hebrew tradition of gematria, was the secret to decoding the cryptic messages from the anonymous military officer who went by the code name Q. Negative 48 was an offshoot of the larger QAnon movement, a splinter sect with its own leader: Michael Brian Protzman. He was a gray-haired man who wore flowy American flag pants and posted his numerology lessons on Telegram, another alternative social network.

One Negative 48 member was a woman named Kelly Heath. When she found Protzman's teachings on Telegram, they rang true to her because she'd developed an interest in satanic rituals since

1998, when she was living in Holland and heard about children being hunted. Later she lived in Napa, and her friends who worked security at wineries told her there were caged children in the cellars. "Some people call QAnon a cult, but I like to spell it cult with a Q, Q-U-L-T, because it's hard to find people that are on our same page," she said from under a black brimmed hat. "We think there's a bunch of dead people that are still alive, that are here to represent truth and righteousness, and that somewhere along the line, things went wrong…We have a complete disaster of a world. We have shots that are mandatory. We have an illness—it's like a flu that people are afraid of, to go outside the house with. And we've been muzzled. And it's ugly. It's just an ugly world we have. And we can't have this world. "

Protzman had brought his Negative 48 group to Dallas in November 2021 to witness the resurrection of JFK Jr., who'd died in a plane crash in 1999. When JFK Jr. didn't show, the group decided to start attending Trump rallies. There they discovered they could also apply gematria to divine messages from Trump's tweets, with their curious misspellings and capitalizations, or from the repeated phrases in his speeches. There could even be hidden meanings in the famous rally playlist, "YMCA" and *Phantom of the Opera*, Elton John and Elvis. They would link up arms and dance in the aisles (*"We're caught in a trap / I can't walk out…"*). It would get them in trouble with the event staff, a crew of bodybuilders bulging out of their silky green polos and tight black pants. (*"Why can't you see / What you're doing to me…"*) The rollicking group started raising nerves on Trump's team, which was always on the lookout for disturbances, intent on pulling off frictionless experiences. What were they doing there? What did they want? No one was sure. They wouldn't say exactly.

"The truth needs to come out," was all one group member, Julie McDaniel, would answer, speaking from behind big black mirrored sunglasses. The truth, to her, meant "all the deceit from the government and the theft of an election. And the beauty of all this: all these patriots out here together showing, after everything we've been through, that we still absolutely believe in that man." She said she was a lapsed Catholic, and this was her church now.

"We're standing for the 2020 election," offered another member, Melissa Cole, who had traveled with her two thirteen-year-olds and a Cavalier King Charles spaniel in a stroller. "It was stolen from us. And so it's important to us to represent all of those that have been tricked into believing that we just move past it. It's been a hard journey to be in this and understand what's happened. We studied all the evidence, went through all the processes to see what really happened. And then people don't even want to talk about it...He tells us, 'Never give up.' And that's what we don't do."

"I know things," said Alan Andrews, a Negative 48 member who held a twenty-two-year-old Congo African gray parrot leashed to his pinkie finger by a purple rope. (Yes, the parrot did talk, but she was being shy right now. At some rallies, the Secret Service wouldn't let Alan bring her in, so he'd have to sit outside and wait for the rest of the group.) "I can't say. Because it hasn't been released to the public...Those who are the enemy of the people will be dealt with by the military. You do know that the NSA has everything on every one of us? Our cell phones, our smart TVs, our smart refrigerators, our smart dishwashers, our smart meters. All tied together, everything being listened to by the NSA surveillance...The media's all lies. Television. They put it in our face at the beginning—they called it a television—and we didn't realize it because we thought it was one word. It's three words: tell a vision...to program the mind, to control the thoughts."

"Military tribunals are already happening—people are already being executed for the crime they've committed against humanity, the treason. And it's all happening already," said Micki Larson-Olson, an Air Force veteran who traveled around with Negative 48 wearing a skin-tight Captain America jumpsuit and sequined peaked cap. She was about to be convicted of defying police orders to leave the Capitol grounds on January 6. Six officers had to physically remove her as she fought and screamed and called them "traitors."* "Those were domestic terrorists inside our Capitol...our Congress," she said. "Execution for being traitors, that's what our Constitution demands."

When the spooky music came on at the end of that rally in Ohio, Kelly Heath pointed to the sky. Julie McDaniel pointed to the

---

* After her release, Larson-Olson traveled to New Hampshire to meet Trump on the campaign trail, where he embraced her and signed the backpack she said she carried with her on January 6.

sky. Soon everyone was doing it. Kelly said they were pointing to God. "That's why he says, 'We will not bend, we will not break, we will never, ever, ever back down. And we will bow to God and God alone,'" she said. "And that is what the problem is with this world, where we're bending to the government or bowing down to all things that aren't us...We shouldn't wait for a savior. We need to know that God is within...We need to have heaven on earth right now. So it's very important to remind ourselves that God exists. And that's what Donald Trump does."

The mysterious hand gesture creeped out Trump's staff. Online, viewers surmised the pointed fingers (a number 1) stood for the QAnon slogan, "Where we go one, we go all." Some people compared the outstretched arms to a Nazi salute. Then it turned out the same piece of stock music that Trump was playing had, back in 2020, been ripped off by a Finnish man who made YouTube videos of himself wearing a teddy bear mask with sunglasses and put the track on Spotify with the title "WWG1WGA"—as in, "Where we go one, we go all"! QAnon followers concluded this had to be another coded message—that Trump was signaling his support for their movement.

Trump's team went into damage control. They swore the song's alter ego was a coincidence, a case of mistaken musical identity. Trump didn't want to ditch the song (especially not in a way that would look like giving in to pressure), nor did his team want this distraction. New orders went out to the event staff, the bodybuilders in green: they started stopping people from bringing QAnon signs and apparel into Trump's rallies, and Protzman had to instruct his group not to raise their hands again.* The next time Trump played the song to end his speech, at a rally in Wilmington, North Carolina, a few scattered attendees tried pointing one finger to the sky, and the green men promptly went over to tell them to stop.

"Look at those cameras," Trump would often say at these rallies, pointing to the media riser. *"I say turn them around, all the way back as far as the eye can see. Turn them to see the people."*

Now the people listened as Trump wrapped up his speech in North Carolina by saying, *"Our MAGA—Make America Great Again—*

---

* Protzman died in a dirt-biking accident in July 2023.

movement [is] by far the greatest political movement in the history of our country, probably in the history of almost all countries. Together we are standing up against some of the most menacing forces, entrenched interests and vicious opponents our people have ever, ever seen. Despite great outside dangers from other countries, our biggest threat remains the sick, sinister, and evil people from within our own country."

The crowd, joyous for most of the warm, bright day, was suddenly hushed and rapt. *"But no matter how big or powerful the corrupt radical left Democrats are, we are fighting like nobody's ever fought before,"* they heard Trump say. *"I really believe that right now we are fighting like nobody has ever fought before. And you must never forget: this nation does not belong to them. This nation belongs to* you." He spread his arms to point all around, then turned to point behind him too. *"Belongs to you,"* he swept a finger around, *"and you. Belongs to you."*

SALLEIGH GRUBBS SHOWED up late to the Cobb County Republican Party headquarters, in a Marietta strip mall next to a charity shop. She had been checking out an event space and gotten stuck in traffic; she was always running around these days. She hurried into the drab windowless room where that night's poll watcher training was being held, under the gaze of life-size cardboard cutouts of Donald Trump and Ronald Reagan.

As soon as she entered, the group clapped for her, but Salleigh was disappointed. The turnout was smaller than she'd hoped for, smaller than the crowd at the last two trainings. She was aiming to recruit and train five hundred, enough to cover every shift at every polling location — her own local version of the Virginia model and the RNC's Election Integrity Task Force.

Georgia law required poll watchers to be trained, but the content and conduct of the trainings were up to the county parties. This session, in April 2022, was being run by Salleigh's friend Pam Reardon, who developed the course in collaboration with people she declined to identify, except to say they were experts on the state's new voting law, known officially as SB 202. The law was known to its critics as Jim Crow 2.0, for how its restrictions seemed designed to disproportionately burden voters of color. The law, passed after the 2020 election, reduced the time to request absentee ballots, heightened ID requirements, outlawed mailing ballot applications to all voters, all but eliminated drop boxes and mobile voting centers, gave the Republican-controlled state legislature more power over election administration, made it harder to extend voting hours for the inevitable glitches that arise at polls, and banned serving refreshments to voters waiting in line. This last provision was one after Salleigh's own heart; during the 2020 presidential election and 2021 Senate runoff, she'd posted photos and videos of people from "nonpartisan" but obviously left-leaning groups that were going around with boxes of snacks or even serving people out of a food truck. Salleigh thought that should be illegal, and now it was.

The trainees were there to learn all their new powers under the law. They received long, detailed checklists of all the steps they were supposed to take to ensure no "irregularities," down to inspecting the serial numbers on the zip ties used to secure the doors of the ballot carriers. Salleigh was now, in her official party capacity, training Republicans to be better equipped to catch fraud and prove it than she had been when she'd haphazardly chased the shredding truck. She advised the trainees to expect the election officials running the polling locations to be leery of them. "They're afraid of us, I think, and they're wary that we're gonna attack 'em or something," she told the group. "And that's not the case. We just want things to be right. And that's really a nonpartisan issue, right? I mean, everybody should want fairness in voting and everything to be legal and right. So one thing I do wanna say is: smile. You know, one of the things that was really terrible during the 2020 election is we're all wearing masks and everything, and you lost so much of the human component of smiling. Or maybe there *was* somebody that really wanted to like, knock you in the head, and you thought they were smiling or something. So try to smile and have a good demeanor, a pleasant demeanor. Be courteous. We're not anyone's enemy" — she paused briefly for comic effect — "except maybe the food truck people."

Pam Reardon played a slideshow that painted a wholesome picture of bipartisan harmony inside the polling precinct: "Pizza and laughs, Democrats and Republicans." But the trainees that night didn't sound like that was the experience they were looking forward to. Pam emphasized that the poll watchers were not allowed to interfere with anyone while voting. "Take a picture of their car — as much evidence as we could get," she said. "But do not talk to them, do not ask them questions, do not confront them, do not talk to any voters."

"Question," one of the trainees, a man in his early seventies named Mike Wilkins, piped up. "I'm guessing that there are certain precincts that are probably more prone to problems than others. Will there be a mechanism in place to make sure that those precincts are always staffed? 'Cause I'd love to do one of those."

"Yeah, we'll notify you where we want you to try to go," Pam said. There were some precincts where the party knew they'd have friendly poll workers, so they wouldn't need Republican watchers there. But others... "I mean," Pam said, "if you live in north Cobb" (the whiter, richer part of the county), "and we want to send you to south Cobb" (the more diverse part, where Republicans used to not even bother), "and you don't want to, that's fine."

Mike Wilkins did want to. "I'm just thinking that there are certain precincts that probably need watching more than others," he said. "I'm glad there will be a mechanism."

Another trainee asked if the Democrats also sent poll watchers. Pam said she hadn't seen any in her experience.

"They were all under the tables," someone joked.

"It depends on what George wants," another said, meaning George Soros, the Hungarian-American megadonor to Democratic causes. "George is gonna pay them fifty dollars an hour. They'll be there."

"They get twenty dollars an hour," Salleigh corrected him, "was the going rate in 2020."

"I heard it was up to forty dollars," Mike Wilkins said.

"For watchers?" Pam asked.

"For absentee ballots."

"Oh yeah," Salleigh said. "Forty dollars for an absentee ballot."*

"Has anybody here in their neighborhoods seen 'em doing ballot harvesting?" Mike Wilkins asked. "I did."

---

* It is routine for both parties to pay door knockers. The going rate for Republicans is $15 an hour (more than $20 after Labor Day) or $3.50 per door. The market rate for a new voter registration is $45 to $55, sometimes as high as $60, with bonuses if the voter successfully casts a ballot.

"Did you really?" Salleigh said.

"A young man was wandering around our neighborhood," he said. "And he parked at the end of our cul-de-sac. And he was wandering around and I stopped him."

"Good for you."

"And I said, 'Excuse me, what are you doing?'" Mike continued. "And he said, 'Well, I'm here talking to people about voting.' And I said, 'Well, tell me specifically what you do.' He said, 'Well, I just go to different houses and I ask them if they need help with their voting, and if they need help with their voting, I'll go ahead and I'll help 'em fill out the ballot. I'll take it with me and I'll vote for 'em.' And then I go, 'What a great idea!'"*

"And then I get paid!" Pam mocked.

"But that never happened!" Salleigh said sarcastically.

"I'll tell you," Mike said, now that they were talking about what did or didn't happen in 2020, "if it had been me at one of those polls and they asked me to leave, downtown, they would've had to arrest me. I would've interfered."

"OK, let's not do that again," Pam sighed.

"I'm just saying!" Mike insisted. "In the spirit of this election, we are trying to be — we Republicans want to be the 'nice people,' right? That's why our country is so screwed up — because we still want to be nice. *You can't be nice to the Democrats!*"

"OK, so lemme just say," Salleigh jumped in. "This is a free speech zone. But look, the ballot is the most important thing that we have in this country. There is no doubt about it. That's how our voices are heard, is through our ballots. And that's why we have a constitutional republic — right? — is that we get to have our voices heard. We should have our republic operate the way that the Founders intended. The problem was, it's Republicans' nature to say, 'I'm gonna live my life. You live your life. What works for you works for you. What works for me works for me. Let's not talk about politics or religion at the same table.' And here we are. It's apathy. And it's blind trust that we put in people that did not deserve it."

"I'm not apathetic," Mike said.

"And I hear you, and I'm glad you're not apathetic. Woo!" she

---

* In Georgia, only family members, household members, and caregivers are allowed to return another voter's absentee ballot.

cheered. "But that's why you're here. And we hope that more people will be here."

"The feeling that I get from this poll-watching thing," another trainee in his seventies, Jerry French, said, "is that we're watching a mugging and all we're doing is taking a description."

"Yes!" Mike agreed.

"We're just describing the assailant and being able to turn it over to the police — "

"Who aren't gonna do anything about it," Mike interjected.

" — an hour later and then hope that they do something," Jerry continued. "But if this is what we're here for, if this is the definition of this job of watcher, where we are noting and declaring and documenting, then I get it."

"It's not," Pam tried assuring him. "If there's a problem, we can address it right away. We have attorneys, and we are not gonna wait for a lame secretary of state to not do anything. And now we can go and we can file a report and we can go to the sheriff."

"Let me clarify," Salleigh added. She felt their frustration. She understood it. She had been that person before, back in 2020, when she and Susan Knox chased the shredding truck, and all they could do was call 911 to make a report and wait for something to happen. But nothing happened. There was a feeling of helplessness, of nothing making sense, and nothing to be done. That moment changed both Salleigh's and Susan's lives, but it set them down different paths. Susan had been the one to encourage Salleigh to run for county chair, but Susan wasn't there that night; she wasn't involved in the county party.

To talk to Susan those days was to hear about how the person in the White House was a body double or a clone wearing a Joe Biden mask (like in *Mission Impossible II*); or how Trump was working to bust a global human-trafficking ring, to rescue children from tunnels where they were being harvested for adrenochrome; or how the Rockefellers and the Bilderbergs and the thirteen families who owned everything staged the "plandemic" to take down Trump, and sterilize soldiers through COVID vaccines, injecting people with microchips to make us "transhumans"; and when FEMA started opening detention centers, they were gonna come for her first. Susan let her professional networking business atrophy while she spent hours a day scrolling through Telegram and researching on the internet. She opened her home to election fraud hunters like Jovan Pulitzer and Patrick Byrne, opened her wallet to True the Vote, a group using cell-phone location data to find ballot fraud; and when they'd all come and gone, the proof they sought still eluding them, Susan was left feeling used, taken advantage of, and let down. Susan had given up on politics. She was looking for something else now, something bigger, maybe supernatural. "The only way that I'll ever feel comfortable," she said, "and this is in my heart of hearts, which helps me to keep going, is I believe that Trump is coming back very soon. I believe that this election is going to be decertified. I believe we are going to a quantum voting system, which is on a blockchain technology that cannot be penetrated by artificial intelligence, and I believe we are going through an entire transformation of the whole world. I believe the Federal Reserve is going away, we are getting rid of fiat currency (gold-backed standard), and the pendulum will swing back to older times that were more conservative — that were about family, and about God, and about helping your neighbor, and about harvesting. It is biblical, and that's what I believe is getting ready to happen. And I believe it's going to happen in the not-too-distant future, based on everything I've read, all my research. And that's when I'll believe that we've won."

Salleigh Grubbs wasn't waiting for a miracle. She was never giving up on politics. Even when it meant long nights in her windowless office at the Cobb GOP headquarters, with her signed Marjorie Taylor Greene yard sign and her poster mapping out the spiderweb connections between Karl Marx and Barack Obama, titled the AGENDA GRINDING AMERICA DOWN. That feeling of helplessness that she remembered from 2020 was exactly what the party was now organizing to overcome, by fielding poll watchers to gather evidence to file lawsuits, she told the trainees now. "There's nothing to say that if there is something egregious — I don't know that it's been done before — that you can't run to the county courthouse and say, 'This is what happened, we need you to rule on this and that,'" she said.

Salleigh wasn't troubled by the zealous words from Mike and Jerry in the safety of a room with like-minded friends; she trusted them in public to keep their cool. "Do not worry about tomorrow, because tomorrow has troubles of its own," she said, quoting

Matthew 6:34, over dinner the next night with a friend from the party. "It means to me that we can't be inactive because we're afraid somebody might be confrontational. We can only be responsible for ourselves. We can only do what we can...And we're all going to do the right thing. I have yet to see anybody become confrontational at all." At the same time, she said, "if you see somebody doing something wrong with ballots on a mass scale, do you not think that's worthy of confrontation?" That was her account of what happened on January 6: as she'd said in her testimony at the State House, it was "a failure to redress grievances. You can't ignore a populace that's saying something happened, something happened, something happened — you can't ignore that and not expect people to become frustrated." Salleigh was done trusting the system, and she didn't think anybody else should either. "I think that this has been a long time coming in America, where people have gotten complacent, Democrats or Republicans...And if We the People don't look at what's going on, and hold people accountable, it will happen over and over and over and over again." There was nothing she could imagine that would convince her to trust elections again. There was no going back.

CHAPTER 9

The Abyss

THE RESULTS FROM the opinion research into the term "MAGA" came back in early 2022, and the findings surprised Navin Nayak. Even though testing the MAGA brand had been his idea, he'd been skeptical that it could work as a theme for attacking Republicans. He'd expected that the acronym wouldn't be widely recognizable, that no one would know what it meant. That was the case for Trump's other mantra, "America First." But the surveys found that practically everyone—more than 80 percent of voters—said they were familiar enough with the term "MAGA" to have an opinion about it. Even more striking, for a full 50 percent of voters, that opinion was unfavorable.

"MAGA" was even more repugnant than "Trump," because even though Democrats didn't like to admit it, Trump did have some positive associations for a lot of people. He remained extremely popular with Republicans. But none of those positives seemed to carry over to the name MAGA. It seemed to capture everything Navin was hoping to convey about today's Republicans: that they had changed, that they were power-hungry, divisive, extreme, and dangerous. "MAGA actually was really well known, much better known than we realized, and with an incredibly negative connotation," Navin would say later. "It was very credible to voters that they were pushing an extreme agenda that involved taking away rights and harming the middle class." Geoff Garin, the pollster working with Navin, observed that the term evoked the racism, sexism, and assault on democracy that many voters associated with the movement, but it wasn't as loaded as using those terms themselves. They could call Republicans MAGA without risking the blowback from calling them racist or sexist, but the subtext still got the point across.

Despite the research, some Democratic operatives mocked the idea. They said MAGA sounded like Hebrew or baby babble; voters wouldn't get it. But in the spring of 2022, Navin's partner on the project, Anita Dunn, arranged for Navin to come to the White House and brief one of the president's top aides, Mike Donilon. Donilon liked the MAGA message and said it fit well with the president's own beliefs. Biden prided himself on working across the aisle, but he also saw how today's Republicans were not like the ones he'd grown up with, and he'd premised his 2020 campaign on a "battle for the soul of the nation."

Biden soft-launched the new buzzword at a DNC fundraiser in April 2022. "This is not your father's Republican Party, by any stretch of the imagination," he said. "This is the MAGA Party. Not a joke." The next month, he went further, in a White House speech on the economy. "Let me tell you about this ultra MAGA agenda," the president said. "It's extreme, as most MAGA things are."

Navin winced as pundits ridiculed "ultra MAGA," as though it was the stupidest gimmick. "Is it kind of like when Hillary Clinton called this same Trump base deplorable?" CNN reporter Alex Marquardt mused on the air. Trump supporters responded by gleefully turning the dig into swag, just as they had done after Clinton used the awkward phrase "basket of deplorables" to characterize them in 2016. They made ULTRA MAGA hats and ULTRA MAGA flags. Trump sent a fundraising email about it and started selling SUPERMAGA shirts. Elise Stefanik, who replaced Liz Cheney as the third-ranking House Republican, told reporters, "I am ultra MAGA, and I'm proud of it."

But Biden didn't let that deter him, and the more he and other Democratic elected officials adopted the MAGA branding, the more Navin saw it resonating online. In his data monitoring social media and news coverage, Democrats were more frequently talking about "MAGA Republicans" than Republicans were talking about "radical socialist Democrats." The beauty of the MAGA Republican brand was how natural it was: it was not a name the Democrats had invented and needed to make stick—it was already part of the mainstream political vocabulary. They just had to amplify it.

"The more the conversations centered on 'MAGA extremism' and 'MAGA Republicans,' this was the power of it," Navin would recall. "If the negative is just about Republicans, everyone goes to their corner. But by talking about 'MAGA Republicans' and just this wing of the party, there's a lot of Republicans who wanted a permission structure to say, 'Yeah, I'm not comfortable with that wing of the Republican Party.'" His team's polling found that 48 percent of voters said they would be less likely to vote for a self-identified "MAGA Republican," including 58 percent of independents and 17 percent of Republicans. "We wanted something that the choir is comfortable spreading and repeating, and that the more the middle heard it, the more uncomfortable it made them," Navin said.

Calling Republicans the party of the rich worked well enough on economic issues, but the MAGA rubric proved more adaptable. Later in May, a teenage gunman killed nineteen children and two adults at an elementary school in Uvalde, Texas. To attack Republicans as extremists for resisting gun regulation, the MAGA label stuck. The next month, in June 2022, the Supreme Court overturned *Roe v. Wade*. Striking down the constitutional right to an abortion had been a stated goal for decades of Republican politicians, and no one was as explicit about it as President Trump. But overturning *Roe* or banning abortion remained unpopular with a majority of Americans. To attack Republicans as extremists for wanting to take away women's rights to control their bodies, the MAGA label stuck. And throughout that summer, the House January 6 committee held public hearings, providing a visual, visceral reminder of what the MAGA movement was capable of. "All of it laddered up to the same story of this extreme wing that was going to harm the American people and take away rights and freedoms," Navin said. "So it's just one consistent story, no matter what the topic."

Matt Canter, the pollster on the project, would do conference calls with the House Democrats' super PAC where he'd pound the MAGA theme, and in response they'd make fun of him and call him "MAGA Matt." But the group's director, Brad Komar, came to appreciate how powerful the message proved to be: in focus groups, voters would bring up the term "MAGA Republican" without prompting from the moderator. The super PAC, which can raise and spend unlimited amounts of money, and was focused on boosting Democrats in the most competitive House races, poured resources into ads that emphasized Republican candidates' extremism. In a competitive Virginia race against a Republican candidate who said the people who stormed the Capitol were "persecuted patriots," the PAC aired an ad showing a mustachioed retired cop saying that "makes me sick." In an Ohio district that was redrawn to lean right, the Republican challenger had himself gone to the Capitol on January 6. To help defend the incumbent Democrat, the super PAC ran an ad with a retired Marine saying the MAGA candidate "should be in jail, not in Congress." In North Carolina, the super PAC attacked a Trump-endorsed Republican candidate by using clips of him on Steve Bannon's and John Fredericks's shows vowing to be a "MAGA warrior." "We were hunting for a proxy for Trump that would keep moderates in the tent, excite our base, and not incite backlash," Komar said. "This checked all three boxes."*

The Democratic candidate who emerged as the most forceful early adopter of this new approach was Josh Shapiro, the Pennsylvania attorney general who was running for governor. His Republican opponent, Doug Mastriano, was a state lawmaker who'd led the effort to overturn the 2020 election results in Pennsylvania and also attended the January 6 rally in Washington. Between the November 2020 election and the insurrection, Mastriano became a

---

* The ads didn't always use the word "MAGA" to make their point about Republicans' extremism. According to Komar, the best case for the effectiveness of the strategy, and for the importance of protecting democracy to voters, was how much the Democrats outperformed in places where they used this message. Nationwide, in the 2022 midterms, Republican House candidates won the popular vote by two percentage points, but Democrats won 90 percent of the toss-up races where they put money behind the extremism message. Democratic candidates running against election deniers for secretary of state also performed better than other Democrats on the same ballot in states such as Michigan, Nevada, and Minnesota.

fixture on Steve Bannon's podcast, raising his profile in the MAGA movement and propelling him to win the Republican primary in May 2022. During the campaign, Mastriano pledged to use his powers, if elected governor, to decommission electronic voting machines and force all voters to reregister, in defiance of federal law. News reports uncovered an old photo of him, as a faculty member at the Army War College, posing in a Confederate uniform. For his own master's thesis, written as an army officer in 2001, Mastriano imagined America falling to a left-wing "Hitlerian putsch." He openly embraced Christian nationalism and supported banning abortion without exceptions, going so far as to suggest that women who underwent the procedure could be charged with murder.

Shapiro began hearing an urgency from voters as he campaigned around the commonwealth — a desperation that he *had* to win. He began speaking directly to that anxiety by emphasizing Mastriano's extreme views and reclaiming for the Democrats a value that Republicans had tried to monopolize. "He loves to cloak himself in the blanket of freedom," Shapiro said of Mastriano in his general election campaign kickoff. "But hear me on this, it's not freedom. It's not freedom when he tries to tell the women of Pennsylvania what they can do with their own bodies. That's not freedom…It's not freedom when he tells you, you can't join a union. That is not freedom. It's not freedom when he tells you what books your children can read. That's not freedom. And it sure as hell isn't freedom when he tells you, you can vote, but he'll pick the winner. That's not freedom."

Shapiro's framing of the race started making headway with Republicans, too. Candidates have long tried to enlist surrogates from the opposite party to pitch themselves as moderate and bipartisan. Shapiro's outreach was next level. He was racking up endorsements from prominent Pennsylvania Republicans: former congressman Charlie Dent, former Homeland Security secretary Michael Chertoff, several former state lawmakers, former Trump White House lawyer Jim Schultz, and even a sitting elected county commission chairman. "I'm only saying what I think a lot of Republican officials across the state are thinking," the chairman, Morgan Boyd of Lawrence County, said in a joint local news interview with Shapiro. "They might not come out publicly and say that they're supporting Josh, [but] when they go into the voting booth in November, he's the box they're checking." Whereas other Republicans settled for refusing to support Mastriano without actively endorsing Shapiro, Boyd said that for him, "This race was too important to sit back on the sidelines."

Another of Shapiro's Republican backers, former congressman James Greenwood, started a PAC specifically to persuade moderate Republicans to cross party lines. The effort wouldn't be visible on TV ads and billboards; the goal was to identify and directly contact the narrow slice of Republicans whose votes could be in play. "What we're going to be doing is very, very tightly targeted," said the PAC's director, Craig Snyder. Snyder had been a former aide to the late senator Arlen Specter, who'd represented Pennsylvania as both a Republican and a Democrat. In a tight election, even a small sliver of Republicans voting for the Democrat could make the difference. "In a more normal world, in a more normal time, Mastriano wouldn't have a chance in Pennsylvania," Snyder said. "We don't live in normal times."

Other anti-MAGA efforts from within the GOP did appear in broadcast ads and on billboards. Sarah Longwell, a well-known anti-Trump Republican strategist, was running a ten-million-dollar nationwide campaign built around testimonials from real-life Republican voters who said they couldn't support this year's MAGA candidates. "There's this group of Republicans who feel alienated from the party despite having been Republican voters for their whole lives," she said. "There's a very specific lament that they have, which is, 'I can't believe what's happened to my party.'"

Longwell herself grew up in a Republican family in central Pennsylvania, worked on Senator Rick Santorum's book tour, and apprenticed with Richard Berman, an eminent Republican lobbyist and communications consultant. By 2016, Longwell had become the first woman board chair of the Log Cabin Republicans, the most prominent conservative LGBT group, and insisted that the organization refrain from endorsing Donald Trump. Her wife went into labor during that year's Republican National Convention, and Longwell remembered holding her newborn baby boy and watching Trump's acceptance speech on the hospital room TV, thinking, "This can't be happening."

A little more than a year later, with Trump's presidency already engulfed by special counsel Robert Mueller's investigation into Russian interference, Longwell linked up with a semisecret meeting of more famous Never Trumpers, such as Bill Kristol, the former chief of staff to Vice President Dan Quayle; Steve Schmidt, a top strategist on John McCain's 2008 presidential campaign; Eliot Cohen, a State Department adviser during the George W. Bush administration; and Max Boot, a prominent conservative writer. Their occasional meetings led to the formation of Defending Democracy Together, an umbrella group for raising and spending money to oppose Trump from within the GOP.

Over the years, Longwell built a massive database of disaffected Republicans, and she gradually worked to convince them to record an interview or put their face on a billboard. She knew that was a lot to ask and an act of bravery in this vicious political environment. But she also believed that it was the one thing that would be most effective. From polling and focus groups, Longwell discovered that the perceived credibility and relatability of the person talking mattered more than what they said. "In this era of low trust, you ask people, 'Who do you trust?' Their number one answer is 'People like me,'" she said. "Oftentimes, the things that test the best—it's less about the exact thing they say and it's more about, like, do people look at that person and think, 'Oh, I trust this person, this person feels like somebody I know'?"

Longwell had used this approach against Trump in 2020, and now she adapted it to his endorsed candidates in the midterms. The voters in her ads always had specific objections. "Doug Mastriano's position on abortion is unbelievably over-the-top," Cathe from Pennsylvania said in one. "We just don't need a crackpot in the governor's office, we really don't. We don't need a dangerous man in there," Wendy from Pennsylvania said in another. "Tell the big lie over and over again and people will believe it—that's what Kari Lake is doing," offered Tom from Arizona. What mattered was their palpable anguish. "Our message is the messenger," Longwell said. "Whatever their reason is that as a conservative or as a Republican, they are not going to vote for this candidate—that's the message. A lot of the experience that Republicans are having who've been lifelong Republicans who do not identify as Democrats, they have a struggle. They struggle with voting against the Republican candidates. They struggle voting for Democrats. And so when the voices of the people reflect that that's an actual tension, those are the things that perform the best from a persuasion standpoint."

There were other, state-specific efforts to rack up crossover endorsements: a hundred and fifty "Republicans for Whitmer" endorsed the Democratic governor of Michigan running for reelection; and in Idaho, fifty past and present Republicans, including a former governor, supported the Democratic candidate for attorney general.* Still more popped up spontaneously, organically. In Nevada, a veteran Republican strategist and former state assemblyman named Pete Ernaut wrote an op-ed endorsing the incumbent Democratic senator, Catherine Cortez-Masto. The article compared Cortez-Masto to the late Republican governor Paul Laxalt, and pointedly never mentioned her MAGA Republican challenger, who happened to be Laxalt's grandson.†

In Tennessee, a lifelong Republican and former political director of the state party named Randy Stamps published an open letter on Facebook endorsing the Democrat in his district's congressional race. Stamps said he'd heard out the Republican, Andy Ogles, by listening to him speak in person no fewer than nine times; each time, Stamps had found Ogles full of anger, yelling about masks and COVID instead of issues that Stamps viewed as more important, like inflation. "Candidly, as a longtime member of our party, I'm concerned about the direction we're heading in," Stamps said. "I absolutely do still consider myself a Republican, and as a Republican, I should still have the right to opt out of voting for one of our Republican nominees every once in a while...It's the temperament of Andy Ogles that disturbs me. It's his apparent lack of desire to ever listen to people who have a different viewpoint. And that is a growing phenomenon in the Republican Party that I would like to discourage."‡

In Washington State, David Nierenberg was one of the largest

---

* Whitmer won reelection by more than ten points. In Idaho, the Republican, Raúl Labrador, won the attorney general's race.

† Cortez-Masto won reelection with 48.9 percent of the vote, to Adam Laxalt's 48 percent.

‡ Ogles won the election with more than 55 percent of the vote. In 2023, reports in local news and the *Washington Post* revealed he had misrepresented his educational credentials, business career, and law enforcement background.

donors supporting his Republican congresswoman, Jaime Herrera Beutler, in one of the country's most competitive House races. In August, Herrera Beutler lost her primary to Joe Kent, a Trump-endorsed election denier who'd targeted her as one of the ten House Republicans who voted to impeach Trump (the second time) for inciting the insurrection. After a period of "mourning," Nierenberg said, he, his wife, and their son reached out to the Democrat, Marie Gluesenkamp Perez, to invite her to meet. She impressed them with her intelligence, moderate views, and upbringing in a Republican, rural part of the state. To Nierenberg, she demonstrated an ability to work across the aisle like Herrera Beutler had.

Nierenberg had grown up outside New York, in a liberal Democratic family that he rebelled against by casting his first vote for Ronald Reagan. After law school, he went to work for the consulting firm Bain & Co., whose CEO, Mitt Romney, became a mentor and friend. When Romney ran for governor of Massachusetts, Nierenberg was a top fundraiser, and he later served as one of the national finance chairs for Romney's 2008 and 2012 presidential campaigns. Now Steve Bannon called Nierenberg a "RINO Romney blowhard" for working against Joe Kent, but Nierenberg wore that as a badge of honor. Closer to home, Nierenberg knew that publicly endorsing a Democrat for Congress would not endear him to all his neighbors. But as a descendant of World War II veterans and Holocaust survivors, Nierenberg felt an obligation to defend what they had fought and suffered for: freedom from authoritarianism and bigotry. "People who are election deniers, people like Joe Kent, who say what happened on January 6 was constitutionally protected free speech, which in my view was an attempt at a Reichstag fire—with those points of view, I cannot support him," he said. Nierenberg heard history rhyming in the fact that when his family immigrated through Ellis Island, the congressman who'd led the effort to close the borders to Jews fleeing Eastern Europe held the same congressional seat that Kent was now running for. "A full century later, here we are with another nativist bigot running to represent this district, and I will not tolerate that," Nierenberg said. "I will do everything I can to defeat that kind of nastiness and incivility."*

---

* Kent lost the election by less than one percentage point. He has announced he is seeking a rematch in 2024.

In Mesa, Arizona, the city near Phoenix that was about to host one of Trump's final rallies of the midterm campaign, the elected Republican mayor, John Giles, endorsed the Democrats running for governor, secretary of state, and Senate. "I set a really low bar," he explained. "I, like most Americans, have been really bothered by the Stop the Steal election denier movement that, without any evidence, seems to be committed to turning its back on the Constitution. I see it as an existential threat to our country. I am a Republican, but I can't get over that hurdle.

"Saying nothing is acquiescing. Obviously I will pay a political price for the positions I'm taking, and I'm a hundred percent OK with that, because the situation we're in is more compelling than 'What's John Giles's political future?' Silence was not an option." Online, the response to his endorsements, he estimated, was ten-to-one people calling him a "traitor," or worse words he wouldn't repeat. But in person, it was ten-to-one the other way—people coming up to him and thanking him for giving them a voice. He was disappointed that more Republican leaders weren't speaking out. "You're not a good leader if you lack courage," he said. "If you're seeking the path of least resistance, that's not leadership. Mainstream people have got to reclaim the Republican Party if it's going to have a future at all."

KATHY PETSAS SAW a clip on Twitter from Kari Lake's speech at CPAC, where she'd gloated, "We drove a stake through the heart of the McCain machine," while making a stabbing motion. Kathy, who still put a McCain sign out on her lawn every year on his birthday, thought that was a hideous thing to say about the late senator and war hero—and also not a smart thing to say three days after winning the primary, when Lake now needed to unite the party to win in November. "Is it unity or not?" Kathy tweeted before going to bed.

In the morning, her phone pinged, alerting her to a reply from the official Kari Lake War Room campaign account. "Kathy," the tweet said, "You're exactly the type of demographic that we feel no need to appeal to. The Republicans who willfully cheered for Joe Biden to win because they vindictively hated this party moving past them."

Kathy was stunned. It was so petty, so personal, singling her out like that, by name, in public. Clearly whoever wrote that didn't know who she was, she figured, since she'd never voted for a Democrat for president, and she'd never voted for a Democrat for governor. She'd worked tirelessly to elect Republicans in elections for nearly half a century. Now she felt like she had no one to vote for. For governor, there were two candidates who'd supported Obama, one of them (Lake) now a Trump convert. She had no choice for secretary of state. She had no choice for attorney general (the Republican nominee was another MAGA election denier). She'd never lived through an election like this.

She obviously wasn't going to go door to door for candidates she couldn't defend. She wouldn't go campaigning for Democrats either. The campaign of Kari Lake's opponent, Katie Hobbs, asked Kathy if she would publicly endorse Hobbs, but she declined; she said she wasn't so much for the Democrats as she was against the MAGA Republicans. There were some local Republicans she'd support, like candidates for the water board and county attorney. But that was far from her usual campaign-season routine.

Still, Kathy did not quit the party. Despite what she'd muttered on primary night ("That was the pinot grigio talking," she'd later say), she remained a precinct committeewoman. She kept going to legislative district meetings and gritted her teeth through tirades and more censure resolutions against fellow PCs. She took out her frustration by needlepointing because she needed to stab something a thousand times. (The canvas she brought to one party meeting was a design sold by Bad Bitch Needlepoint, depicting a Greek diner coffee cup reading WE ARE HAPPY TO SERVE YOU.)

Under Kathy and other previous chairs, the meetings used to start with inspiring quotes from former Republican presidents and elected leaders. Now they started with a prayer. But it was not the type of prayer Kathy would say in church. One time, Kathy refused to go in until after the "prayer" was over, and her husband, Bill, who was also a PC, insisted on going ahead without her. "OK," she told him, "you'll see." The prayer turned out to be all about delivering the Republican candidates from the demonic Left. "Then I realized," Bill recounted later, "how smart my wife is."

For the next meeting, Bill didn't attend but promised to save Kathy some wine for when she got home. "You might need a little bump," he said.

"I'm gonna need more than a bump," she sighed.

That night, there was a cop stationed outside the church where the LD met. Dan Farley, the new district chair, had just gotten into a physical scuffle with members of the Patriot Party, a fringe group to the right of the GOP. They used to be Farley's allies, but now that he was the district chairman, they were accusing him of being an incompetent sellout. At a meeting in a different district the week before, they'd blocked Farley from entering the doorway until he pushed past them, then accused him of assault and called the police. "It's interesting that it didn't take very long for them to implode," Kathy muttered that night while washing dishes. "I really thought it'd take longer." She wasn't sticking it out just for schadenfreude, though: she was confident the party was about to blow it in November, and when that happened, she wanted to be there to pick up the pieces and rebuild. She'd been there for cleanup duty before, and she was ready to do it again.

As early voting started in Arizona, Kathy saw reports of people camping out to guard ballot drop boxes. The drop box fixation had been popularized that year by a movie called *2000 Mules,* produced by the right-wing media personality Dinesh D'Souza, whom Trump had pardoned for a 2012 campaign finance violation. The movie used cell-phone tracking data to identify people who repeatedly passed by drop boxes and accused them of being "mules" who stuffed the boxes with thousands, maybe millions, of phony ballots. But the drop boxes were intentionally placed in busy areas where they would be most accessible to voters, so plenty of people might have repeatedly passed by them for any number of unrelated reasons, such as on a commute or a delivery route. The movie claimed to use surveillance footage to catch people dropping off ballots while wearing gloves to hide their fingerprints (rather than because it was cold outside or they were worried about coronavirus exposure). Republican officials had examined the cell-phone tracking data earlier in 2022 and concluded it amounted to nothing. Yet now people were coming out to monitor drop boxes with cameras and dogs and even guns, sometimes wearing camo and tactical gear.

Kathy thought these people needed better hobbies. They could try needlepointing! They were like living, breathing manifestations of all the conspiracy theories and misinformation that had been swirling and spreading for two years now. She joked that she ought to show up wearing a Mardi Gras mask with a whole stack of empty envelopes just to mess with them. But in all seriousness, she worried that the vigilantes would make people afraid to vote, or that they would harass election workers so they couldn't do their jobs. She didn't really want to think about it.

Around that time, Kathy got a call from a blocked number. She was driving, so she couldn't record it in time. The call was vague but clearly threatening, and clearly because of her political activism. It happened twice. Kathy didn't spook easily, never had; it was just how she was wired. But this freaked her out. It got a little too close. The local Greek festival was coming up, always a highlight of Kathy's year, but this time she didn't want to tweet about it, concerned about publicizing her whereabouts, in case someone out there might try to take advantage of a time when they knew she wouldn't be home.

A few weeks before Election Day, Kathy got a chance to meet a personal hero. She was invited to a private lunch with Liz Cheney. The Wyoming congresswoman, the most famous of the ten Republicans who'd voted for impeachment, had lost her primary in August. Cheney had been the third-ranking Republican in the House until the conference ousted her in May 2021, fed up with her refusal to stop criticizing Trump over January 6. She went on to become vice chair of the House committee investigating the attack on the Capitol, though in practice she operated as the panel's chief: she led the sharpest, most direct condemnations of Trump, keeping the committee's hearings and eventual report laser-focused on Trump's culpability, and concluding that he should never hold office again. Her role bolstered the committee's credibility, both in public and with the witnesses they interviewed; and she deliberately stacked the committee's hearings with testimony from her fellow Republicans, making them the messengers for the most damaging descriptions of Trump's conduct and mindset. Trump's own campaign aides told her how they'd advised him against declaring victory on Election Night 2020. Trump's own attorney general and White House counsel told her there were no credible allegations of fraud that could affect the outcome. Republican state officials told her how they'd refused Trump's demands to overturn the results. Trump's own White House aide told her the president had wanted to lead the mob to the Capitol and didn't care that people in the crowd were armed. His own vice president's lawyer explained for Cheney how Pence lacked the power to reject the Electoral College votes. A widely respected retired conservative judge testified that Trump and his movement posed an ongoing "clear and present danger to American democracy" — and "not because of what happened on January 6," the judge, J. Michael Luttig, said. "It's because to this very day, the former president, his allies, and his supporters pledge that in the presidential election of 2024, if the former president or his anointed successor as the Republican party presidential candidate were to lose that election, that they would attempt to overturn that 2024 election in the same way they attempted to overturn the 2020 election, but succeed in 2024 where they failed in 2020." Kathy watched the hearings, and saw Cheney as an inspiration.

The lunch, at a resort in Scottsdale, had about sixty people, all Republicans. They asked Cheney what the heck they were supposed to do now. She told them not to give up, to remain courageous, that you cannot win if you're not in the fight, and the country needed a functioning two-party system. Kathy took a picture with Cheney and shared it with close friends and family. In the past she would have proudly posted it online, but now she didn't; she was worried about provoking more threats.

For Kathy, the most memorable part of the lunch came when someone waved Cheney over to a group of people saying something like "We don't bite." Cheney replied, "You don't have to worry about my courage." It was just an aside, not even a real remark, but to Kathy it said everything.

After the lunch, Cheney went to the McCain Institute at Arizona State University for a public speech. She began by recounting her work on the January 6 committee, and she made sure to emphasize, "It was courageous Republicans who withstood pressure from the former president at all levels and who have been willing to come forward and tell the truth about what happened. So if anybody says to you, 'January 6 wasn't all that bad, the institutions held,' please tell them they only held because of people, and because of Americans who stepped forward."

Her main message that day was that the danger was not over, the threat had only grown, and Arizona was on the front lines. "You have a candidate for governor in Kari Lake, you have a candidate for secretary of state in Mark Finchem, both of whom have said — this isn't a surprise, it's not a secret — they both said that they will only honor the results of an election if they agree with it," Cheney said. "If you care about democracy and you care about the survival of our republic, then you need to understand, we all have to understand, that we cannot give people power who have told us that they will not honor elections."

Toward the end of the hour, Cheney took questions from the audience. "For Republicans who feel alienated by the Trump tilt of the Republican Party," a man asked, "what is the best avenue for them to pursue, to promote good change? Is it to join a third party with moderate Democrats? Is it to stay within the party and work to affect change within? What do you see as the best avenue for those Republicans?"

"I'm not ready to say we're going to allow Trump and those who are at war with democracy to hijack our party," Cheney answered. "I'm not ready to give that fight up...Individually, Republicans need to be engaged in battling for the precinct chairmen and -women's seats. If you look at what the antidemocratic forces in the Republican Party are doing, they have a very concerted effort underway to take control at a local level, at a state level, and to fundamentally turn the Republican Party into something that is anti-American. And I think that those of us who love the ideals and believe in the ideals the party has stood for have to be engaged on the ground in that battle to challenge them, to fill those seats, to make sure that at a state level we don't watch this slip away.

"I go back to the choice that Arizona voters have this election cycle," Cheney went on. "And I say this as somebody who, my first vote I ever cast, I was eighteen years old and I voted for Ronald Reagan. So for almost forty years now I've been voting Republican. I don't know that I have ever voted for a Democrat. But if I lived in Arizona now," she said, as if speaking directly to Kathy Petsas, "I absolutely would.

"The country's at the edge of an abyss," Cheney said. "That's not overstating the danger we're facing. And if we don't decide that we're going to pull back from that, that we're going to vote for the serious people, that we're going to hold our elected officials accountable, that we aren't going to accept appeasement of antidemocratic forces, then we're going to go over the edge...It's going to be a battle for a long time. But those who are fighting to unravel our democracy need to know, absolutely, with total clarity, that those of us who are fighting to maintain our freedom, to maintain our constitutional republic, are stronger and more dedicated and have more determination than they do, and that we're going to win."

CHAPTER 10

The Trump Machine

ELECTION NIGHT IN Arizona started like a replay of the primary. In the governor's race, Katie Hobbs, the Democrat, posted an initial lead based on mail ballots and early votes. But Kari Lake had the advantage with voters who followed Trump's instruction to vote in person on Election Day. Would Hobbs's lead be enough to hold? Not that Kathy Petsas was rooting for Hobbs. She'd knocked on so many doors of independents who didn't like Katie Hobbs but couldn't stand Kari Lake. More than anything, Kathy was eager to turn Lake's own phrase against her and declare, "We drove a stake through the heart of the Trump machine."

By morning, Hobbs was still on top, but her lead had narrowed to less than one percentage point. Too close to call. Kathy hung on every update of every batch of ballots as they were posted online, analyzing where they came from and what method of voting they were to extrapolate the trend. As it became clearer how many Republicans like her were defecting, the statewide races were starting to look like a Democratic sweep. By Saturday, Kathy was still not ready to celebrate, but she did delight in a tweet she saw from David French, a prominent Never Trumper: "Turns out the GOP base actually needed some of the folks that it mocked, scorned, and bullied right out the party."

The Associated Press finally called the race for Hobbs on the following Monday. Kathy felt vindicated. She had been right — "in a huge F'ing way." Hobbs beat Lake by thirty points with independents, and even won 11 percent of Republicans.

The results were consistent across the country. The MAGA Republicans all went down. This should have been the moment Kathy had been waiting for: the GOP had done a full belly flop in the midterms; the MAGA extremists had been repudiated at the polls. It should have been time for her and her allies to retake the party and steer it back toward sanity.

But Kathy understood something fundamental about the people she was dealing with, about human psychology in general. She understood that admitting a mistake can be so embarrassing that people would rather accept ever-more-fanciful excuses and rationalizations. "People at a certain point, when they believe something, their minds cannot be changed," she said. "Because they're so bought in, and to change their minds means they were wrong. And that is the hardest thing for some people."

Those were the people who controlled the party now. In Arizona, they were the PCs who'd been elected in the August primary—back when Kathy had been trying to recruit moderates to take back the party and had struggled to motivate them because they'd thought the party looked like a hopeless case. Now that the election results validated what she'd been saying all along, it was too late. The incumbent PCs were the people least inclined to learn their lesson from the midterm results and course-correct. The electorate had spoken, but the fringe still controlled the party.

A few weeks after the election, the county board of supervisors met in Phoenix to officially certify the results. Kathy didn't attend in person, but she watched the whole thing streaming live on YouTube. The chairman, Bill Gates,* began the meeting by recognizing the county recorder, the official in charge of the voter file and early voting.

The recorder, Stephen Richer, was a Republican, and when he'd been elected to the position, in 2020, he still had a full head of hair. For a while after the election, Richer went around speaking to Republican groups, answering their questions, and reassuring them that the election was legitimate. He'd figured these were fellow Republicans he knew and who knew him, and they could talk it out. At one of these

---

* No relation to the Microsoft founder.

meetings, in 2021, someone asked Richer if the tabulation machines were connected to the internet, and in that moment, Richer understood that if he told the truth (that they were not), he would lose the room, and the rest of the meeting would not go well for him. He recognized the politician's impulse, maybe a human impulse, to want to be liked; he drew no joy from being reviled in front of a crowd. But once he told the truth, knowing it would make him unpopular, that the machines weren't connected to the internet so they couldn't be hacked by a foreign power to flip votes to Biden, he couldn't get another word in. He gave up holding more Q and A sessions.

Now, speaking at the board of supervisors meeting to certify the 2022 midterm results, Richer went over again how his office authenticated mail ballots. "I know you all have heard me describe this a million times…There is no use of artificial intelligence," he said. "These conversations need to focus on real issues. We can spend the next two years as we've spent the last two, fighting over conspiracy theories promoted on social media by people who know nothing about—"

The crowd interrupted him with booing. Gates reminded them to be respectful and let Richer speak; they would have their turn. "The world is watching," Gates said, which only prompted more talk-back from the crowd. "I'm getting very close to calling a recess here and I don't want to do that," he calmly insisted.

Richer started again. "If we spend all of our time on stuff like Splunk logs, fractional voting, and ballot mules, then we won't be addressing the questions that all Arizonans care about, such as how can we speed up the time it takes to process Election Day early ballot drop-offs, or how can we prevent third-party groups from confusing voters by masquerading as a county entity," he said. "This is my first foray into elected politics, and it's been an eye-opener. But if we make some of these real improvements to our election system over the next two years, then it will be a worthwhile endeavor, and it will be something that we'll all be proud of, both elected and Arizona citizens alike."*

* In June 2023, Richer sued Kari Lake for defamation, alleging her false accusations about his administration of the election cost him relationships with friends, family, and supporters and took a physical and emotional toll. "My name continues to be dragged through the mud in front of millions of her online viewers in various platforms," he told the *Washington Post*. "And I felt that I needed to take the only recourse left."

Richer finished, and Kathy watched for hours as her friend Thomas Galvin, Bill Gates, and the other supervisors, like hapless C-SPAN hosts during a call-in segment, sat solemnly and listened to a parade of two-minute comments from the audience members.

"I'm the chief election denier, I'm the person he talks about as far as a conspiracy theorist," said a right-wing podcaster from Colorado named Joe Oltmann. "The fact that we can gaslight the American people like we did with COVID, like we did with gender fluidity, like we did with all sorts of other things that we started to uncover during the pandemic, is just wrong...You can't outvote a machine," he concluded. The crowd clapped in response, which Gates politely reminded them not to do.

"I came here today to get an up close and personal look at the seven traitors to the United States Constitution sitting at that desk," a woman named Kathy Roscoe said, pointing to the supervisors one by one. "Interference in an election in the United States of America, Mr. Gates, is a capital offense...Those who make peaceful revolution impossible make violent revolution necessary!"

"If this election is certified, the only parties that will benefit from this are the cartels," said Ben Bergquam, a correspondent from Real America's Voice, the right-wing network that carried Bannon's *War Room*. "They've taken over Mexico, and sadly they've taken over many politicians in America. What we saw on Election Day was outrageous, and to say that it was anything but that is either you think we're stupid or you're just that arrogant...If you certify today, the only thing you'll be certifying is your corruption." Since Gates had asked for no cheering or clapping, people stood and fluttered their hands to show support in American Sign Language.

"This is a war between good and evil, and you all represent evil," said Chris Hamlet, a bald, bearded veteran who'd just lost a race for the Mesa school board. "God-fearing men and women out here need to understand that and get up every day and start donning your body armor before you step on this battlefield. We cannot continue to fight this war with these earthly weapons and continue to talk on deaf ears."

Several people spoke about specific, personal experiences of encountering long lines and rejected ballots. In truth, there had been some real glitches on Election Day: the county used heavier paper and longer ballots than in earlier tests, causing some printers and tabulators to jam. Voters were instructed to go to a different polling site or leave their ballots in a secure drawer. Ultimately, an independent review concluded that there was no malfeasance. Elections are hard, people are human, and something almost always goes wrong. But at this hearing, voters demanded to know how the supervisors could certify a result with so many problems. One man cited the fact that a Republican candidate for state treasurer got a hundred thousand more votes than Kari Lake as proof of fraud (as opposed to evidence that the state treasurer candidate was more appealing to moderates and independents than Lake was). One woman used her two minutes to read from the Book of Psalms, asking God to tear out the fangs of the sinners. Another demanded a revote with hand-counted paper ballots. Another played a clip that she said was a man testifying to a judge about his work rigging elections, and she pointed jerkily from her phone to the audience as it played. There was a woman wearing a green beanie who spoke with a thick accent, recounting how her family had lost everything in Venezuela because of Dominion voting machines. Kathy had met that woman before; sometimes her story was that she was from Russia, or Ukraine, or Romania.

Kathy thought this hearing made convincing testimony for increasing mental health spending in Arizona. She was not being glib — she thought this spectacle attested to a mental health crisis. She felt for Bill Gates, who had to literally go into hiding because of threats to his life after the election. Months later, Kathy would be out with friends when one of them got a text message: Gates had just announced he was suffering from PTSD and wouldn't run for reelection. Kathy and her friends all broke down in tears.

Two days after the certification hearing, Kathy's legislative district was set to choose representatives to the state party convention, known as state committeemen. The state committeemen would go on to vote for a new state party chair at the state convention in January. As Kathy had feared, Dan Farley was making a run for state chair. So was Steve Daniels, his old Patriot Party ally turned adversary, the guy who'd accused him of assault. (They both now had temporary restraining orders against each other.)* Kathy's district

---

* Later, at the state convention, Farley helped stave off Daniels by withdrawing from the race and endorsing Jeff DeWit, a former state treasurer, as a consensus choice.

was allotted more than a hundred state committeeman slots, but Kathy knew it'd take a miracle for her to get one. There would be no proxy votes allowed for any PCs who couldn't attend in person. When Kathy had been chair, she'd held proxies for members of her precinct who'd given her permission in their absence, which was normal parliamentary procedure. But the proxies had become one of the complaints from the new PCs who accused her of shutting them out. Now other districts still allowed proxies, but not Kathy's LD. Kathy thought it was not fair to exclude active party members just because they had a scheduling conflict on a given night. For example, her husband, Bill, was going to a Phoenix Suns game. Another friend was in the symphony orchestra and had a dress rehearsal. Or people were ill. People had lives. She viewed this new rule as a form of disenfranchisement. "That's just one way that somebody like Dan Farley can fix a race," Kathy said, "if he limits who can vote to his true believers." Sure enough, Kathy did not win a slot, and Merissa Hamilton texted a reporter to rub it in. "I am now elected State Committeeman," she said, "and Kathy Petsas is not."

Even though Kathy would not be able to vote at the state convention, she was still a PC, meaning she could still attend district meetings and the county meeting. The county meeting was held in January 2023 at a megachurch in northern Phoenix. To help her get through it, Kathy brought a needlepoint canvas depicting a Nantucket clutch. She was sitting quietly working on her needlepoint, as the county chair, Mickie Niland, went through the formal resolutions that had been proposed for the county party to consider adopting. She came to Resolution Seven: "Censure of Republican members of the Maricopa County Board of Supervisors and Republican Maricopa County Recorder Stephen Richer."

"Oh God," Kathy groaned. A man sitting nearby called out, "Hit the road." The crowd cheered. Mickie started recognizing people to speak for and against the resolution at microphones set up in the aisles.

"Here's the problem," one PC said. "Maricopa County is effectively 62 percent of all of Arizona, and it's run by the four most crooked SOBs." People laughed and clapped and screamed, "Yeah!" "I'm tired of this," the PC who was speaking added. "They need to be held accountable. They need to be censured, frankly, every opportunity we have. We cannot wait until 2024."

"This is not the Board of Supervisors, this is the Board of Criminals," the next speaker said. "Stephen Richer lied to every single one of us. He's not a Republican. I personally showed him IP addresses of flipping way back in January of 2021. That man saw this. He lied, he continues to lie. Every one of these are liars, criminals. Censuring is not enough."

That was it. Kathy had had enough of keeping quiet. She thought about a time in 2016 when the Republican Senate candidate had spoken to her LD and insulted John McCain; Kathy had cut off her microphone. Now she looked around the room and saw people who she knew opposed this lunacy and could have said so. If they wouldn't, she would.

As soon as Kathy took her place at the microphone and announced her name, the room erupted into boos — the loudest boos she'd heard all day. "I will stand here," Kathy said. "My name is Kathy Petsas, I'm from LD 4."

"The proxy queen!" a man jeered from the audience, cutting through the booing.

"Censuring has no purpose in this body," Kathy continued.

"Bullshit!"

"It does not build our party. It does not gain us more people. And I stood here two years ago and said to you, by censuring these individuals, *you* will give us Governor Katie Hobbs — "

"BOOOOOOOOOO!"

" — and that's exactly what your actions did."

"GO HOME!" "YOU gave us Hobbs!"

"Bill Gates, Richer, Sellers, Hickman, Galvin," Kathy shouted into the microphone, reciting the names of the recorder and the Republican supervisors, "these are all upstanding individuals — "

The boos were so deafening she had to stop. *"SIT DOWN!" "GO HOME!"* It was as if she were now physically confronting all the people from all 132 coffees, multiplied by all twenty-seven districts in the county, here to drown her out and shut her up. Friends would ask Kathy afterward if she regretted going up there. She would answer that what she would have regretted was if no one had said anything. Other people could have spoken against the resolution. What was stopping them? They were afraid of being booed? By these people? Kathy had seen so many Republicans sell their souls. She decided she couldn't live with herself if she'd said nothing, if she didn't stand up for the true Republicans who were defending democracy.

No one else rose to speak against the resolution, so Kathy asked to go again. *"NOOOOOO!"* the crowd bellowed. Before she could, she was beaten to the microphone by Brian Ference. He was another of the Patriot Party guys who had gotten into the scuffle with Dan Farley. "I'm going to speak against this," he said sarcastically, as if he were taking Kathy's side. Then he proceeded to stand silently and waste his whole allotted minute as the audience burst into laughter and applause, and finally into chants of *"USA! USA!"*

Passing Brian Ference on her way back to the microphone, Kathy told him, "He didn't punch you hard enough." She tried to speak again, but the heckling completely buried her. Kathy was mindful that there was a camera trained on her, projecting her face onto two giant screens above the stage. *Just keep smiling*, she thought to herself. *Don't let them see them getting to you.* They did not need to worry about her courage.

AS THE CENSURE resolution passed, elsewhere in the megachurch auditorium sat Dan Schultz, wearing his big white PC button. He was there with one of his sons, who'd driven down from Flagstaff. His daughter was also a PC but had an emergency at her work as an engineer, so Dan would be her proxy vote (which, in this vote, was perfectly permissible). Dan was not an active participant at the county meeting, but he was used to people coming up to him and telling him that his *War Room* interview was the reason they were there. His own LD's new chairman was one of those people.

And yet. Despite all the new PCs at this county party meeting, despite how the GOP had been transformed in Arizona and across the country, Dan was not feeling optimistic about the future of America. He still thought things were going to get a lot worse. It was like he always said: "I can't guarantee you that if we carry out the Precinct Committeeman Strategy that we're going to save the republic. Can't guarantee that. But we have a shot if we do." For the past hundred years, since the turn of the twentieth century, Dan believed, the communists had been trying to take over America without firing a shot. "They're getting really close, aren't they?" he said now. "I want my kids to grow up in the America that I grew up in, thank God, in the sixties and early seventies." One of his sons had come home from his freshman year in high school, saying they'd had a lesson on political participation. The teacher had asked, "What can you do to get involved in changing things politically?" No one raised their hand, until Dan's son did and suggested, one thing you could do is become a precinct committeeman for the political party of your choice. The teacher looked back at him and said, "What's a precinct committee?"

At the county party meeting, the proceedings broke down into a drawn-out and chaotic fight over the rules, with some PCs demanding to get rid of the electronic tabulation machines and insisting on hand counts for the election of county party officers. The eventual compromise was to verify the machine counts with hand tallies after the fact, but the debate took so long that they didn't finish voting before the church kicked them out. Dan hoped that next time, at the state convention two weeks later, they would eliminate the machines entirely. He wasn't sure whom he'd support for state chair; all five candidates claimed to be conservatives, and he struggled to sort out who really was. He thought about nominating himself from the floor ("What the hell?"). Other times he wondered if he should just "go Galt" — make like the hero of Ayn Rand's *Atlas Shrugged* and go on strike from productive society, withdraw into isolation, and wait for the government to crumble.

He asked himself whether there were enough good, decent Americans left to save the republic. There were so many reasons to get pissed off that he hoped he could use to motivate more people to become PCs: rising gas prices, higher taxes, federal spending, the national debt...He still wanted to get rid of voting machines. He wanted to see Nuremberg-style trials imposing the death penalty on the people behind the COVID vaccines, because he believed the vaccines were bioweapons meant to depopulate the planet. He wanted porn out of schools — picking up on widespread right-wing backlash against library books and educational programming about gender and sexuality, what Dan called "the transgender nonsense, the drag queen crapola." As a former intelligence officer, Dan seethed at the FBI and CIA officials who spoke out against Trump, and who warned during the 2020 campaign that Hunter Biden's laptop looked like Russian disinformation, even though the trove of embarrassing and incriminating materials turned out to be genuine.

And still the president's son walked free,* while Trump was staring down multiple criminal investigations, including separate federal probes into his handling of classified documents and his efforts to overturn the 2020 election. Trump was calling it a two-tiered system of justice, where Democrats could get away with crimes and Republicans got persecuted. Dan was reminded of the famous scene in *The Outlaw Josey Wales*, when Clint Eastwood's character tells his besieged band of misfits, who are hiding out from bounty hunters and Union soldiers, "Now remember, when things look bad and it looks like you're not gonna make it, then you gotta *get mean*. I mean plumb, mad-dog *mean*. 'Cause if you lose your head and you give up, then you neither live nor win. That's just the way it is."

For about a half hour every day, usually while he waited for his son to get home from school, Dan recorded a podcast going over the same slides with the same case for why conservatives needed to take over the party by becoming PCs. His office looked unchanged from the first time he'd appeared on Bannon's *War Room*: diplomas on the walls, skis in the corner, books about communism on the shelf, PC button pinned to his shirt. He posted the podcasts on the alternative video-hosting site Rumble, using the username Cold-Warrior1978. On a good day he broke a hundred views. Maybe the next one would be the one to go viral. He occasionally threatened to stop doing these podcasts, but he never did.

DAN DIDN'T GO on Bannon's *War Room* anymore, but that did not mean Bannon had given up on the Precinct Strategy. "The Precinct Strategy is the mechanism for how it's gonna happen," Bannon said. By "it," he meant completing the Republican Party's transformation into the party of MAGA. Bannon couldn't have agreed more that Republicans lost the midterms because they nominated MAGA candidates who alienated moderate Republicans. Arizona was a perfect example. Moderate Republicans defected from Kari Lake, worked

---

* President Biden's son Hunter was later indicted, in September 2023, by a federal special counsel for allegedly making false statements and illegally possessing a handgun. The charges came after a plea deal to two misdemeanor tax violations fell apart in July 2023. In December, a federal grand jury in California indicted Hunter Biden on nine felony tax violations.

against her, and cost her the election. But that was Bannon's point: that was *their* fault, not MAGA's. He wasn't interested in winning those people back. He didn't think that made any sense. "You're not going to get those establishment Republicans," he said.

"The only thing that held this thing together was tax cuts and deregulation," Bannon explained. "Anti-communism bound it together until the eighties, Reagan's Revolution. What bound things together was tax cuts and regulations that the donors would do this and hold their nose as long as they got their tax cuts." But that bargain had broken down, the coalition had unraveled, become untenable. "The country-club elites are against, socially, everything that MAGA believes. They think it's too far right," he said. "What the establishment Republicans want as far as unity goes, they want the Grundoons* to just shut the fuck up and just ring doorbells, give small-dollar donations and show up to vote. This party is not going to have unity. There's not going to be a party that has both the working-class nature of it and the donor class. They're incompatible. This is populist, nationalist, America First, antiwar, anti–the World Economic Forum / globalization. The big power elites, the corporate interests, and the Chamber of Commerce is just adamantly opposed to that. There's not a big tent to have."

Instead of winning back establishment Republicans, Bannon's vision for the GOP's future was to expand the MAGA movement. He believed there were more working- and middle-class Americans who had yet to be recruited or who didn't reliably vote. He liked his chances better of converting far-left Democrats, such as supporters of Vermont senator Bernie Sanders or California congressman Ro Khanna, than going back to Republicans who'd supported Karrin Taylor Robson in the Arizona gubernatorial primary.

Bannon knew the Democrats would love his strategy, that it would make the Republican brand more toxic to the suburban women who decided elections. That didn't faze him. "They also thought my formula in '14–'15 was idiotic," he said. "I was talking populism and nationalism before Trump—the force of nature—came on the scene. Go back and look at that: 'It's ridiculous, it's

* Bannon's term for mindless grunt workers, taken from the diapered groundhog character in the *Pogo* comic strip.

Nazism, it's white nationalism, it's crazy.' It worked in '16. And quite frankly, it did turn out 74 million *real* votes in '20."

Since the midterms, MAGA grassroots uprisings had only spread to more states — South Dakota, Nebraska, Washington State, Kansas, Texas, Pennsylvania. "There's a massive sea change," Bannon said. "The awakening has come. This is the revolt." The establishment was planning to ride it out, still hoping the fever would break, Bannon said. But the MAGA grassroots had developed a taste for blood after dominating the 2022 primaries. Now he was bringing the fight to the pinnacle of the party pyramid: chairman of the Republican National Committee.

CHAPTER 11

The Waldorf and the Nuthouse

THE RESIDENCE INN San Juan Capistrano was a bright orange and yellow stucco building next to the interstate, with pullout sofas and kitchenettes in the guest rooms and a tiny Astroturf putting green by the pool. In a beige, carpeted conference room, under a low hung-tile ceiling, about a hundred people from the surrounding areas of Orange County, in Southern California, answered the call from Steve Bannon's *War Room* and John Fredericks's radio show to attend the only public debate for the RNC chairman's race. Across the creek and a couple of miles down the road, past the Italian cypress trees and gated subdivisions, the 168 members of the Republican National Committee were gathering at the Waldorf Astoria Monarch Beach. The Waldorf had a sprawling, destination golf course, a private beach club, a garden adorned with classical statues, a regular pool and a saltwater pool, and a light-drenched lobby perfectly positioned to catch the sunset over the Pacific. Here, in two days, on the last Friday in January 2023, the party's central committee would vote on whether to reelect Ronna McDaniel (née Ronna Romney) as their national chair.

McDaniel was seeking a record fourth term as chair. The position embodied the harrowing, perhaps impracticable, and often thankless task of holding together the party's fractious coalition. McDaniel had a special knack for it. Her direct constituency was the RNC's 168 members—a party chair and two other delegates from every state, D.C., and five territories, known in the club as the One Sixty-Eight. She tended them dutifully. But in this race, she was vulnerable. She had detractors from the middle who thought she was too pliant to Trump: she'd been his pick for chair, in 2017, and even changed her own name at Trump's request. And she had detractors from the right who thought she was not MAGA enough— they still remembered that she was a Romney! She had talked a big game about a blockbuster election integrity initiative with thirty thousand poll watchers and as many poll workers across all the key battleground states, and what did they have to show for it? The election integrity team showed up to this RNC meeting with a report recommending investing further in the initiative, with more trainings, volunteers, and lawsuits. As evidence of success, the report cited higher Republican turnout in the Georgia Senate runoff, omitting the fact that the Republican lost.

In the race for chair, McDaniel faced two challengers, who were both vying for the mantle of overthrowing the establishment and speaking for the party's furious grassroots activists: an RNC member from California named Harmeet Dhillon, who as a lawyer had advised the campaigns of Donald Trump in 2020 and Kari Lake in 2022; and the MyPillow guy, Mike Lindell. At stake was control of the RNC's extensive resources: hundreds of staff, more than a million volunteers, hundreds of millions of dollars, a prominent public platform, and considerable behind-the-scenes arm-twisting clout.

Now, two days ahead of the vote, Fredericks had convened this debate, unsanctioned and unofficial, on the periphery of the formal meeting. He was broadcasting it live on his show from the Residence Inn, which was, he said, "where *real people* come in order to hear from their candidates...people that can't afford to go to the Gestapo thing they got going on right now, the RNC, at the Waldorf." Here at the Residence Inn, the parking was free, not seventy dollars like the Waldorf's valet. At the Residence Inn, breakfast was included, not a hundred and twenty dollars like Fredericks and his wife had paid at the Waldorf. Even though the RNC had gotten a block rate at the Waldorf that brought the nightly cost under two hundred dollars a room, to Fredericks the exclusive atmosphere epitomized everything that was wrong with the whole affair: a spirited grassroots movement that, when it came time to elect a party leader, got cut out by elites who pretended the movement didn't exist. "We've asked you for two years to become involved — Precinct 2.0," Fredericks said on the air. "You've done that. Thank you. And now we've basically been locked out…That's why we're bringing the action back to you."

Before kicking off the debate, Fredericks took a moment to thank his sponsor, MyPillow, now offering 80 percent off with the promo code GODZILLA. Then he introduced the moderator, Virginia state chair Rich Anderson, who presented the candidates, starting with Mike Lindell. Representing Harmeet Dhillon was her campaign manager, Caroline Wren, who blamed the candidate's absence on having to attend a committee meeting on election integrity, suggesting that this scheduling conflict was some form of willful establishment subterfuge.

Wren, wearing a red dress and a gold elephant pendant, was a Republican fundraiser who finished her phone calls with, "MAGA, bye." She was one of the organizers of the January 6 rally on the Ellipse that led to the riot at the Capitol, and she resented being identified in every news article since as one of the organizers of the January 6 rally on the Ellipse that led to the riot at the Capitol.

Next to her, representing the incumbent, Ronna McDaniel, was an empty chair, because depending on whom you asked, she either never got an invitation or never RSVP'd.

Lindell spoke first. After two years of promising to deliver proof that the 2020 election was stolen, hosting conferences, producing films, touting hand-delivered Supreme Court petitions that never happened, showing up as an uninvited warm-up act for Trump rallies, and propping up thousands of right-wing talk shows and podcasts with pillow ads, he said he decided to run for RNC chair because of Kari Lake's loss, when the RNC didn't back her demand to hold a new election. Lindell said the Republican Party had a branding problem, and he was the master marketer they needed to turn around their image. "This country is 70 percent red," he said. "If you remove all the garbage and all the corruption and everything, it's 70 percent red, and it's getting redder every day."

Caroline Wren went straight after the incumbent. "We have had underperformance, if not outright failures, in 2018, 2020, and 2022," she said. "If you owned a football team and you lost three seasons in a row, you would fire the head coach…We have the same head coach and we're expecting a different result. And that's the definition of insanity." Republicans like Mitch McConnell were blaming the midterm losses on nominating bad candidates, including Kari Lake, whom Wren worked for. "It doesn't really actually matter with candidate quality, because you cannot explain to me that Katie Hobbs was a good candidate, or John Fetterman, who was brain dead and got elected," Wren said.* "They can elect a cucumber because we don't have real elections in this country...It was not bad candidates, it was not-real elections. And we have to recognize that and either play the game the Democrats are playing"—the audience started clapping—"or fold up shop and go home."

The lesson from Arizona, Wren said, was Republicans put all their eggs in the Election Day basket, so on the day of, when there were printer problems and machines went down, that disproportionately impacted Republican voters. Democrats were banking ballots for forty-five days of mail and early voting, while Republicans piled into just one day. Fredericks agreed, calling it "the most insane strategy in the history of politics."

Whose strategy was that? Who'd gotten up at every rally and told his supporters to vote only in person on Election Day because somehow that would prevent theft? Still, Fredericks did not blame Trump; he said the party chairman should have been telling people to vote by any method they wanted. Actually, McDaniel had been saying that—on Bannon's *War Room*, of all places—but clearly Republicans had listened to Trump instead. Now, in the aftermath of the midterms, Republicans were increasingly acknowledging the reality that no matter how much they distrusted early voting and mail ballots, they couldn't afford to boycott them. "We will play the game that they play until we can get our people back into office and finally clean up our elections," Wren said in the debate, threading the needle. "The goal has always been to vote on Election Day in person, but we are not there right now, and so we have to weaponize, the same way the Democrats are doing it. Harmeet Dhillon, as an attorney, is the right person to do that. Ronna McDaniel seems like a nice enough person, but you do not get to run for

---

* Fetterman suffered a near-fatal stroke in May 2022 and continued to experience difficulty understanding oral conversations.

reelection after three failed election cycles with no actual plan to move forward.

"The Republican Party is facing an existential crisis right now," Wren went on. "And if you do not listen to the grassroots and what they want, which is change in leadership, then we will lose our party. Every single grassroots organization that I know, they're sending thousands of emails to the RNC 168 members saying, 'We don't want change, we are *demanding* a change.'"

There was indeed a deluge of emails, but they were not especially persuasive to many of the RNC's 168 members. "Moronic, sad, pathetic," one member said — mostly robotic copy-paste jobs, and many of them vulgar or rude. While Wren and Dhillon were out collecting automated emails and Fox News monologues and Twitter likes, McDaniel and her team were playing the inside game: working over the One Sixty-Eight individually with phone calls and meetings and relationships. In the chairman's race, the One Sixty-Eight were the only votes that counted.

Dhillon had made her own job harder by attacking the people whose votes she needed, accusing them of being bought off, calling them "elite...cronies [with] contempt for grassroots." It played well on Fox News and Bannon's *War Room*, but not with the One Sixty-Eight. "Your words have damaged the institution you claim to want to lead," Iowa's party chair, Jeff Kaufmann, said in an email to the group. Then Dhillon showed up at the Waldorf with Kari Lake, and grimaced as Lake hogged the cameras to talk about her lawsuit challenging the Arizona election, rather than Dhillon's candidacy. Wren, as her campaign manager, was not necessarily endearing herself to the committee members either. She went around the resort telling one contractor she would cut off her finger to cross his name off the vendor list in blood (she said she was joking!), promising party officials who voted for Dhillon that they would get fundraisers with Kari Lake, and, late on the night before the vote, boisterously accosting Vernon Jones, a former Georgia state legislator who was supporting McDaniel, by calling him a "fucking sellout."* But perhaps the greatest obstacle Dhillon faced was needing to run around McDaniel on both flanks, appealing to ultra MAGAs and

---

* Wren denied using the term "sellout," saying she told him, "The grassroots is not going to forget this."

Trump skeptics at the same time, a tough trick to pull off (and one that previewed the challenge facing Florida Governor Ron DeSantis as Trump's main challenger in the presidential primary). Lindell had his own issues; according to one RNC member present for the closed-door candidate's forum, Lindell gave a rambling speech that mentioned his battle with crack addiction and left the audience unable to rule out a relapse. By Friday he would receive four votes, Dhillon fifty-one, McDaniel one hundred eleven.

Fredericks never really expected to topple McDaniel at this meeting. But Fredericks remained impressed they'd come this far, this fast, since 2021. "I never thought we'd be here, we're way ahead of ourselves. I thought it would be four years before we could get competitive," he said over a glass of wine, after migrating from the Residence Inn to the Waldorf's bar, overlooking the ocean. "It takes a long time to get from joining the party, to precinct captain, to county chairman, to vice chair of the party, to running for state chairman or being a [national] committeeman. Now, half these people you see," he said, gesturing to the RNC members scattered around the lobby, "we're voting them out. We'll get new people. It's going to take time, but we're going to rise up. We have to take the party over from the bottom up. Can't take it from the top down. Gotta take it from the bottom up. Two years from *now*, half these One Sixty-Eight you're seeing? Are gone. Quote me on that. They're gone."

ON THE SAME day as John Fredericks's debate, in January 2023, snow was falling near Lake Huron, where the thumb meets the palm of Michigan, as the Saginaw County GOP met in the lodge of a gun club. At the front of the slant-roofed room, a screen displayed a desktop background photo of Mar-a-Lago. The chairman, Curt Tucker, called the meeting to order.

A stocky man with close-cropped gray hair who ran a company that manufactured high-performance seat belts for race cars and military vehicles, Curt had taken over the county party the previous fall with a group of newcomers who called themselves "America First precinct delegates." They were part of a wave of Precinct Strategy–inspired recruits sweeping into county parties across this pivotal state. One of Curt's allies, a woman from the area named Debra Ell, was one of the most prolific recruiters of precinct delegates, not only in Saginaw County but all over Michigan. She'd described her objective as building an "America First army" to take over the state party, and that's exactly what they'd done.

In Michigan, the precinct delegates choose the party nominees for attorney general and secretary of state, rather than holding an open primary. The America First delegates used their positions to vet candidates through their own questionnaire. The prompts included "Define a RINO in your own words"; "What do you believe happened on Election Day, November 3, 2020?"; "Should Dominion Voting Machines be removed?"; and "What do you believe happened at the U.S. Capitol on January 6, 2021? Were you there?" At the nominating convention in 2022, the precinct delegates selected Matt DePerno for attorney general and Kristina Karamo for secretary of state. Both candidates were political novices who had risen to prominence by spreading election fraud claims. DePerno's activities had earned him a criminal referral from a Republican-led state senate committee. Karamo swore an affidavit claiming she'd personally witnessed illegal vote counting as a poll watcher and insisted the January 6 insurrection was the work of far-left infiltrators. In November 2022, DePerno lost by almost nine points, and Karamo lost by fourteen. The Democrats won unified control of the state government for the first time since the 1980s.

For decades Michigan Republicans had been the model of mainstream moderation, in the tradition of George Romney and Gerald Ford. If just one state GOP was going to learn its lesson from the 2022 midterms, you might think it would be this one. The opportunity to course-correct was here, in these county party meetings, as the members chose their delegates who would go on to elect a new state party chair at the upcoming state convention. Here in Saginaw, a backlash was brewing to Curt Tucker's America First clique. This meeting was poised to be a clash with a rival faction, aiming to give Curt and his crew their comeuppance for how they were marching the party off a cliff. Both sides had tipped off the local police that it might get heated.

As the meeting got started, Curt could barely finish leading the Pledge of Allegiance before someone was already shouting, "Mr. Chairman, point of order!"

The voice came from Josiah Jaster, a ruddy-faced twenty-year-old wearing khakis, a navy blazer, shirt, and tie, the most dressed-up person in the room. Josiah had finished high school at sixteen and double-majored in applied math and computer science at a college in Flint. Now he worked as an insurance actuary and, with his mastery of parliamentary procedure, had run the earlier convention that elected Curt and his America First cohort. But in just a few months, Josiah had soured on the America First bloc, and he'd come to tonight's meeting with a plan.

"Mr. Chairman, there was a delegate that was not permitted to gain his credential under MCL 168599," Josiah said robotically. He then quoted another provision, MCL 168941, warning of criminal penalties for breaking the meeting rules in the presence of a law enforcement officer — and the chief of the city police department was in attendance as a party member. "I would ask that this be fixed so that the law enforcement officer is not *forced* to institute criminal proceedings," Josiah said, returning to his seat.

"It wasn't intentional, certainly," Curt said from the podium. He felt pained to see Josiah doing this. They had gotten close, and he liked him personally. But he thought the young man was being misled by the county party's previous officers, the old guard whom the America First delegates had overthrown.

Josiah called out another point of order, and Curt relented, "So let's give him a credential, that's fine."

But Josiah wasn't done. He said there were guests seated among the delegates so you couldn't tell them apart. Curt said they would move when the voting began. Josiah said there were guests with delegate credentials. He named names. "Again, I may remind the chairman of MCL 168941, which requires police officers to institute criminal proceedings," Josiah repeated.

"Mr. Josiah," Curt sighed, "please keep your voice down. We can all hear you. You don't have to shout."

"Another member just said they can barely hear me, but I will try to keep my voice down."

"Your point has been heard and now you're overruled."

"Mr. Chairman, I appeal the ruling."

Someone called out: "I make a motion that Josiah be silenced."

"Out of order!" a chorus shouted back.

"We're gonna take a vote on having you sit down," Curt said to Josiah.

"NOOOO!" he and his supporters cried while Curt's supporters clapped.

"You're out of order," Curt kept saying, banging his gavel.

"I appeal the ruling," Josiah kept saying back.

Curt said he'd given Josiah three warnings and would have to call the police to have him removed. "Please do," Josiah said.

"He did not do nothing wrong," one of his allies called out.

"You're out of order as well!" Curt said, with another smack of his gavel.

"Say 'Point of order,' then speak," someone coached him.

Debra Ell, the precinct delegate recruiting machine, took the microphone to support Curt. "Anybody that claims to be a real Republican in this room and you're talking over everybody?" she huffed. "Come on."

"I resent being called that type of Republican!" someone shouted.

"You're no Republican," someone else yelled back, "you're just an ass."

Curt called a recess while they waited for the cops. The officers came but stood in the back and did not intervene. During the interlude, it became clear that Josiah had the majority support of the members present. He and Curt worked out a deal. When the proceedings resumed, one of Josiah's allies proposed removing Curt as the chairman of the meeting. The motion passed. Curt gaveled a motion to elect Josiah as the new chair, and the group applauded as the young man took over the podium.

Then the meeting ran smoothly, and in a few more minutes, they'd elected their thirty-seven delegates to the state convention. All but one were from Josiah's bloc, putting them in control of helping decide the Michigan GOP's future. The party was in shambles. The MAGA movement was in flux. It would be up to people like Josiah to choose the path forward. The race for Michigan's state party chair would be an early test case for the new dynamics that would shape the primary for the presidential nomination in 2024. Trump was officially running now, and his campaign dispatched operatives to Michigan to help make sure the state chairman's race went Trump's way.

When Josiah made the hour's drive to Lansing a month later for the state convention, he showed up like a walking embodiment of the party's future, not only for how he brought down the average age in every room he entered (barely old enough to have voted for

Trump in 2020), but because of his willingness to say out loud what many Republicans were thinking: that as much as they all agreed on the policies of Trump's presidency, it was time to move on from blind, unthinking loyalty to Trump the man. Josiah was not, for instance, letting Trump's endorsement determine his decision on who to support for state party chair. That did not make him a Never Trumper. That dichotomy was obsolete.

Trump had endorsed Matt DePerno, the failed AG candidate. In 2022, Trump's endorsement probably would have been the end of the discussion. But now, in 2023, it was more complicated. The power of the Trump endorsement had been cheapened in Michigan, specifically, by a perception that his picks there had been brokered by the outgoing state party cochair, Meshawn Maddock. Maddock had come into the position as a MAGA darling. In April 2020, she'd helped organize protests in Lansing against pandemic restrictions, leading two weeks later to armed protesters pushing inside the State Capitol, paralyzing the legislature. After the election, Maddock had helped mobilize Republicans to mob the Detroit convention center where ballots were being counted. She tried to disrupt the meeting of the state's Electoral College delegation and signed onto a phony certificate, claiming to be an elector casting one of Michigan's sixteen electoral votes for Trump.* She helped organize nineteen buses to Washington for January 6 and spoke at a warm-up rally near the White House the day before. After the insurrection, some older party officers wanted to kick Maddock off the ballot for cochair, but she won overwhelmingly. Now, just two years later, this grassroots hero was on her way out as a grassroots villain. She was supporting DePerno but keeping a low profile at the convention.

DePerno also had the backing of Mike Lindell and Kari Lake, who was billed as his special guest for a party the night before the convention at a bar across the street called the Nuthouse. Guests were supposed to RSVP by texting "NUTHOUSE" to DePerno's campaign. But Lake didn't show; her aides said she couldn't make the schedule work (which is what politicians usually said when they meant they'd rather be clipping their toenails), but the rumor

---

* In July 2023, the Michigan attorney general charged Maddock and the fifteen other phony electors with election law and forgery felonies. She pleaded not guilty.

around the convention center was that she had to go to Washington because the Supreme Court was taking up her election challenge.

Josiah's candidate for state party chair was a software engineer named JD Glaser, who said Trump was cheated in the 2020 election, and campaigned on empowering the precinct delegates. Another candidate was the star of a TLC show about a twenty-five-member, three-generation family living under one roof. No one knew who the frontrunners were; there weren't any polls, it depended on word of mouth, and that depended on who you talked to.

There was a lot of buzz around Kristina Karamo, the failed candidate for secretary of state, now running for state party chair as well. The night before the convention, she spoke to a "patriot" group in the nearby town of Charlotte by emphasizing her master's degree in Christian apologetics. She played a slideshow featuring images of full-frontal nudity in the presence of children, instructing her audience, "Don't be offended that the images are being shown, be offended by the depravity of our society." She said Miley Cyrus "represents our degenerate culture" and called Darwinian evolution "one of the biggest frauds ever perpetrated." She condemned the Enlightenment philosophers for moving Western civilization toward secularism and argued that Republicans needed to make Christianity core to their politics. "When we start talking about the spiritual reality of the demonic forces, it's like, 'Oh, my God, this is crazy, we can't go there,'" she said. "No. It's like, did you read the Bible? Didn't Jesus perform exorcisms? Scriptures are clear. And so if we're not operating as though the spiritual realities of the world exist, we're going to fail every time. This is a spiritual battle. How many of us have heard this phrase, 'The greatest trick the devil ever played was making people think he doesn't exist'? But it kind of makes sense if you think about it from Satan's perspective. His goal is to destroy us. If they start seeing manifestations of demons and things of this nature, what would happen? They would go, 'Oh my God, I guess that Bible is real.'" She got a standing ovation.

As the leader of the Saginaw County delegation, Josiah spent the convention hectically guiding around his delegates and alternates, huddling with them to go over the meaning of every motion and helping instruct them on how to cast their votes. The convention quickly went awry as delegates objected to the voting method. They fought over whether the "tellers" who counted the votes needed to be randomized, to prevent people from exercising favor within their own counties, or even whether to hold roll calls of the two thousand delegates. Many said they didn't trust the votes to be recorded on laptops and transferred on flash drives. "How many of us got in this fight because of flash drives and laptops?" a delegate from Kent County said to cheers, demanding a tally that could be audited manually.

"We're in the nuthouse now," someone grumbled on the convention floor.

After two hours, the rule change received 64 percent support, just less than the two-thirds needed to pass. The candidates for state chair started giving their speeches. DePerno, instead of speaking live, played a video endorsement from Trump. Some delegates viewed that as a cop-out. And around the convention hall, many of the precinct delegates said they'd ruled out supporting DePerno because, after making his name in the election denier movement, he'd conceded his loss in the November election. Karamo never conceded, as she reminded everyone in her speech. "Why would I concede to a fraudulent process?" she shouted, to roaring applause. "Conceding to a fraudulent process means agreeing with the fraud, which I will not do."

In the first round of voting, Karamo led, closely followed by DePerno, but no one reached a simple majority, so the top three finishers advanced to a second round. Josiah's pick, JD Glaser, was eliminated. Glaser endorsed DePerno in exchange for becoming his policy director, a deal that was transparently prearranged, since the DePerno campaign already had printed up signs announcing it. Josiah didn't take Glaser's loss too hard. "It's a vote," he shrugged. "That's the way it works." He hadn't come prepared with a second choice, so now he tepidly picked DePerno. The second round did not produce a majority either, so the vote went to a third ballot, a runoff between DePerno and Karamo.

The delegates lined up to vote amid competing shouts of "Trump endorsed DePerno!" and "Power to the delegates — Karamo!" Either way, the Michigan GOP was clearly not going to tack toward the center, and a few scattered delegates were disappointed to see the party blowing that chance. On the other side of the convention hall from Josiah and the Saginaw delegation, a woman named Marla Rieli Braun stood in line to record her vote as an abstention. "I'm going to abstain because the party has to know that what we have put forward here is not acceptable," she said. "I am an old-school Republican. I grew up in Jackson County, the birthplace of the Republican Party,* and I'm going to tell you something: these fucking hillbillies have got to be taken out and shot."

Josiah wasn't sweating the runoff. He stuck with DePerno, but he said he'd be OK with Karamo too. She'd always been among the three candidates he'd been deciding between. "I like Kristina's policies," he said. "I'd be OK with Kristina."

What, then, had been the point of staging the revolt at the gun lodge, of overthrowing Curt Tucker and Debra Ell's America First ring? Every member of the Saginaw County GOP had a slightly different explanation. Josiah's account focused on violating the bylaws, failing to file treasurer reports, changing the county party logo—little-p politics. "There is not an ideological difference," Josiah said. "We're both America First. We all agree on the same points that what Trump has done was good for the country. We agree on Trump's policies a hundred percent."

"We definitely believe in election integrity and that the election was stolen in 2020," one of Josiah's allies, Andrea Paschall, agreed. They could take Trump out of the equation, and they'd still be MAGA.

The results in the chair's race appeared on a spreadsheet displayed on two giant screens next to the stage, and people started gathering close to read. The last few districts hadn't reported yet, but it was already clear Karamo was going to win.

"Are you ready for this?" a reporter asked Meshawn Maddock, the outgoing cochair who'd arrived as too extreme for the incumbent party leaders and was now preparing to hand off the gavel to someone too extreme for *her*.

"Not really," Maddock said. "No one is."

---

* Jackson, Michigan, was the site of the first official Republican convention. The party's birthplace is more commonly attributed to Ripon, Wisconsin, where the GOP's first public meeting was held and its name was chosen.

CHAPTER 12

Complete MAGA Takeover

SALLEIGH GRUBBS COULD not contain her excitement when she received the official announcement from the Georgia GOP that Donald Trump was coming to speak at their state convention, three weeks away, on June 10, 2023. "Happy," she texted thirty times over. "I am so happy." Not only would Salleigh get to hear Trump speak in person again, she knew there was a chance that, as the party chair in the county with the most Republican voters in the state, she would get to actually *meet* him backstage, for a handshake and a photo.

It was thrilling to have something special to look forward to after a full year of setbacks. Back in May 2022, Salleigh had fielded her legion of specially trained poll watchers to monitor early voting in the primary, and they got buried in glitches. Because of the once-a-decade redistricting after the census, there were all kinds of problems with candidates not showing up on the right ballots in the right places. Then there were all the usual snafus: poll pads that needed software updates, tabulation tapes that misprinted because the memory cards were removed from scanners that weren't shut down properly. Thanks to all her poll watchers in position, Salleigh was able to report the problems in real time to the secretary of state's office. Then officials announced the problems were quickly fixed and that overall the primary election had run smoothly. That didn't sound right to Salleigh. Instead of spending primary night at victory parties, she camped out at the board of elections, waiting for the last batch of votes that didn't come in until one thirty in the morning. Four precincts' results failed to upload and had to be recertified. "It was a hot mess," Salleigh said. And though Salleigh, as a party official, was officially neutral in primary races, it was no secret that most of her regulars in the Cobb GOP were rooting for the Trump-endorsed candidates for governor, David Perdue, and secretary of state, Jody Hice. Both of them ran by emphasizing how if they'd been in office in 2020, they wouldn't have certified the election results. But the incumbents, Governor Brian Kemp and Secretary of State Brad Raffensperger, won those primaries handily. Salleigh blamed crossover voters — Democrats voting in the Republican primary — though independent analyses didn't support that theory. Salleigh wasn't sure what to believe anymore. She went back and watched an HBO documentary from 2006 about how electronic voting machines could be tampered with.

As summer turned to fall in 2022, Salleigh went all over the campaign trail with Herschel Walker, the Heisman Trophy–winning running back whom Trump had handpicked to run for Senate against the Democratic incumbent, the Reverend Raphael Warnock. She cracked up when Walker would recount the plot of the horror flick *Fright Night*, then rolled her eyes at viral out-of-context tweets making fun of him for going on about vampires and werewolves. In October, the race was roiled by news reports that Walker, who was supporting an abortion ban without exceptions, had himself, years earlier, paid for a girlfriend's abortion. Walker denied it, and Salleigh didn't believe the stories. He'd sent the woman a "get well" card but the card didn't say abortion. There was a receipt from the clinic and a bank transfer in the same amount, but they didn't say what the money was for. "There's no absolute proof," Salleigh said. "At the end of the day, she's the one who had an abortion, not Herschel." Salleigh took seriously Walker's own account of his troubled past, his struggles with mental health and violence; she saw him as "a sinner saved by Grace." And she said there were other people in office who'd done much worse but never made the news; she wouldn't specify who or what. She sneered at the outgoing lieutenant governor, Geoff Duncan, for purporting to speak for her when he told CNN host Don Lemon, "Even the most staunch

Republicans, I think, are rattled." "What self-respecting conservative goes on CNN with *him*?" she demanded, meaning Lemon. Salleigh cheered as part of the live studio audience for Walker's Fox News town hall with Sean Hannity, and she wasn't allowed to cheer when she sat in the audience for Walker's debate with Warnock, even when Walker pulled out a badge to defend his claim that he was an honorary cop, which the moderator scolded him was against the rules. "He killed it," Salleigh said. "TKO."

But it wasn't a technical knockout. Come November, Walker did worse than Kemp and Raffensperger. They campaigned by ignoring Trump and avoiding the MAGA label, and that amounted to a five-point difference. They won, while Walker's race went to a runoff. And then he lost the runoff. Salleigh was at the campaign's party. An impromptu prayer circle formed, and Salleigh saw some young campaign staffers jump in and out, in a mocking way, as if this was all a joke to them. She was *disgusted*. She felt like they weren't really committed to the cause, and that meant she would have to work even harder now.

Salleigh had to decide whether to run for county chair again when her term was up in March 2023. She assumed she would; she thought it was what you were supposed to do. Then in January, her younger son had a terrible motorcycle accident. He broke an arm, broke his leg in four places, and fractured two ribs and three vertebrae. His heart stopped for a moment and he had to be resuscitated. He needed two blood transfusions and would have to learn to walk again. But he survived, and for that she felt blessed. She kept grisly photos of the injuries and X-rays on her phone, along with a picture of him in the hospital bed, hugging a giant soft drink, which she joked could have been an ad for RaceTrac, the Georgia convenience store chain. After that, a rumor went around that Salleigh was not going to run. That might have been understandable, given all that she was dealing with in her personal life, but it seemed more like the rumor was meant to undermine her, because one version of it went that she would run only to resign and appoint her replacement. She refuted that one by saying it couldn't possibly be true—the bylaws didn't work that way. She was shaken but she decided to stick with running for chair, and she was moved to tears at the county convention in March, when someone who wasn't even her biggest fan moved to reelect her by acclamation.

After the county convention, Salleigh's next step in the party reorganization process was the convention for her congressional district. There, the party members chose delegates to send on to the state convention. There was a little bit of controversy because Salleigh appointed someone who was a member of the Georgia Republican Assembly. The GRA was an outside activist group descended from the California Republican Assembly that had formed back in the sixties to help get Barry Goldwater the Republican nomination. The group existed to rebel against the official party's prescribed neutrality in primaries and make endorsements for Republican candidates who were honest-to-God conservatives. Now, in Georgia, the GRA had two priorities for the upcoming state convention. The first was to pick delegates who were first-time participants, empowering grassroots volunteers rather than following the custom of handing out delegate slots to current and former elected officials as courtesies. Salleigh was all for that.

The second item on the GRA's agenda was to pass a so-called accountability rule, creating a mechanism for the state party convention delegates to block a candidate from appearing on the Republican Party's line on the ballot. Typically the Republican nominee would be whoever won the primary, but this measure would effectively give the state party delegates veto power over the primary winner. Everyone understood the proposal as a shot at Kemp and Raffensperger. The proposal was, in some ways, a logical extension of the Precinct Strategy: a way for party leaders to enforce ideological compliance on the party's candidates. Salleigh, though, was skeptical. She supported empowering the grassroots, but she didn't like the idea of overriding the results of a primary election. She also worried that the rule could be abused if a different faction took control of the party and used it to block MAGA candidates.

The other drama at the district convention was over whether to censure their member of Congress, Barry Loudermilk, for supporting a deal to raise the federal debt ceiling in exchange for moderate spending caps. Salleigh disapproved of Loudermilk's debt ceiling vote because she opposed Washington backroom deals and thought federal spending was out of control; but she also opposed the censure resolution. She'd learned from her own experience, from the backlash to her party committee's censure resolution against Governor Kemp in 2021, that it wasn't the most productive way to express disagreement. Being in party leadership gave you a voice and a seat at the table, and with that came ways to show displeasure, but a public, formal censure only served to shut down the conversation. Salleigh knew she was sounding like a real insider, and she was sure there were now hard-liners out there dragging her behind her back. But the truth was she had learned from her time as party chair. She'd seen how much more complicated things are, how much you couldn't see from outside, how there are always unintended consequences. She had to be more strategic.

Even though Salleigh was an insider now, she had a way of relating to the grassroots folks (who usually called themselves patriots, like she used to). The key was to make them feel heard, to give them a voice, because that's what they wanted. That's what she'd wanted when she'd been one of them. But even as Salleigh needed to shore up her right flank, she had to mind the middle too. She wanted to become the leader of Georgia's largest thirty-two counties, in an election to be held at the state convention. The position was called the over-eighties chairman because the counties included each had more than eighty thousand people. Combined, they were home to more than 7 million people, the vast majority of the statewide population. The over-eighties post would bring more responsibilities and further raise her profile in the state party. There was one other candidate, and Salleigh had heard that person was running because of the view that Salleigh was too "far-right." (She hated being called far-right!)

The state convention would consist of various committee meetings, party leadership elections, an exhibition hall, a banquet, and speeches, culminating with Trump's. It would be held in Columbus, a historic mill town turned college town along the Chattahoochee River, a two-hour drive from Marietta. A few days before, Salleigh got the call she'd been hoping for: the Secret Service needed to run a background check on her for a VIP meeting with President Trump. She couldn't wait. She got to town on Thursday, earlier than most of the general delegates, for an executive session of other county chairs and state committee members. In the meeting, the outgoing state chairman, David Shafer, updated the committee on the state party's finances and the record-breaking attendance for the convention, doubtlessly boosted by Trump's appearance.

Even though Georgia was the one state where primary voters in the midterms had bucked Trump by rejecting his endorsements for governor and secretary of state, the state's party organization was disproportionately, overwhelmingly MAGA. Shafer himself had alienated Kemp and Raffensperger when he helped organize the slate of electors claiming Trump had won the state in 2020, an effort now under investigation by the district attorney in Fulton County.* The convention skewed so intensely toward Trump that Kemp declined to attend; and he made plans to bypass the party apparatus altogether by forming his own political committee to raise and spend money on the 2024 elections. Raffensperger wasn't even invited to the convention.

As soon as Salleigh left the executive session, her phone started blowing up. *"The corrupt Biden Administration has informed my attorneys that I have been Indicted,"* Trump announced on his Truth Social website. He had already been indicted, in March 2023, in New York for hush money payments before the 2016 election. Now, in June, came the first *federal* indictment, accusing him of mishandling classified documents taken from the White House to Mar-a-Lago.

Friends were texting Salleigh saying this was insane, that the country was out of control, that everything Trump had been saying was now ringing more and more true. They'd all suspected this indictment was coming, but still, now that it was actually happening, sadness washed over Salleigh. She felt like every day we were losing the things that made America America. "I feel like the body's dead but it hasn't quit twitching," she said. "I mean, did you read *1984?*"

She got one text message from a friend saying, "Trump is the most persecuted man since Jesus Christ." Salleigh understood the idea, with all the allegations and constant attacks, all the arrows he'd taken, like in a medieval painting of the martyrdom of Saint Sebastian; but she didn't really agree with the comparison. She loved President Trump. She did not worship him. He was not a god. He was a man, just like the rest of us. What he was, to Salleigh, was

---

* In August 2023, the Fulton County DA indicted Shafer, alongside Trump and seventeen others. Shafer smiled in his official mugshot and made it his profile photo on X, the online platform formerly known as Twitter. He pleaded not guilty.

a symbol of standing up for the little guy against power-hungry forces that wanted to crush American freedom. Trump had hubris, she got that, but she also got what he meant when he always said, "They're not coming after me, they're coming after you, and I'm just standing in the way." She knew liberals scoffed at that, like, *Yeah, if you paid off a porn star or stashed classified documents in your bathroom, the feds could come for you too.* But if you believed Trump when he said that these charges had been ordered up and concocted by his political opponents, that the evidence against him had been planted, that the full power of the federal government was being weaponized against him, then you could understand the fear that if they could do that to him, with all his power and resources, what chance did you stand? Salleigh personally knew people who'd been subpoenaed or searched for their involvement in January 6, for what she considered exercising their First Amendment right to peaceably assemble, to protest a stolen election. She felt like she, too, had a target on her back for being a politically active Republican. It made her think twice about what she said publicly, and that was an affront to her God-given liberty.

Salleigh left the convention center for the Marriott across the street, where the state committee members were having a cigar party on a back patio. John Fredericks, the radio host, was a spon-sor. His Trump-wrapped tour bus was parked out front. Fredericks had traded out his signature suit and tie for a polo shirt, revealing tattooed forearms, and he was in a buoyant mood. The loudspeak-ers on the patio were blasting the iconic Trump rally playlist, and Elvis's "Suspicious Minds" had just come on when a reporter broke the news to Fredericks of the Trump indictment, by reading him Trump's Truth Social posts. Fredericks took a moment to gather his thoughts, as if allowing himself a moment to wind up his outrage. "Game on," he said. "Indict away. Every indictment, we get more emboldened. We get stronger. We get more votes. Because working people in this country are on to their game. Trump will be the nominee, and he will win an overwhelming victory, regardless of the number of witch-hunt indictments that the communists and the liberals try to push on him."

He broke back into a broad smile. "Is that good?"

Then Fredericks decided he wasn't finished. He wanted to talk about this Georgia GOP convention, what was happening in this state party. "What you're going to see on Saturday — write this down — what you're going to see here on Saturday is the complete takeover of a major state Republican Party by MAGA forces from top to bottom, A to Z, from chairman to assistant secretary. Never been done before. Was done in three years. We're gonna take over every single state party — this is the model. And then we bang down the door at the RNC, and the next time we go there, we're going to kick it and take the whole thing over. This is a MAGA revolution. Seventy percent of the delegates are new, they've all joined up since we inspired them to go and join their units. And now we're gonna see Saturday, the culmination of MAGA America taking over an entire state apparatus in one day. And it's a beautiful thing. And it's a blueprint to go forward.

"This is what started when we started telling people to get involved. Precinct 2.0. Join your local unit. You gotta get off the sideline, gotta get off the couch. Join your local unit. Join the party. Deal with the nonsense. Become a precinct chairman. Become a delegate. They're all MAGA. They're all Trump. Our slate is going to romp. Our bus is here. It's gonna be a stunning victory. That's why Kemp's not here. Raffensperger's not here. DeSantis isn't here. Pence isn't here. None of them are here, because it is a rout. This is a MAGA rout. And it is the beginning of what's to come."

He smiled again. "How's that?"

The sun was setting and the cigar smoke drifting around the patio was doing little to keep the mosquitoes away, as word was still spreading about the indictment. Laurie Wood, from Forsyth County, had been in the hotel elevator when she got a text alert and thought, "Here we go again." She was a first-time delegate who became a precinct chair after hearing about Dan Schultz's Precinct Strategy on Steve Bannon's *War Room*. "It's a hit job," she said of the charges against Trump. "Why do you wanna take someone out that's a voice for the people? But we know why. This is the Washington Swamp."

"Trump tries to get fair elections in Georgia and he gets indicted," said Sam Carnline, a car dealer from Grady County, near the Florida Panhandle. Another first-time delegate, Sam said he got involved in the party after watching all ten hours of the state senate hearing about the 2020 election—he remembered Salleigh's testimony about the shredding truck. "There's a lot of people that had no reason to lie," he said. "And in that hearing you could hear in their voice their sincerity about what they were saying. They believed what they were saying. So therefore I believed what they were saying.

"Republicans, elected people in this state, didn't uphold their oath of office. What they shoulda done is said, 'OK, boys, hold the fort, we got a problem down here in Georgia, and we gonna check it out before we certify the election.' January 6, by the way, if I was going to go take over the Grady County Courthouse and try to take over the Grady County government, I'd take more than a broomstick and an umbrella. So we're getting fed a bunch of stuff that's just not right."

Nearby, Salleigh was chatting in a circle with some friends from the party who were still gradually learning about the indictment. "I'm not surprised," said Jim Tully, the party chairman in Paulding County, next door to Cobb. "Fulton County's coming next, too, and that's a sham."

"Don't start me with that," said Orien Roy, a Georgia field representative with the right-wing youth group Turning Point Action. "I was just at the county commissioners' meeting yesterday," he said, referring to the Fulton County commissioners' rejection of a Republican nominee for the election board who had challenged the eligibility of thousands of voters.

"The American conservative is about to erupt," Jim said. "We have had enough of being bowled over in our lifestyle, our religious beliefs, our work ethic, and our responsibility. This is an attempt to intimidate us."

A loud train went by, blaring its horn, and Jim asked to take a picture with Salleigh "before you get too famous and won't talk to me anymore."

In a far corner of the patio, Jackie Harling ("like Darling with an H"), the new party chairwoman from Walker County, on the Tennessee border, found refuge in an Adirondack chair because she'd had two drinks and her feet were hurting. "Literally nothing shocks me anymore," she said. "I would be more shocked if they *didn't* indict him for something. Literally. The truth is coming out in so many ways that it literally actually was a witch hunt. And it continues. The proof just keeps coming out...He is so obviously targeted because he was crazy enough to tell the truth about all the corruption. He became the world's most dangerous politician because he was willing to actually tell the truth. Every time he is unfairly targeted or indicted by some DA that was funded by God knows who, it makes him so much richer. Watch and see how much money is raised off of this. It never hurts him when this kind of thing happens to him, because everybody knows it's politically motivated and not real, and it literally only invalidates the people who are going to pursue that, not him. It makes him look better, puts him on a pedestal. It makes him a martyr. You'd have to be living under a rock to not see all the corruption for the last few years."

Jackie was a lifelong Republican, but it wasn't until after the 2020 election that she'd become involved in the party. "Everything, every official narrative from every government organization since COVID has been proven untrue," she said. "Every narrative. The CDC, everything they said ended up being not true. Everything Dr. Fauci said ended up being not true. Everything that the corrupt people that are going after Trump — it ends up being untrue...If you shut out the gaslighting and the crazy conspiracies of what Trump did or what he is or whatever, all it is, all it was, is gaslighting. It's just lies and propaganda used to feed people's emotions. When you feed people's emotions and you make them afraid, they are easy to control."

The playlist was repeating itself now. Elvis was crooning again. *"We're caught in a trap..."* Salleigh left for bed. She was tired and had to report to the nominating committee at seven forty-five in the morning.

SALLEIGH SPENT ALL the next day in a private conference room with the nominating committee, responsible for interviewing the candidates for state party officer positions and voting on whom to recommend to the full convention on Saturday. While this select group met behind closed doors, the rest of the delegates were free to roam around the exhibition hall, checking out booths for Georgians for Truth, advocating for paper ballots under a giant PAPER PLEASE sign; swag shops with NOT GUILTY shirts and honey in Donald Trump–shaped bottles; a clinic selling hyperbaric chamber treatments; the right-wing artist Steve Penley, a neo-impressionist painter of nostalgic Americana; and, for the first time anyone could remember at the Georgia GOP convention, the John Birch Society. There was also a booth for Never Back Down, the super PAC supporting Ron DeSantis's presidential campaign, that was being staffed for part of the day by Jason Shepherd, Salleigh's estranged predecessor as Cobb County chair. As chair, Salleigh had to stay officially neutral in the presidential primary, and she'd checked out a DeSantis event in March, when he'd come to speak at a gun store just south of Marietta. DeSantis was still on a "book tour" then, but everyone understood he was running for president. He drew a pretty good-sized crowd, but the visit became probably best known for a viral video from a young man in the audience (whom Salleigh knew) who held up a huge Trump banner and got escorted out by the security staff, or, as he called them, "the Meatball goon squad." As for the speech itself, Salleigh thought it reminded her of how Trump sounded in 2016. She viewed DeSantis as cribbing Trump's talking points, as if Republican consultants were trying to present him as a candidate with the America First policies without the mean tweets. But for Salleigh, the mean tweets were the point: Trump's personality was how he struck tough deals and got great results for America.

While the committees conducted their business, the rest of the delegates to the state convention could attend two sessions about election fraud. The first was led by Seth Keshel, or Captain K, a retired Army officer turned traveling showman who punctuated his presentation on how to change election laws by shouting "SLIDE!" Keshel was followed by Garland Favorito, a gray-haired IT consultant in a double-breasted blazer and loafers who was like an election-fraud hipster: he liked it before it was cool ("All the way back in 2002, I wrote a letter..."). When he finished speaking, after about an hour, and took questions, a man in a Trump hat named Leonard Perez stood up and told a story about his son who took a video of poll workers counting ballots in a back room.

"It's all supposed to be public," someone said.

"It was not," Leonard insisted.

The crowd broke into murmurs. Favorito moved on to another question.

"The state is turning our country upside-down and it's all corrupt," said Richard Schroeder, who lived north of Atlanta. "I've become a poll worker after being at Trump's rally in March of 2022. I worked the primary elections. The paper is the only thing that's real...They used to go in a black bag. It had two zippers. It came together. You put a wire tie around those two zippers with a number on it. It's documented on a spreadsheet. It's called chain of custody...Now, watch what happens in the midterm election, November '22, and three days of training. No black bag. What the heck is going on here? No black bag in the building. No black bag. They took the votes to the election office in a gray bag. The gray bag only had one zipper. They've done away with the chain of custody, with a wire tied to two zippers in the black bag."

Favorito thanked him for his "question." Before finishing, he called on two more people (who happened to work for him) whose "question" was to encourage audience members to donate to Favorito.

Meanwhile, in another private conference room, the rules committee was meeting to decide the fate of the Georgia Republican Assembly's proposed accountability rule, the measure about blocking candidates from appearing on the ballot as Republicans. Making the case to the committee was the GRA's president, Alex Johnson. Alex had been a nuisance to the state party since 2009, when he got involved in the local party as a law student in DeKalb County. He could still pass for a college student today, with snug suits, a boyish face, and occasional bedhead. But he was well versed in parliamentary procedure and the party bylaws, and he spoke fluidly, well practiced from having presented at county parties around the state. "Oftentimes we have Republicans, the Republican delegates and Republican voters, saying, 'Hey, how do you vote for the lesser of two evils?' And I think that it's about time that most of the leaders of the party actually make sure their brand is maintained," he said now to the rules committee. "For example, somebody has a really horrible voting record or is saying things that make the party look absolutely terrible — the state delegates by majority vote could just say they cannot qualify as a Republican."

The other committee members raised several objections. The rule, if adopted, was sure to be challenged in court, by candidates who could argue the party delegates lacked the authority to disqualify them. The litigation would stick the party with expensive legal fees. The party had insurance coverage that could help cover litigation costs, but this lawsuit could cause them to lose their coverage or pay higher premiums. Kemp's allies in the state legislature would pass a law to overturn the rule, as they had done to create a vehicle for Kemp to raise and spend money outside the state party. A cell phone rang, making a "womp womp" sad trombone sound.

"That was serendipitous," someone joked.

"My question is," another member asked, "so if I don't like you, I can just bring your name to the floor and say, 'I don't like John Smith, so let's vote him [off the ballot] because he's not Republican enough'?"

"Then you would have a debate over it," Alex agreed.

"You're asking two thousand people or sometimes less," another member said (meaning the convention delegates), "to make a recommendation, or say this person did that, when there are millions in our state" (meaning the primary voters) "that are going to be pissed at us because they want a certain candidate, and we're saying no because we don't like that candidate, you can't be on the ballot."

"Who determines if you're Republican enough?" another asked. "We can't get twenty Republicans to agree on anything."

Alex made his closing pitch. "We need to really think about what it means to be a political party," he said. "What we need to recognize is that we are an organization. And when it comes down to who determines what a Republican is, I mean, I know it's scary, but it's *us*. Like, that's why we go through this. We don't do this process just to listen to politicians speak, say we love the Republican nominee, and go home. I mean, we can do that. I've seen a lot of people do it. I did, a few years of the convention process...I urge everyone to think that we are the ones in charge. The party *matters*. Elected officials, if they want to run under our banner, they have to go with our philosophies and policies. If they don't like it, they go somewhere else. But I think that we need to reimagine our role. We are the leaders — "

"Wrap it up," the committee chairman interrupted.

"That's it," Alex said.

"Can I just say one more thing?" another member, a woman, asked, before they took a vote. "Alex *is* the future of our party," she said. "Alex, you've poured [your] heart in this. Tweak it, do whatever you've gotta do. I think it does have merit in some places." Alex was the only vote in favor.

The rules committee still had thirty-five other proposals to consider, preparing the rules and agenda for the convention's general session the next day. The work stretched on for hours. Over in the nominations committee, Salleigh went through slate after slate of candidates, and they were still voting past five o'clock. At that time she had to duck out and go to the election of the over-eighties caucus.

She arrived late, wearing American flag–printed sneakers that her treasurer had given her. She wore her hair white and straight now, with bangs. There were twenty-six county chairs present, and the outgoing caucus chair, Alton Russell, an old hand from Columbus-Muscogee County, called on first-timers to stand; there were eleven.

Alton called up Katherine James, the chairwoman from rural Lumpkin County, to present about a program they were starting, focused on the next election. "There is an initiative that we have kicked off called Unite the Right,* and you guys need to know about it," she said. "It takes what the Democrats have done, turns it around, and does it better. And legally, because we've got to do that. We cannot keep doing the things that we used to do, because we will lose…If we do, like in my family, traditional voting only on Tuesday, kids get sick, cars break down—you're going to lose that vote…If we don't understand the difference between ballot harvesting and ballot tracing and ballot curing, we will lose."

Ballot chasing was the new "it" thing for Republican groups: whereas last cycle, the fixation was on election integrity, finding fraudulent Democratic ballots or preventing them from being cast, now the focus was on making sure Republicans got around to casting their votes. The right-wing youth group Turning Point Action proposed raising $108 million to build a "ballot chasing army" of 1,650 full-time staff in a single year. In Arizona, Kari Lake launched her own ballot-chasing initiative, and hired as its director Merissa Hamilton. The RNC started running its own effort called Bank the Vote, and officials begged Trump to endorse mail ballots. He eventually would give lip service to mail voting, but in interviews

---

* Party officials later changed the program's name to United Saves America to avoid echoing the name of the 2017 rally in Charlottesville, Virginia, that featured neo-Nazis and white nationalists, one of whom killed a counterprotester with his car.

he almost always hastened to add that mail ballots were full of fraud and couldn't be trusted.

"Unite the Right brings us together by targeting marginal voters, new voters, and voters not active in their own GOP," Katherine James continued at the caucus meeting. She said they were using voting data to identify top targets and developing scripts for talking to different kinds of people, from students to churchgoers. As in Bannon's vision for the future of the party, they were hoping to activate new voters who weren't registered or didn't reliably vote, rather than trying to recapture Republicans who were reliable but weren't MAGA. They were going after the high-hanging fruit.

"We're working with executives at the RNC because then we will roll it out nationwide," Katherine James said. "In closing, y'all remember what Catherine Engelbrecht said in the movie *2000 Mules*? She said, 'We know they're going to cheat. They just can't cheat too much because they'll get caught.' We've got to show up in numbers that will make a difference to move the needle. This group here will make that difference."

Aside from Katherine's proposal, the main agenda item for the over-eighties caucus meeting was to elect the caucus chair. Now Alton called for nominations.

"I nominate Salleigh Grubbs," said Eddie Caldwell, the chairman from Whitfield County, up north.

"Second," a bunch of people called out.

"I had my hand up first," Jim Tully joked, and the group laughed. Then someone else nominated Donna Sant, the chair from Houston County, in the middle of the state. Alton decided to hear from the candidates in alphabetical order, so Salleigh went first. She stood and walked to the front of the room.

"So I apologize for running in a little bit late because I was on the nominating committee, and so I just basically told everybody who I was gonna vote for. So if you hear anything, it was a lie," she joked. People chuckled. Salleigh went on, "I hate doing this kind of stuff. And so I just want to thank you for the opportunity to run for over-eighties. The thing that I wanted to say is, that what I want to do is, I think we need is, the over-eighty counties, our thirty-two counties make up clearly the majority of the votes in the State of Georgia, and we need to be working together. One of the things I've been working on, the joint election integrity task force, with Marci and Jenny Beth Martin, people in Cobb, Fulton, and some people in Gwinnett, all over the state. And one of the things is that when something's happening in Cobb, is the same thing happening in Chatham County? Is the same thing happening in Muscogee County? We figured out that the machines and that kind of stuff, curious things kind of happen at the same time. And if we're not in communication, we are not aware of what is going on. Election integrity is the big thing, but when the rubber meets the road, it's all about the counties and what we do." She was speaking directly to the importance of the base of the party pyramid, as the Precinct Strategy always emphasized. "We can't hold our breath and wait for the state party to do it," Salleigh said. "Just like with the rest of the country, nobody's going to come to save us, right?"

"That's right," someone called back.

"We have to save ourselves, and the way that we save ourselves is by leaning on each other and relying on each other," Salleigh said. "So I'm actually very excited about the opportunity to win this position, because to a large part I do it anyway just because I'm kind of wired that way."

Now she had to address the opposition. "And then the other thing is," Salleigh said, "I had to laugh because I am an America First conservative. Someone said that they might get somebody to run against me because I'm GRA." (The truth is she joined the Georgia Republican Assembly when she first ran for county chair, but she'd never been to a meeting.) "Well, let me just clear it up right now. I love Brant Frost," she said, indicating the Coweta County chairman, who was in the room, and who was also the GRA's first vice president. "I love the fact that every time I call him and pick up the phone that he will help me," Salleigh said. "But that doesn't mean that I am in the Frost bucket. I love people in the Log Cabin Republicans, but that doesn't mean I'm an LGBTQIA-LMNOP person. I like to get along with everyone, so please know that I'm fully aware that in the Republican Party, all of us represent people from this side to the right side and everybody in between. And so the politics of personal belief shouldn't get in the way of doing our job. So that's how I feel."

"Yes, ma'am," someone said, as people started to clap.

"So vote for me," Salleigh concluded. "Please."

The other candidate, Donna, took her turn to speak next. Then it was time to vote. Alton handed out green slips of paper. "We're not going to count off of spelling," he said, "but if you will, the best way to spell Salleigh is S-A-L-L-Y." Salleigh buried her face in her lap. They all wrote down their votes and passed back the green slips.

"And listen, since we're voting by paper ballot, you'll know the results probably tomorrow," Alton joked. Then he and Brant Frost counted the votes, reading them out one by one, like a tribal council on *Survivor*. "Donna. Donna. Donna. Salleigh. Salleigh. Salleigh. Donna. Salleigh. Salleigh. Salleigh. Salleigh. Grubbs." (Some cheers for that one.) "Salleigh," Brant kept reading… "So eighteen Salleigh, eight for Sant."

"Wait a minute," Alton said.

"There should be twenty-five of us."

"Carmen came in, which makes twenty-six."

"No," Carmen said, "I was here way before you passed them out."

"Let me call the roll," Brant said.

"You can't vote twice," someone said.

"Wait a minute," Brant said. "There's six people absent from the roll. There's thirty-two. So there's twenty-six of you all together. So y'all were correct. Our count was off by one, but you're all legitimate." They called the roll again just to make sure.

"Wait a minute, before we declare a winner, y'all happy with this?" Alton said. "Salleigh, you or Donna wanna come to look to make sure we're good?"

"No!" Salleigh said, laughing. (This experience prompted her to clarify that when she said she wanted hand-counted paper ballots, she was OK with the kind of optical scanners that are widely used on standardized tests.)

"OK, so Salleigh is our winner," Alton announced as they applauded. He called her up as the new caucus chair to have the privilege of adjourning the meeting.

"Thank you all for being here," Salleigh said. "For those of you who voted for me, thank you. For those of you who did not vote for me, thank you, and I'll win you over, I promise."

As the people drifted out, Salleigh made sure to visit not only with her friends and supporters — "thankyou-thankyou-thankyou-thankyou" and "yaaaaaay" — but also with the county chairs who didn't vote for her. "I definitely wanna work with you," she said to the chairman from neighboring Gwinnett County. She cooed to him and another chair, "I just love you guys."

As soon as she walked outside, people were telling her, "Congratulations, Salleigh!" Her friends had immediately started texting out the news. "I'm an idiot," she whispered, thinking about all the additional work she was taking on. "I would like us to be normal. We're not. We're the center of the world right now," she said, thinking about Trump's speech the next day and Georgia's importance as a must-win state for Republicans in the next election.

"Madam Chair," people kept calling out as they came up to her. "Congratulations!"

"Thank you, thank you, thank you." Salleigh would say.

"Congratulations!"

"Salleigh!"

"Salleigh, congrats! Happy for you!"

"Thank you for all your help," she said. She was looking forward to a big glass of wine at dinner, where Kari Lake would be the keynote speaker.

"Hey, Ms. Grubbs!"

"Congratulations! It's great news!"

As she stepped outside to catch her breath and stow her bag in her car, Salleigh sighed, "I've never felt so loved."

THE NEXT AND final day of the convention was the day of Trump's speech. Salleigh got up at five to get ready. She put on a cherry-red bell-sleeved dress, a braided rope necklace, and her flag sneakers, stashing heels in her bag to switch into for the photo with President Trump. The streets around the convention center were blocked off by police, and the line to go through the Secret Service security screening was out the door and around the block. The convention center used to be a munitions factory for the Confederate army, but today it looked like an oversized version of one of those twee barns where millennials liked to get married, a huge hall with exposed brick, weathered wood beams, and string lights dangling from the rafters.

As the county chair leading the Cobb delegation, Salleigh was like the teacher on a field trip, constantly checking to make sure everyone was accounted for. She kept studying a printed-out spreadsheet, figuring out which delegates were missing and which alternates would need to be elevated. She had to move her delegates into the convention hall, get them seated with the delegation, make sure everyone was OK. Did everyone have what they needed? The fire marshal was eager to get the crowd seated, so Salleigh came up with a game to keep people occupied, asking them to name their most obscure political memorabilia. Salleigh's was a one-dollar bill signed by Francine I. Neff, the thirty-fourth treasurer of the United States, during the seventies.

Even though the hall was packed, the AC was cranking, so it was as frigid as a meat locker. At the front of the room hung a giant American flag, whose broad stripes were each almost as tall as the lectern where Trump would speak.

But first it was Salleigh's turn. She went up to offer a tribute to the outgoing state party chair, David Shafer.

"Helloooo, patriots!" Salleigh bellowed. "I have a question: do we have any new people in the house?" A cheer swept over the din of the crowd. "We see you back there and we love you," Salleigh said.

"If you're new, there are some things that you may not know, and I'm going to share a few things with you right now about David Shafer." She briefly recounted Shafer's biography and his success in turning around the state party's finances. "David Shafer stood with the alternate electors in the election for President Trump in 2020," Salleigh said, to more cheers. "David Shafer ensured that the alternate electors had legal representation for carrying out their duty for all of Georgia Republicans...And he also has not backed down with the threats by a weaponized Justice Department, even after being offered immunity to testify against President Trump...You also might not know that David worked with Dinesh D'Souza on *2000 Mules*." More applause.

Salleigh was reading from prepared remarks and had to pause once to flip the page, but her delivery became more natural as she struck a more personal note. "I met David Shafer in 2020, after the recount at Jim Miller Park, and let me tell you, we did not start out on a good foot, at least on my part. He talked to me for an hour and a half, and he made sure that what was going on was corrected for as much as we could. I've come to love David Shafer very, very much, and I hope that you will join me in thanking him for his service to the Republican Party." The audience clapped and cheered as she presented him with "an original Penley," a painting of the Statue of Liberty's head.

As Salleigh walked offstage, the convention's first order of business was to adopt the agenda and rules. The version that had been approved the day before by the rules committee would effectively shut out the GRA's accountability rule from standing any chance of passing. Now there was a motion from the floor to amend the rules, to reopen a path for considering the accountability rule. The proceedings were being presided over by Barry Fleming, a bearded state representative from the Augusta area. He called for a vote on the rules. The two thousand delegates voted by standing or sitting, and to many observers, the split was far too close to judge with the naked eye, in a hall almost as long as a football field. But Fleming eyeballed the crowd and announced that "clearly" the ayes had it: the rules were adopted as written. That meant the accountability rule was toast. The crowd booed, and delegates lined up to protest, arguing that Fleming's call for the vote was out of order, or that he couldn't see how many people were standing in the back. Fleming allowed a vote on whether to overturn his ruling, conducted the same way, by eyeballing how many people were standing or sitting. Then he confidently announced his ruling was upheld.

The proceedings broke down into points of order, motions for amendments, and debates over *Robert's Rules of Order,* making Salleigh feel like she'd rather have a sharp stick in the eye. But as she watched Fleming dispense with the challenges from the delegates, many of whom she knew were there for the first time, she sympathized with how they seemed to be getting railroaded and denied a voice. Later, as the convention dragged on into the night, the delegates would register their disapproval by voting down almost everyone who'd been active in the party before 2020. Salleigh was on the right side of that line, but she still left feeling furious and disappointed, because some of the candidates she'd recommended out of the nominating committee had been rejected, and she thought the delegates were applying an overly simplistic litmus test that didn't select the best people. It was another example of how things looked different to her now from the inside, and as long as people on the outside felt dejected and ignored, their fury toward whoever they perceived as "establishment" would only keep escalating.

But now Salleigh had to leave the convention hall, weave through the long line for lunch boxes (she never got hers) and find the rendezvous point for the receiving line for Trump. One of his aides met her there and brought her around the corner and under the stairs, like going around your elbow to get to your knee. She came to a big room on the other side of the exposed brick wall from the main convention hall. There was a stanchion set up for people to stand in line, probably twenty-five of them. Salleigh was number sixteen. She recognized a lot of the people in line: the parents of state party secretary candidate Caroline Jeffords; Stan Fitzgerald from Veterans for Trump, and his wife, Donna; Florida fundraiser Meredith O'Rourke; Atlanta Tea Party founder Debbie Dooley; and Tea Party Patriots cofounder Jenny Beth Martin. Part of the room was cordoned off by a royal-blue curtain, where the pictures would take place.

Salleigh waited there for more than an hour. She spent the time texting with her party officers about what was going on out on the convention floor, where they were scrambling to find alternates for no-show delegates. Salleigh had set up a group chat on the encrypted messaging app Signal, but some people weren't keeping up with their messages. Kari Lake walked through with Caroline Wren, and Salleigh paused her work to take a picture with her.

She could tell Trump had arrived in the building by how the temperature in the room changed. Suddenly there was a flurry of activity, more people moving around. She caught a glimpse of one of Trump's top advisers, Susie Wiles, whom Salleigh had met at the Walker-Warnock debate in Savannah. As the line started to move, they had to empty everything from their hands and pockets onto a table, including a business card Salleigh had been hoping she could slip to him.

Finally the staff brought her behind the blue curtain and there, between an American flag and a Georgia state flag, both hemmed with gold fringe, stood Donald Trump. Tall. Broad. Blue suit. Red tie. White shirt. Tanned skin. Dark eyes. Golden hair. Gigawatt smile. There was so much Salleigh wanted to tell him, and she didn't know how much time she'd have. She remembered what she'd learned from her father, the trial attorney: he always made her get to the point. State your business.

Trump greeted her warmly. She told him how he'd called her

when she'd first been elected county chair, and he said yes, he remembered. It seemed to Salleigh like he really *did* remember; he wouldn't lie about that. She had no idea how many other county chairs he might have called to congratulate. She didn't know why she was special. When she was a girl, she'd always revered presidents. Back then it was Richard Nixon. Her class did an exercise where they wrote a letter to the White House. To her amazement, Salleigh received a reply. It came in a big manila envelope addressed to *her*. Inside there was a letter signed by the president. She was so excited to show her mom and dad, and she remembered her dad laughing, unable to conceal what she was too young to understand, that it was clearly a form letter with a photocopied signature, one of millions of identical letters just like it. But the phone call was different. This meeting was different. This was a real personal connection. "Who am I?" she thought. "I am nobody. I'm just, for years, a single mother raising two children. Doing it all, cleaning house, going to doctor's appointments, taking care of my mom. And now I'm standing in a room with President Trump. How does that happen?" Salleigh knew how lefty lawyers and professors and pundits on MSNBC were always saying that Trump took and took from his supporters because he really only cared about himself. How did that fit with her story, everything he'd done to uplift her life? It was surreal. She felt like that scene in *Notting Hill*: "I'm just a girl..."

Salleigh told Trump he'd also sent her a gift box, and he said he remembered that too. The box had been full of Trump swag: hats and T-shirts, a couple of pens and golf towels and golf balls, and a beautiful pin. She'd shared some of the merch with her friends, but the rest remained in the box it had arrived in. Some day she planned to display those items in a place of honor—on a bookshelf with her great-great-grandmother's baby shoe and a cast-iron clothes iron that had been in the family forever—if she ever had the time to clean up and get her life together. She went from one thing to the other and never had a break. She felt like she hadn't had time to think since November 2020, much less get her house organized.

Now Salleigh told Trump she was worried about the 2024 election, worried about the Republicans' ground game. They needed help. He said absolutely, he would get them what they needed. He called over Marjorie Taylor Greene, who was standing nearby. She came over and hugged Salleigh.

Trump and Salleigh posed for a photo. She hoped she didn't blink. She wished she'd gone on a diet. Trump gave a thumbs-up. Salleigh did, too. Then it was time for her to move along. She stepped away and chatted with Greene for a moment. They hugged again. Alongside the birth of her children, her grandson being born, and her son surviving his accident, it was one of the happiest days of her life.

And with that, she was back out on the convention floor, back to checking in on her delegates, seated at the front of her delegation like the teacher at the head of the class, one county delegation out of a hundred and fifty-nine, one face in a room of more than two thousand. Before long, a campaign ad played on the giant video screens, and then a male voice announced: *"Ladies aaaaaand gentlemen, please welcome the next president of the United States: President Donald! J.! TRUMP!"*

The audience screamed and leaped to their feet. A thousand cell phone screens glowed below a thousand string lights. Trump appeared stage right, from behind an American flag, standing as tall as three of the stripes on the giant flag behind him. His walk-on music blared, *"And I'm proud to be an American, where at least I know I'm free..."* Trump mouthed "WOW!" at the hooting crowd. He nodded, mouthed "Thank you," pumped his fist, clapped his hands. He pointed to someone, mouthed "Thank you" again. He approached the lectern, rested his hands on it, adjusted the microphone.

The music started to fade, preparing for him to begin, but then he withdrew. He was not ready to start. The song was not over. The ovation was not finished. People started chanting, "USA! USA!" "TRUMP! TRUMP! TRUMP!" He did a jerky little dance to the music for a bit, pointed again, then stood still, hands at his side, smiling, nodding, brow low, chin high, breathing it all in. *" 'Cause there ain't no doubt I love this land / God bless the USA!"*

"Wow," Trump said, returning to the podium at last. "Thank you very much. You have a record crowd here today." He thanked the fire marshal and police. He thanked David Shafer and the great state of Georgia. He called out Marjorie Taylor Greene and a few other lawmakers who'd endorsed him for president. Then abruptly, he finished the acknowledgments and started reading from the tele-prompter. He got serious. The crowd got silent.

"For seven years," Trump said, shifting from side to side, "we've been engaged in an epic struggle to rescue our country from the sinister forces within who *hate* it." He growled out the word *hate*. "They hate our country. And who want to destroy it. Can be no other reason. These forces are far stronger than Russia, China, North Korea, and Iran all put together. Think about that: from within is worse than from without…

"Together, we stand up to the globalists, we stand up to Marx-ists, we stand up to the RINOs. You know, the RINOs are pretty bad," he said, as the crowd both cheered and booed. He ad-libbed, "With the RINOs, you don't exactly know where they're coming from. The others, you know, but with the RINOs, sometimes you find out. We've got to stand up to the RINOs."

Back to reading, in his singsong way. "Communists and envi-ronmental extremists. You know, you have environmental extrem-ists, too," he interrupted himself, as if surprised by his own text. "We stand up to the open borders fanatics, the radical left Demo-crats. Their lawless partisan prosecutors. *Prosecutors*," he shook his head. "Every time I fly over a blue state, I get a *sah-pee-nah*."

The crowd erupted in laughter. "Trump, we love you!" a woman shouted.

"And on November 5, 2024," Trump said, straightening his spine as he leaned his arms on the podium, "we're going to stand up to the corrupt political establishment," he said. "We're going to evict a totally corrupt President Joe Biden from the White House — "

The crowd roared. Then Trump, facing them, under the bright stage lights, saw his next words crawl onto the teleprompter: "And we're going to FINISH WHAT WE STARTED!"

The People's Republic of MAGA

"LOOK AT THIS fruitcake."

Saturday, September 30, 2023, was a perfect fall day in Washington — sunny, seventy-two degrees — and Steve Bannon was spending it in the basement of his townhouse, the old Breitbart Embassy, now the command center for the MAGA movement, with the lights off and the shades drawn. His famous podcast studio was in the next room, but he was not on the air now. He was watching C-SPAN, as the House of Representatives was about to vote on a last-minute stopgap measure to avert a government shutdown. Bannon had stayed up the night before watching the debates until three or four a.m., and monitoring comments and chat rooms to see the real-time reaction from his *War Room* audience. Now he was glued to the proceedings again, as Connecticut congresswoman Rosa DeLauro (a Democrat) appeared across his giant TV screen, wearing a yellow blazer and scarf, chunky rings and oversized glasses, a shock of purple in her cropped black hair.

"I love it," Bannon said. "She's so great. We highlight her every time she's on. She's *so* radical. And she looks like something from the Addams Family, right? She's smart as shit. But dude, I just — here we go..."

"It's really not so clean a continuing resolution as it has been portrayed," DeLauro said on the TV, speaking about the seventy-one-page bill to keep the government open that House Speaker Kevin McCarthy was now rushing through to a vote. *"This strikes the member pay*

193

prohibition, in effect giving members a pay raise," she said. *"Now let me just explain..."*

"Whoa! You see how good that is?" Bannon reacted, as if the TV were screening a movie and he was the director. "That's a great shot right there."

Bannon sat at a glossy wooden dining table surrounded by stacks of books (*The Case for Christian Nationalism* by Stephen Wolfe; an oral history of the Trump presidency called *The Method to the Madness*; *March to the Majority* by Newt Gingrich; *Unafraid: Just Getting Started* by Kari Lake), a poster of Rudy Giuliani, and a bust of Bannon himself. He put his feet up, clasped his hands and rested them atop his paunch. He was, in a black collared button-down over a black T, the image of a scofflaw, an American classic, like the Outlaw Josey Wales: convicted criminal, sentenced to four months in prison for defying a congressional subpoena. But he had yet to serve a day, since the judge had suspended his sentence while he exhausted his appeals. All the while, he was forging ahead with his project to transform the Republican Party into an institution for the MAGA movement.

"Our audience does not hate these people," Bannon said of DeLauro and the Democrats. "They don't think they're Americans. But they *hate* the RINOs. So right now, when they hear that, they're like, 'Fucking burn it down! McCarthy gave himself a pay raise!'"

McCarthy had won the speaker's gavel in January after a humiliating fifteen rounds of voting. His difficulty was a direct result of the party's shortcomings in the midterms: with no red wave to deliver a commanding House majority, McCarthy had no room to lose even a handful of votes. If there was one Republican pleased with that outcome, it was Matt Gaetz, the Florida congressman whose self-professed devotion to Trump extended to taking his call during sex. Bannon saw Gaetz as one of the few House Republicans who could actually be effective; and Gaetz had told Bannon, in the summer of 2022, one floor up in this same townhouse, that he didn't want a twenty-seat majority—he wanted a five- or eight-seat majority, because then he'd have more leverage.

The Republicans had ended up with an eight-seat majority, so Gaetz and a handful of other agitators used their leverage to impose painful conditions on McCarthy's leadership. They demanded that he pass twelve separate appropriations bills to fund different parts of the government, rather than forcing everyone to accept a single, comprehensive, up-or-down package—a process change that the hardliners hoped would empower them to force steep spending cuts. And if McCarthy failed on this commitment, a mere five members could call for his ouster, through a maneuver called a motion to vacate. "The drama that happened in the fight in January, the speaker fight—it was over the most obscure shit in the world," Bannon said. But the *War Room* posse couldn't look away. "People were into it, and now they understand how important the rules are. We're having a civics lesson here. We're exploding, and the reason we're exploding? We're really getting into the granular, and people can't get enough of it."

In the nine months since, the House had passed four individual funding bills and moved two more out of committee. That left six to go, and the Senate still hadn't taken up any of them. Now they were out of time: the government was set to run out of funding at midnight on September 30. McCarthy was asking for a forty-five-day extension. Bannon was rooting for a shutdown. Without the support of Gaetz and the other Republican hardliners, McCarthy would have to rely on Democratic votes to pass his extension. And that, to Gaetz and Bannon, was unforgiveable. It would be the last thing McCarthy ever did as speaker.

The Democrats were stalling for time while they reviewed the text of McCarthy's bill and decided whether to support it. DeLauro used her floor speech to call out the Republicans for sneaking a congressional pay bump into the bill. *"Page seven, line thirteen,"* she said. *"In essence, what they have done is provide themselves with a pay raise."*

"See how good she is?" Bannon said.

"Come on!" House Republicans objected from around the chamber, complaining that DeLauro was breaking the House rules by disparaging them directly. The presiding Republican, Steve Womack of Arkansas, banged his gavel.

"See?" Bannon chuckled.

"The gentlelady will suspend," Womack interjected. *"The chair would like to remind his colleagues that, in keeping with the proper decorum on the floor, please direct your comments to the chair."* Bannon translated: "Don't bring up when you caught us giving us a pay raise!"

DeLauro then passed off the podium to the Democratic leader,

Hakeem Jeffries of New York. The Democrats stood to clap and cheer. "And Nancy right in back of him," Bannon observed. "Isn't that a great optic?"

"*I rise today to have a conversation with the American people,*" Jeffries began.

"How good is this?"

"*We want to talk about why we are here at this moment on the brink of a shutdown that was entirely unavoidable—*"

"No, avoidable," Bannon corrected him.

"*—and has been brought to us by the extreme MAGA Republicans—*"

Bannon slapped the table with delight.

"*—who have decided that, rather than pursue the normal legislative process of trying to find common ground—not as Democrats or independents or Republicans, but as Americans—they want to threaten the American people with a shutdown, to try to drive their extreme agenda down the throats of the American people.*"

"So good!" Bannon beamed. "He's framing this perfect for him. They've got their narrative: 'extreme.' Very effective. Compare him to fucking McCarthy. Can McCarthy stand up and do that?"

He looked at his phone, reviewing the online chatter. "People are fired up right now. 'The evil deal...' It's just all on McCarthy. They're just shitting on McCarthy nonstop. It's constant." He said he had a hundred fifty thousand people in chat rooms right now, twenty-five thousand people watching last night at three in the morning (figures that could not be independently verified).

Bannon gestured to the TV and said, "If it hadn't been for the Precinct Strategy, you wouldn't have had this." He'd been so busy covering the shutdown fight that he hadn't had Steve Stern on *War Room* in a while, but he brought him back on the show that morning. Stern had a chorus of flag-shirted mannequin torsos behind him as he cheerfully promoted an upcoming conference call and gave out his cell phone number. (Dan Schultz, meanwhile, was on his own podcast, saying he couldn't guarantee that filling up all the vacant PC slots would save the republic, but if not he guaranteed we'd lose it.) "One of the reasons you wouldn't have had it is because people—they know the nomenclature," Bannon continued. "This audience is so savvy now on this shit. Think about this: the MAGA movement, the base of the Republican Party being focused on appropriations bills? The Tea Party never got to this level." The passion had been there—the anger. But what had the Tea Partiers been so angry about? The GOP's biggest donors came in and tried to make the Tea Party about small government and deregulation. But that hadn't been the point at all. "And that's why the Tea Party evaporated," Bannon said. "You know why they never got to this level? The Kochs and the people that put the money up to drive it didn't want it to get to this level."

He was reminded of another book he'd read, back in 2004: *What's the Matter with Kansas?* by Thomas Frank. "Hugely influential on me," Bannon said. "He makes the case that the Kochs and these people throw out these cultural issues to get the working class that support the Republican Party totally voting against their own economic interest. He's one hundred percent correct." The book was actually a *left*-wing critique: Frank argued that the hollowing out of middle America was the fault of laissez-faire economic policies enacted by Republican officials who got elected by tricking voters into caring more about culture war issues such as abortion, homosexuality, gun control, and evolution. Frank went on to become a supporter of Bernie Sanders, and he'd noticed years earlier that Bannon was filching his ideas. He could point out that Donald Trump was just another example of a Republican politician hoodwinking working-class voters, channeling their social grievances into achieving policies that benefited the ultra-wealthy.

But then Bannon would just blame the RINOs and globalist interlopers, like Treasury Secretary Steve Mnuchin, National Economic Council director Gary Cohn, and Trump's son-in-law Jared Kushner. "The fights we had in the Roosevelt Room, over trade policy and tariffs, were the most vicious in the White House," he said. "I mean, there was almost punches thrown." This defense of Trump's record was non-falsifiable: everything good he accomplished was true MAGA; everything else was someone else's fault. Still, it helped explain why Bannon spent so much more time ragging on Republicans than Democrats. To be clear, he thought the Democrats were total phonies, too, when it came time to make good on taxing the rich and helping the working class. But they were off doing their own thing—whereas the Republicans were the ones standing in the way of Bannon's plans. "The first guys that we gotta take down is the Republican Party," he said. "We haven't done that yet. We're getting there. Trump's our instrument. We're getting there. We're not there yet. We're getting there. The Precinct Strategy — major part of it."

Trump's campaign this time around was benefiting from an inside game, a good old-fashioned delegate strategy like Goldwater's in 1964. In 2016, the party insiders had mounted a credible threat to thwart Trump at the RNC. But now the party apparatus was working to Trump's advantage. In Nevada, the state GOP switched from a primary to a caucus, where better-organized Trump supporters were poised to outperform. Michigan Republicans also voted to select most of their delegates through caucus meetings instead of an open primary, again with the expectation that the change would benefit Trump. The California Republican Party decided to award its delegates winner-take-all for any candidate who cleared fifty percent in its primary, which would put Trump in position to claim fourteen percent of the total delegates needed to clinch the Republican nomination. In Florida, Trump supporters in the party organization revolted against requiring candidates to swear a loyalty oath to the eventual nominee in order to get on the ballot, a measure viewed as boosting Ron DeSantis. In Iowa, home of the first nominating contest, the caucus sites would be run by the party precinct chairs, and many of those same volunteers would be doing double duty as "Trump caucus captains," leading the campaign's turnout operation at those same locations. "That's the Precinct Strategy at work," Bannon said. "A hundred percent Precinct Strategy."

But in Georgia, that troublesome must-win Peach State, site of the Complete MAGA Takeover at the June state GOP convention, Bannon worried that the new state chair might have gone soft. The latest flare-up was over a state senator from the rural northwest corner of the state, Colton Moore. He was demanding a special session to remove Fani Willis, the Fulton County DA who was prosecuting Trump for trying to overturn the 2020 election results. The other state senate Republicans argued that a special session wasn't the right move; they preferred to leave Willis to a newly created "Prosecuting Attorneys Qualifications Commission" that they'd established to investigate alleged misconduct by DAs. When Moore responded by impugning his colleagues directly, they said he'd violated their conference rules and voted to suspend him.

Bannon faulted the state chair for not coming to Moore's aid. The Cobb County chair, Salleigh Grubbs, was sympathetic to Moore's cause, but she also understood that the state chair was just trying to stay neutral and repair relations with Governor Kemp. In a "patriots" chat room Salleigh belonged to on the encrypted messaging app Signal, someone shared an article calling on the state chairman to resign, and Salleigh spoke up to defend him, saying this was a distraction and people needed to get past it. In response, Salleigh got called a "RINO" and kicked out of the group. She just had to laugh. She thought Republicans couldn't afford to be at each other's throats like this; it was self-defeating and self-fulfilling. She told the story to a state senator she saw at a fundraiser a few nights later, and he replied that if *she* was a RINO, "there is no hope."

An even bigger problem for the Georgia GOP was the financial drain of covering spiraling legal costs for David Shafer and all the other "alternate" (phony) electors. The money was drying up for the state GOPs in Michigan and Arizona, too. The cash crunch threatened to hamper their ambitious "ballot chasing" and "election integrity" plans for 2024. But what did they expect to happen, after throwing off the moneyed interests? "All these parties, if you go to every one that's had a populist takeover or a Dan Schultz Precinct Strategy–inspired takeover, they're all out of money," Bannon acknowledged. "Maybe Dan and some of the guys hadn't thought it through, but I told them from the beginning, 'Hey, you're not going to walk in and have the Chamber of Commerce write you a huge check. The traditional business interests may think you're a little too unclubbable.'" But those setbacks would only serve to motivate the insurgents more. "Once they join the Precinct Strategy and get involved, they hate the establishment a hundred times more. Immediately. Because the establishment is trying to fuck them," Bannon said. "The problem in Washington with this apparatus gets personified down to your life."

Bannon was not formally or extensively advising Trump, but he loved what he was hearing out of the candidate. Three nights earlier, Trump had delivered a prime-time speech in Michigan, a state that his campaign hoped to win back in 2024. "I'm here tonight to lay out a vision for a revival of economic nationalism," Trump had told a cheering crowd outside Detroit, from a podium with a campaign placard rendered, instead of in the usual, friendly white on blue, in a stark white on black. "The Wall Street predators, the Chinese cheaters, and the corrupt politicians have hurt you. I will make you better. For years, foreign nations have looted and plundered your hopes, your dreams, and your heritage, and now they're going to pay for what they have stolen and what they have done to you, my friends. We're going to take their money. We're going to take their factories. We're going to rebuild the industrial bedrock of this country like it used to be."

Bannon thought it was the best speech he'd heard since Trump's first inaugural, "American Carnage." "That was a throwdown," he said. "That was a tightly argued case for economic nationalism. That's not a Republican speech. It's a populist speech: a populist, economic nationalist speech. It's a shot across the establishment's bow that the second term is going to be ten-X more aggressive on the implementation of policy than the first. I think we're going to do a hundred times more in the second term."

Policy wasn't the only way Trump was planning to be more aggressive in a second term. He was already privately telling advisers and associates that if he returned to the White House, he wanted to sic federal law enforcement on his critics. Among the people he specified wanting to prosecute were some of his own former aides: his former chief of staff, John Kelly, who said Trump called dead service members "suckers"; his former attorney general, Bill Barr, who defied Trump on the 2020 election and called him "a very petty individual who will always put his interests ahead of the country's"; the former chairman of the joint chiefs of staff, Mark Milley, who used his farewell address to affirm, "We don't take an oath to a wannabe dictator"; and his former defense attorney, Ty Cobb, who said, "America must be better than Trump to survive." Trump had demanded prosecuting his enemies before, but Kelly would ignore him until he moved on. A second term would be different. People like Kelly wouldn't be around. Instead, Trump would surround himself with people like Jeffrey Clark, the former Justice Department official who'd wanted the agency to claim it found "significant irregularities" in the 2020 election. For a second Trump administration, Clark was developing a plan to invoke the Insurrection Act on Inauguration Day, empowering Trump to deploy the military against civil demonstrations.*

---

* In January 2024, Trump downplayed the "retribution" theme he'd spent the better part of a year emphasizing. "We're going to have a success that's so great that I won't have, hopefully, I won't have time for retribution," he said during a Fox News town hall days before winning the Iowa caucuses.

The day after Trump's speech in Michigan, Biden had gone to Arizona to deliver a fresh warning about MAGA extremism. "I've met now with over a hundred heads of state of the nations of the world — everywhere I go, they look and they ask the question, 'Is it going to be okay?'" he'd said. "There is something dangerous happening in America now. There is an extremist movement that does not share the basic beliefs in our democracy: the MAGA movement. Not every Republican, not even a majority of Republicans, adhere to the MAGA extremist ideology. But there is no question that today's Republican Party is driven and intimidated by MAGA Republican extremists.

"We can't take democracy for granted. Remember when you were in high school and college, if you took political science, they said every generation has to protect democracy. I used to think that that was just a saying. But here I am, as President of the United States of America, making this speech about my fear of the diminishment of democracy...

"We should all remember: democracies don't have to die at the end of a rifle. They can die when people are silent, when they fail to stand up or condemn the threats to democracy, when people are willing to give away that which is most precious to them because they feel frustrated, disillusioned, tired, alienated. I get it. I really do. I get it."

He did get it. He'd read *How Democracies Die*, a pair of Harvard professors' study of how free societies slide into authoritarianism at the hands of their own elected leaders. He got it like FDR got it — Biden's presidential role model, whose portrait Biden placed most prominently in the Oval Office, who'd resolved that the way to stop the fires of fascism then engulfing Europe from spreading to the United States was to make democratic governance deliver for regular people: "democracy will save itself with the average man and woman by proving itself worth saving." Biden got it even decades earlier, during his first ill-fated run for president; he was plenty flawed as a candidate, but he could work a room. He was electric. He had a touch, he could make a personal connection with every last person, and even when he finished his staff would have to pry him away. He felt the people's need, their hunger to be led, so much that it scared him: *"If I can do this to these folks, what happens if someone comes along who can really SING?"*

He *got* it, but could he *do* it? He had in 2020 — believed he was the only one who could. It's why he ran. It's why he was running again. But the head-to-head polls were awful. His approval rating was worse. And above all, he was no longer the young stud who could find the connection with every person in every room in 1987. He was, at the time of that speech, eighty years old, and he looked it.

In the opinion of one of the few thousand people who would make all the difference in 2024, Kathy Petsas watched Biden's speech online and thought he did great. His heart seemed to really be in it; he, too, remembered John McCain. She still found Biden lacking as a leader, but he was at his best when he was talking about relationships and human decency.

Bannon, too, thought the speech played to Biden's strengths, but only because the MAGA extremism attack was all he had: he couldn't run on the strength of his own policies, because people weren't feeling the benefit in their own lives. "The bottom is actually falling out. And Biden is a perfect representative of that," Bannon said. "The way he speaks, it doesn't grab people. Trump goes right to the solar plexus. He goes right to the heart of the matter. It's an emotional connection. I can understand where they're saying, 'Hey, are either one of these guys fighting for us?' Whoever captures that *feeling*, and I think the MAGA movement's doing it — whoever captures that feeling, with workers throughout the country, that's the coalition that you put together for — you could govern the country for fifty years."

He turned his attention back to the TV. "Are we doing the thing now?" Yes, the House was voting. "We could definitely get rolled here."

And just then, in case Steve Bannon might have looked like nothing more than some grumpy old man shouting at the TV in his basement on a sunny, seventy-two-degree afternoon, his phone buzzed.

"So what's the word?" he answered.

On the other end of the line, a breathless tenor delivered a report on the latest maneuvers inside the Capitol. *"It looks like the Senate will wait for the House,"* Matt Gaetz told Bannon over the phone, *"after which you'll see it signed into law. And then all we're waiting for then is basically, once that puppy's signed into law, we go drop the motion to vacate."*

"Perfect," Bannon said. "That'll be tomorrow or Monday? 'Cause they'll sign it tonight."

"*Motion to vacate Monday, probably,*" Gaetz said.

"OK, perfect," Bannon said. "Let's come in hot. That's perfect... We're gonna smoke this fucker out. We got him."

"*He has put on the floor a bill with Democrats . . . used Democrats to advance Joe Biden's agenda . . .*"

"And Pelosi. It's perfect. It's perfect. It's awesome . . . How many no's will it have? . . . Womack and these guys can't be that nuts . . . We gotta primary that fuck . . . Unreal . . ."

"*Is it better if I do it alone? Is it better if I get one of my proxies to do it?*"

"No, it's historic. You gotta drop it."

"*Should I go alone or should I have like —* "

"No, you should go down with your Praetorian Guard."

"*Five, six, seven?*"

"Yes, but you drop it . . . OK, cool. I'm around. Bye."

The next day, Gaetz would go on CNN to publicly announce his plan to topple McCarthy, plunging the House back into chaos, with no one having close to enough votes to become the new speaker. Kathy Petsas would be watching CNN on the TV in her kitchen, while needlepointing a decorative cursive *Ciao*. At the sight of Matt Gaetz's smug face on her screen — the high slicked-back hair, the arched eyebrows, button nose, and big chin — Kathy would scoff that she wished she "could stitch his mouth closed."

After three weeks and three failed speaker nominees, Republicans would elect Mike Johnson, a little-known Louisiana backbencher. After the 2020 election, Johnson had recruited 125 colleagues to sign a Supreme Court brief arguing to overturn the results. The DNC would swiftly attack the new speaker as an "election denying, anti-abortion MAGA extremist." The Biden campaign, picking up the theme, would announce, "MAGA Mike Johnson's ascension to the speakership cements the extreme MAGA takeover of the House Republican Conference." That night, Trump would chime in with a social media post, cheering, "MAGA MIKE JOHNSON!"

Whether the MAGA Mike branding would work with someone so obscure, and whether the MAGA Republican attacks would work for Democrats in an election with Trump's name on the ballot, and the impact of multiple indictments and maybe even convictions of Trump — there was no way to predict. For now, Bannon hung up the call with Gaetz and watched the votes appear on his TV. "Come on, baby," he said as the no's ticked higher. "Just give me ninety-two, ninety-three..." A few months earlier, there'd been seventy Republicans against raising the debt limit. Every vote more than that was a win. "It's not bad," Bannon said. "I'm in high cotton." The final tally was ninety-one, a pick-up of twenty-one.

"Are we gonna have some losses?" he said. "Fuck yes. We're going to get fucking rolled. And we may get rolled today. But that's OK. At every defeat, there's enough seeds of other victories that are there. People just gotta stay on it, understand that we're winning more than we're losing. That's why—a revolutionary vanguard. This has happened before in human history, right? We have to take over and we have to rebuild it. Remember, it's a Fourth Turning. We have to rebuild these institutions. That's not my job. That's all to come. I've got a task and purpose. That's for others behind me and others that are at the vanguard of taking this on and tearing it down to rebuild. It will have to be rebuilt. That's gonna be huge. We're not going to be rebuilding any time in the foreseeable future. We're going to be taking things apart.

"They say Trump's a divider. This is what I keep saying on the show—what's my mantra? One side's going to win, and one side's going to lose. No compromise here. You're at one of those deciding moments. You can't compromise. One side's gonna win, and one side's gonna lose. We can't unite with these guys. Tell me what's to unite around. There's nothing to unite around. They believe in a complete different theory of government, a complete different theory of the republic than we do."

He stood up. "I gotta go back to work here," he said. "We gotta figure out next steps."

Acknowledgments

The first person who encouraged me to take on this challenge was Marilyn Thompson, an invaluable mentor and dear friend for many years. As my editor at ProPublica, she spotted the potential in my initial reporting on the Precinct Strategy to grow into a book-sized story. Marilyn remained a crucial source of advice and support throughout the process, including as one of the first pairs of eyes on the draft manuscript.

Thank you to Steve Engelberg, Robin Fields, and Eric Umansky at ProPublica for supporting the first Precinct Strategy story, and to Doug Bock Clark, Anjeanette Damon, and Alexandra Berzon for helping with the reporting in South Carolina, Nevada, and Michigan. Mollie Simon is an incredibly talented researcher. ProPublica colleagues Ken Armstrong and Dave McSwane were generous with their advice on conceptualizing a book and finding an agent, as were Adam Davidson, Ken Vogel, Scott Higham, Margy Slattery, Steve Brill, David Shimer, Joshua Foer, Emily Bazelon, and Anne Fadiman. Anne, who taught me how to write, told me, "The book needs to be written, and you're the right person to write it." The incomparable Fred Strebeigh helped prepare me to think through Voice and Structure and connected me with Burkhard Bilger, who took a chance on me by introducing me to Elyse Cheney.

Elyse and her brilliant associate Isabel Mendía believed in me and the project from the beginning and pushed me mercilessly to expand, improve, and refine the proposal. Pronoy Sarkar at Little, Brown immediately saw the potential and shared my vision for the book, and he was endlessly patient with editing a first-time author through multiple false starts, title changes, delays, and resets. He never said no to any of my out-there ideas, not even a complete history of the United States or a sound collage of January 6; he just queried me to death until I thought better of it. Special thank-yous as well to the whole Little, Brown team who turned these words into a real book: Alyssa Persons, Bryan Christian, Chris Nolan, Melanie Schmidt, Mike Noon, Darcy Glastonbury, Albert LaFarge, Allan Fallow, Maria Espinosa, and Katharine Myers.

A decade ago, another college writing professor, Jack Hitt, kindly offered to help if I ever wanted to write a book. When I finally took him up on it, I never dreamed he would become such an exceedingly generous and prolific supporter. It is no exaggeration that none of this would have been possible without his help. He patiently edited and coached me on early pitch drafts that are embarrassingly unreadable to me now. As if that weren't already above and beyond, he then recommended me to Emanuele Berry, who surprised me with a phone call asking if I was familiar with *This American Life* (!) and then paired me with the true rock star Zoe Chace. Zoe taught me how to radio and covered for me when my flight to Phoenix was canceled. Ira Glass agreed to say my book title on the air even though he expected it would change, and he was right, as always. Thank you to the entire *Washington Post* audio team for accommodating us in the studio with last-minute retracks.

My colleagues at the *Post* make every day an honor and a party. Michael Scherer was the first to welcome me in and help me with sourcing for my very first story as the kind and generous colleague he always is. Josh Dawsey sprinkled magic dust on every story we did together, and covered for me all month in the Berkshires. Amy Gardner ran interference in Columbus. The indefatigable Hannah Knowles found the Saginaw drama. Dylan Wells didn't judge when I booted in the middle of dinner during *White Lotus RNC*. Catherine Valentine taught me how to do my own makeup. Isaac Stanley-Becker made everyone think I was twice as productive. Robert Samuels told me to just worry about writing a good book. Tyler Pager caught errors others missed! Yeganeh Torbati provided moral support in taking the book plunge with me. Martine Powers made my *Post Reports* dreams come true. My campaign trail ride-or-dies Jabin Botsford, Vaughn Hillyard, and Kate Sullivan made every trip something to look forward to. My editors Tim Elfrink, Dan Eggen, and Sean Sullivan always said yes, and higher-ups Phil Rucker and Matea Gold were invariably supportive throughout this project.

Dan Balz, an all-around icon and role model, lent his careful eye and sage advice. Marilyn Thompson supplemented her smart line edits with hilarious one-line takeaways on every chapter. Jose Del Real taught me that even book chapters need sneaky nut grafs, and reassured me in moments of doubt caused by Robert. Eric Randall came up with the best title we never used, and the other title we almost used. Margy Slattery's edits were *always* right, and she *only* made right edits. Tom Stackpole, my blood brother in bookwriting, offered smart and sensitive edits on multiple drafts of the proposal long before there was a manuscript, and I can't wait to return that generosity with his book.

My in-laws crashed their weekend to set up a proofreading sweatshop in their dining room. My mom is always first to tell me where my articles appear in the paper. I wish my dad got to read this book.

Lastly, and most of all, to Liz, the only opinion that matters: thank you for supporting me through all the time this took me away from you, because it was for you, as is everything, always.

Notes

Prologue: The MAGA King in Exile

xi   modeled on: Laura Litinsky, "The Mar-a-Lago Club," *Florida Design*, vol. 15, no. 4, 105.

xi   dreamed: Maggie Haberman, *Confidence Man: The Making of Donald Trump and the Breaking of America* (New York: Penguin Press, 2022), 7.

xi   all passed through: Josh Dawsey and David A. Fahrenthold, "GOP Candidates Are Flocking to Mar-a-Lago to Pay Trump for the Privilege of Hosting Their Events," *Washington Post*, December 16, 2021.

xii   cocktail napkin, and a dinner menu: Devlin Barrett, Mariana Alfaro, Josh Dawsey, and Jacqueline Alemany, "FBI Searches Trump Safe at Mar-a-Lago for Possible Classified Documents," *Washington Post*, August 8, 2022.

xii   "the last election": Jess Bidgood, "'The Last Election': In Arizona, the Guardrails of Democracy May Be About to Fall," *Boston Globe*, November 4, 2022.

xiii   Kristina Karamo: Lauren Gibbons, "Kristina Karamo: What to Know About Michigan GOP Secretary of State Candidate," *Bridge Michigan*, September 26, 2022.
        far-right religious group: Clara Hendrickson, "Sec. of State Candidate Karamo Uses Religious Talk, Church Militant to Find Supporters," *Detroit Free Press*, August 23, 2022.

xiii   Doug Mastriano: Rosalind S. Helderman, Isaac Arnsdorf, and Josh Dawsey, "Doug Mastriano's Pa. Victory Could Give 2020 Denier Oversight of 2024," *Washington Post*, May 18, 2022.

xiii   Tim Michels: Patrick Marley, "Candidate Promises Republicans Can Take Permanent Control of Wisconsin," *Washington Post*, November 1, 2022.

xiii   *going to announce*: Isaac Arnsdorf and Josh Dawsey, "Trump spooks GOP with abandoned talk of presidential launch on eve of vote," *Washington Post*, November 7, 2022.

xiii   "not at all ANGRY": Donald Trump, Truth Social, November 10, 2022.

xiv "Two more years!": Isaac Arnsdorf and Josh Dawsey, "One Likely 2024 GOP Contender Triumphed on Election Night. It Wasn't Donald Trump," *Washington Post*, November 9, 2022.

xiv "America First": Bradley W. Hart, *Hitler's American Friends: The Third Reich's Supporters in the United States* (New York: St. Martin's Press, 2018), 160–87.

xiv Trump may not personally have been aware: Haberman, *Confidence Man*, 238.

xiv deliberate revival: Nicole Hemmer, *Partisans: The Conservative Revolutionaries Who Remade American Politics in the 1990s* (New York: Basic Books, 2022), 257.

xv loosely defined: Hemmer, *Partisans*, 1–14.

xv harsh pessimism: Hemmer, *Partisans*, 1–14.

xvii two-thirds of Republican midterm voters: AP VoteCast, Nov. 8, 2022.

Chapter 1: True Believers

4 "I'm a Leninist": Ronald Radosh, "Steve Bannon, Trump's Top Guy, Told Me He Was 'a Leninist,'" *Daily Beast*, August 22, 2016.

4 revolutionary party: Victor Sebestyen, *Lenin: The Man, the Dictator, and the Master of Terror* (New York: Pantheon, 2017), 139–44. Blurbed by Radosh.

4 clash of civilizations: Joshua Green, *Devil's Bargain: Steve Bannon, Donald Trump, and the Storming of the Presidency* (New York, Penguin Press: 2017), 51.

4 obsessed with history: Green, *Devil's Bargain*, 5, 74.

4 *The Fourth Turning*: Neil Howe, "Where Did Steve Bannon Get His Worldview? From My Book," *Washington Post*, February 24, 2017.

5 wanted to be an agent: Green, *Devil's Bargain*, 204–8.

5 *That's Hitler!*: Jeremy W. Peters, *Insurgency: How Republicans Lost Their Party and Got Everything They Ever Wanted* (New York; Crown, 2022), 187–8.

5 shaped by Eric Hoffer: Steve Bannon, author interview, August 6, 2022.

5 worked as a stevedore: Tom Bethell, "The Longshoreman Philosopher," Hoover Institution, January 30, 2003.

5 "The preliminary work": Eric Hoffer, *The True Believer: Thoughts on the Nature of Mass Movements* (New York: Harper & Row, 1951; reprint, HarperPerennial, 2010), 130–1.

5 "He cannot conjure": Hoffer, *True Believer*, 111–2.

5 fanatics: Hoffer, *True Believer*, xii.

5 "self-renunciation…holy cause": Hoffer, *True Believer*, 12–13.

5 most susceptible: Hoffer, *True Believer*, 24–57.

5 "When our individual interests": Hoffer, *True Believer*, 15–17.

6 Hong Kong: Green, *Devil's Bargain*, 67–83, 145–7.

6 unofficial media partner: Green, *Devil's Bargain*, 161–78.

6 closing message: Green, *Devil's Bargain*, 199–224.

Notes

6 "blue-collar billionaire": Donald Trump Jr., interview by Mark Halperin, "The Circus," *Showtime*, March 21, 2016.

6 Hillary Clinton: Hillary Clinton, *What Happened* (New York: Simon & Schuster, 2017), 10.

6 "new political order": Ryan Teague Beckwith, "Read Steve Bannon and Reince Priebus's Joint Interview at CPAC," *Time*, February 23, 2017.

7 scapegoat: Green, *Devil's Bargain*, xi–xxiv.

7 medieval monastery: Philip Pullella, "Steve Bannon Loses Bid to Start Right-Wing Political Academy in Italy," Reuters, March 15, 2021.

7 SEC's crosshairs: U.S. Securities and Exchange Commission, "SEC Charges Three Media Companies with Illegal Offerings of Stock and Digital Assets," September 13, 2021.

7 There he was: Alan Feuer, William K. Rashbaum, and Maggie Haberman, "Steve Bannon Is Charged with Fraud in We Build the Wall Campaign," *New York Times*, August 20, 2020.

7 Prosecutors accused: *USA v. Kolfage et al.*, 20cr412.

8 Trump shrugged: Feuer, "Steve Bannon Is Charged with Fraud."

8 In truth: Michael C. Bender, *"Frankly, We Did Win This Election": The Inside Story of How Trump Lost* (New York: Grand Central Publishing, 2021), 204–5.

8 Bannon explained: "Arapahoe Tea Party: Steve Bannon—The Plot to Steal 2020," YouTube video, October 14, 2020. Isaac Arnsdorf, Jacqueline Alemany, Rosalind S. Helderman, and Josh Dawsey, "Bannon, Dangling Possible Testimony, Brings New Focus to Jan. 6 Role," *Washington Post*, July 10, 2022.

8 "no downside": Steve Bannon, interview with the author, September 30, 2023.

9 "shred that fucker": Steve Bannon, interview with the author, September 30, 2023.

9 "in the crib": Bob Woodward and Robert Costa, *Peril* (New York: Simon & Schuster, 2021), 207–8. Bannon confirmed this account in an interview with the author on September 30, 2023.

9 "This is more important": Steve Bannon, *War Room: Pandemic*, Real America's Voice, January 2, 2021.

9 "Living history": Steve Bannon, *War Room: Pandemic*, Real America's Voice, January 4, 2021.

10 "cusp of victory": Steve Bannon, *War Room: Pandemic*, no. 636, Real America's Voice, January 6, 2021, (audio) 43:25.

11 "These were *Republicans*": Steve Bannon, "The Next Day," *War Room*, no. 638, January 7, 2021.

11 "he lost his mind": The White House, "Statement on Former White House Chief Strategist Stephen K. Bannon," January 3, 2018.

12 "psyop": Steve Bannon, "*Atlantic* Magazine Meltdown on Rise of the Populist," *War Room*, no. 1,468, December 7, 2021, (audio) 18:13.

12 another Bannon influence: Steve Bannon, author interview, August 6, 2022.

12 a path to self-empowerment: Steve Bannon, "*Atlantic* Magazine Meltdown on Rise of the Populist," *War Room*, no. 1,468, December 7, 2021, (audio) 18:13.

12 Patriot Party: Josh Dawsey and Michael Scherer, "Trump Jumps into a Divisive Battle Over the Republican Party—with a Threat to Start a 'MAGA Party,'" *Washington Post*, January 23, 2021. Jonathan Karl, *Betrayal: The Final Act of the Trump Show* (New York: Dutton, 2021), 331–3.

13 fool's errand: Steve Bannon, "It's All Converging," *War Room*, no. 711, February 6, 2021.

13 uniparty: Steve Bannon, author interview, August 6, 2022.

13 a hundred years: Cheryl Yeh, "Steve Bannon Ranted Outside a Courthouse in DC, Claiming MAGA Will 'Destroy the Democratic Party' and 'Govern for 100 Years,'" *Business Insider*, June 16, 2020.

14 Before bringing Dan Schultz on the air: Daniel J. Schultz, interview with Steve Bannon, "How to Win," *War Room*, no. 712, February 6, 2021, (audio) 5:04. Daniel J. Schultz, interview with Zak Payne, "Dan Schultz and the Precinct Project Joins RedPill78 on the Friday Night Livestream," May 22, 2021, (audio) 1:36:50.

Chapter 2: Extremism No Vice

15 In seventh grade: Daniel J. Schultz, "2021 Person of the Year," *War Room*, no. 1,528, December 31, 2021.

15 more studious: Jeff Baecker, author interview, February 7, 2022.

15 Dan's parents: Daniel J. Schultz, interview by Tracy Diaz, "THIS Is How We Win," *Dark to Light with Frank & Beanz*, February 12, 2021.

15 "city kid": Janet Alvord, author interview, February 8, 2022.

15 Dan and his brothers: Daniel J. Schultz, "Dan Schultz on How GOP Is Cheating Donald Trump & How to Fix It," interview by Robert David Steele, #UNRIG, YouTube video, December 17, 2020.

15 Tom Sawyer: Daniel J. Schultz, personal website.

15 "A government resting": John Dewey, *Democracy and Education* (1916).

16 shifting the emphasis: Rebecca Winthrop, "The Need for Civic Education in 21st-Century Schools," Brookings Institution, June 4, 2020. Charles N. Quigley, "Public Perception and Understanding of the Justice System," American Bar Association Symposium, February 25–26, 1999.

16 "King's Assassin": *Winona Daily News*, April 6, 1968, 1.

16 "Kennedy": *Winona Daily News*, June 5, 1968, 1.

16 "Yippies": *Winona Daily News*, August 26, 1968, 1.

16 worlds away: Daniel J. Schultz, "Precinct Strategy: Your Reconnaissance Mission," Rumble, June 28, 2023.

16 100 percent white: Census Bureau, "1970 Census of Population: Characteristics of the Population," U.S. Department of Commerce, June 1972.

16 annex: *Winona Daily News*, November 24, 1968, 18.

16 soil erosion: *Winona Daily News*, March 7, 1968, 13.

16 basketball team: *Winona Daily News*, February 16, 1968, 14.

16 Prairie Hill Pat Velma: *Winona Daily News*, July 5, 1968, 14.

16 In the civics course: Daniel J. Schultz, interview by Robert Beadles, "Taking Back Our States," *Crypto Beadles*, April 27, 2021, (audio) 2:56.

16 Dan admired him: Daniel J. Schultz, interview by Royce White, "Please Call Me Crazy," no. 97, YouTube video, September 11, 2023.

16 He was twenty-four: Janet Alvord, author interview, February 8, 2022.

17 politically active: Daniel J. Schultz, interview by Zak Payne, "Dan Schultz and the Precinct Project joins RedPill78 on the Friday Night Livestream," May 22, 2021, (audio) 44:30.

17 a copy at home: Daniel J. Schultz, interview by Royce White, "Please Call Me Crazy," no. 97, YouTube video, September 11, 2023.

18 "The decisions made by political parties": H. Rupert Theobald and Patricia V. Robbins, eds., *Wisconsin Blue Book* (1968), 663–8.

18 Mr. Alvord told the seventh graders: Daniel J. Schultz, "Dan Schultz Returns to Talk About the 200,000 Open Precinct Councilman Seats Establishment Republicans Don't Want You to Know About," interview by Brannon Howse, "Brannon Howse Live," *Frank Speech*, November 3, 2021, (audio) 7:26.

18 real organizations: Daniel J. Schultz, interview by Robert David Steele, "Dan Schultz on How GOP Is Cheating Donald Trump & How to Fix It," #UNRIG, YouTube video, December 17, 2020, 5:02.

18 Everyone lived in a precinct: Daniel J. Schultz, interview by Robert David Steele, 5:02.

18 "*actual* power": *Wisconsin Blue Book* (1968), 663–8.

18 chose their leaders: Daniel J. Schultz, "Neighborhood Precinct—Take Back America Call," YouTube video, April 25, 2021, 46:04. Dan Schultz, "Precinct Strategy Discussion," Rumble, June 1, 2022, 10:16.

18 "communist parties": *Wisconsin Blue Book* (1968), 662.

18 Communism fascinated Dan: Daniel J. Schultz, Rumble, September 11, 2023.

19 At the decade's outset: Theodore H. White, *The Making of the President, 1960* (New York: Atheneum, 1961; reprint, New York: HarperPerennial, 2009), 3–62.

19 "There is room": *Wisconsin Blue Book* (1968), 662.

19 dad told him: Daniel J. Schultz, author interview, October 20, 2023.

19 The most important thing: Daniel J. Schultz, interview by Steve Bannon, "How to Win," *War Room*, no. 712, February 6, 2021, (audio) 5:04. Daniel J. Schultz, interview by Zak Payne, 8:30. Daniel J. Schultz, interview by Robert David Steele, 13:08.

19 other students: Jeff Baecker, author interview, February 7, 2022.

19 But for Dan: Daniel J. Schultz, interview by Robert Beadles, 2:56.

20 Meanwhile, Mr. Alvord: Janet Alvord, author interview, February 8, 2022.

20 Crash description: "Alma Teacher Dies in Crash," *Winona Daily News*, December 19, 1979, 3.

20 with a short note: Alma High School River Log, 1980, 2.

21 the dedication page: Daniel J. Schultz, *How to Get Into the Real Ball Game of Politics Where You Live to Help President Donald J. Trump Make America Great Again* (self-pub., 2017), 3.

21 baseball champion: "State Team Championships," Wisconsin Interscholastic Athletic Association. "Alma Tourney Team," *Leader-Telegram* (Eau Claire, Wisconsin), July 27, 1971.

Notes

21 National Honor Society: Alma High School *Annual,* 1974. Carol Wieczorek, email to the author, March 22, 2022.

21 "civics experiment": Daniel J. Schultz, interview by Elizabeth Nader, Facebook, (video) 1:05.

21 wanted nothing: Tom Reiter, author interview, August 10, 2021.

21 rode a bus: Daniel J. Schultz, personal website.

21 thinking themselves: Peter A. Eschbach, "Cold Warriors," *Old Grad Comics* (2018).

21 untouchables: Spencer Klaw, "West Point 1978: What's Happened to the Long Gray Line," *American Heritage,* vol. 29, no. 4 (June/July 1978).

21 Beast Barracks: Klaw, "West Point 1978." Peter Eschbach, author interview, February 13, 2022.

22 Cold Warriors: Eschbach, "Cold Warriors." Peter Eschbach, author interview, February 13, 2022.

22 end of Beast Barracks: Peter Eschbach, author interview, February 13, 2022.

22 "long gray line": Klaw, "West Point 1978." K. Bruce Galloway and Robert Bowie Johnson Jr., *West Point: America's Power Fraternity* (New York: Simon & Schuster, 1973), 17.

22 would not make it: "Graduation Rates," West Point Class of 1978 40th Reunion.

22 "passing the poop": Klaw, "West Point 1978."

22 Dan took seriously: Daniel J. Schultz, "Neighborhood Precinct Committeeman Meeting," *Network America,* June 13, 2021, (video) 2:01:14.

22 Army intelligence: Daniel J. Schultz, interview by Steve Bannon, February 6, 2021, 5:04. Daniel J. Schultz, interview by Zak Payne, 57:31.

22 MICE: J. A. Sheppard, "Reconsidering the Role of Motivation in HUMINT," *American Intelligence Journal,* vol. 36, no. 1, "HUMINT in the 21st Century: Espionage, Attaché Operations, and Other Challenges" (2019), 6–12.

22 One day in spy school: Daniel J. Schultz, interview by Zak Payne, 1:06:14.

23 Dan strained to imagine: Daniel J. Schultz, "*Network America* Conference Call," *Network America,* May 16, 2021, 1:52:44.

23 He felt the horror: Daniel J. Schultz, interview by Robert Beadles, 9:24.

23 While stationed: Schultz, *How to Get Into the Real Ball Game of Politics,* 9.

23 unlikely bestseller: Rick Perlstein, *Before the Storm: Barry Goldwater and the Unmaking of the American Consensus* (New York: Bold Type Books, 2001), 63.

23 Goldwater's vision: Perlstein, *Before the Storm,* 158–60.

23 Fans begged: Perlstein, *Before the Storm,* 84.

23 Goldwater declined to run: Perlstein, *Before the Storm,* 94.

23 fly on the wall: Daniel J. Schultz, "Precinct Strategy Discussion," Rumble, June 1, 2022, 10:16.

23 "honest-to-God conservative": Perlstein, *Before the Storm,* 188.

23 supporters met in secret: Middendorf, *Glorious Disaster,* 13.

24 "We're going to take over": Middendorf, *Glorious Disaster,* 12–17.

24 John Birch Society: Perlstein, *Before the Storm,* 114–9.

24 foot soldiers: Perlstein, *Before the Storm,* 171–200.

24 "extreme reactionaries": Perlstein, *Before the Storm,* 360.

24 had the votes: Middendorf, *Glorious Disaster,* 102.

24 Dan had a memory: Daniel J. Schultz, "Neighborhood Precinct—Take Back America Call," YouTube video, April 25, 2021, 46:04. Daniel J. Schultz, "Precinct Strategy Discussion," Rumble, June 1, 2022, 10:16.

24 The scene was bedlam: Perlstein, *Before the Storm,* 371–84.

25 His campaign's whole strategy: Ari Berman, *Give Us the Ballot: The Modern Struggle for Voting Rights in America* (New York: Picador, 2016), 69.

25 Wallace Democrats: Kevin Boyle, *The Shattering: America in the 1960s* (New York: W. W. Norton, 2021), 146–50.

25 "my fellow extremists": Perlstein, *Before the Storm,* 431.

25 "reactionary takeover": "The Greatest Danger," *Washington Evening Star,* July 15, 1964, 24. Quoted in part in Perlstein, *Before the Storm,* 393.

26 underlined: Perlstein, *Before the Storm,* 391.

26 "right-wing kooks": Middendorf, *A Glorious Disaster,* 133.

26 "stench of fascism": Perlstein, *Before the Storm,* 392–3.

26 "equivalent of Russian Stalinism: Taylor Branch, *Pillar of Fire: America in the King Years, 1964–65* (New York: Simon & Schuster, 1999), 401–3.

26 deliver one speech twice: Perlstein, *Before the Storm,* 230.

26 ten to one: Perlstein, *Before the Storm,* 473–4.

26 "indisputable proof": Perlstein, *Before the Storm,* 513. Boyle, *The Shattering,* 167–71.

26 a thirtyfold increase: Middendorf, *Glorious Disaster,* xi.

26 lifelong bug: Perlstein, *Before the Storm,* xiii.

26 American Conservative Union: Middendorf, *Glorious Disaster,* 235.

26 became "the Moses": Middendorf, *Glorious Disaster,* 265–6.

26 Nixon plotted: Middendorf, *Glorious Disaster,* 243.

27 Nixon, and later Reagan: Hemmer, *Partisans,* 5, 15–41, 43–66.

27 never big on Nixon or Bush: a person close to Schultz who spoke on the condition of anonymity.

27 "America is fundamentally": Barry Goldwater, *The Conscience of a Conservative* (Shepherdsville, Kentucky: Victor Publishing Company, 1960).

27 finished his required active duty: Daniel J. Schultz, interview by Robert David Steele, 0:26.

27 law school: Daniel J. Schultz, interview by Tracy Diaz, 13:39.

27 had it made: the person close to Schultz.

27 ESQKIER: Marital settlement agreement, Los Angeles County Superior Court, January 15, 1992, 1.

27 tore through: Schultz, "Neighborhood Precinct Committeeman Meeting," 2:01:40.

28 trip wire: Daniel J. Schultz, interview by Chuck B, "Live Interview by Dan Schultz from Precinctstrategy.com," *RTT Nation,* YouTube video, 18:39.

28 He was outraged: Daniel J. Schultz, "What Will You Choose to Do?," *The Liberty Pole*, ed. Steven A. Silver, vol. 2, no. 5 (November 1995).

28 His fixation was shared: Jeffrey Toobin, *Homegrown: Timothy McVeigh and the Rise of Right-Wing Extremism* (New York: Simon & Schuster, 2023), 20–28, 63–88.

28 President Bill Clinton responded: John F. Harris, "Clinton Rejects Patriot Claim of Armed Groups," *Washington Post*, May 6, 1995.

28 Dan objected: Daniel J. Schultz, "The Milita of One," *The Liberty Pole*, ed. Steven A. Silver, vol. 4, no. 1 (February 1997).

28 fringe idea: Hemmer, *Partisans*, 139–61.

28 militia movement: Toobin, *Homegrown*, 56.

28 sparsely attended: Cassandra Burrell, "Militia Rally Advocates Paper Ballots, Gold to Solve U.S. Problems," Associated Press, September 1, 1996.

28 they blamed: Joyce Price, "Rally to Protect Bill of Rights Fails to Draw Big Crowd; Organizers Blame Traffic, Media," *Washington Times*, September 1, 1996.

28 The rally included: Burrell, "Militia Rally Advocates Paper Ballots."

29 Dan spoke: Daniel J. Schultz, "The Key: The Constitution," *The Liberty Pole*, ed. Steven A. Silver, vol. 3, no. 4 (September 1996).

29 He quit: Daniel J. Schultz, "Starving the Beast," *The Liberty Pole*, ed. Steven A. Silver, vol. 5, no. 1 (March 1998).

29 volunteered: "Pro 2nd Amendment Lawyers," United States Concealed Carry Association, June 6, 2011 (last updated).

29 He encouraged: Daniel J. Schultz, "The Disarmers," *The Liberty Pole*, ed. Steven A. Silver, vol. 5, no. 4 (September 1998).

29 still searching: Schultz, "What Will You Choose to Do?"

29 law practice: Daniel J. Schultz, personal website.

29 they could still tell: A former coworker of Schultz's who spoke on the condition of anonymity, author interview, February 8, 2022.

29 got divorced: Marital settlement agreement, Los Angeles County Superior Court, January 15, 1992.

29 Dan chose: "Superintendent Diane Douglas Welcomes New Director of Legal/Hearings," Arizona Department of Education, March 21, 2017, 17.

29 in LA: Daniel J. Schultz, interview by Elizabeth Nader, 2:24.

29 autistic: Maricopa County Probate Court, case no. PB2017-092424.

29 The family moved: Daniel J. Schultz, interview by Tracy Diaz, 10:04.

29 He didn't think: Daniel J. Schultz, author interview, October 20, 2023.

29 When Dan joined: Daniel J. Schultz, interview by Zak Payne, 8:48.

29 Dan thought: Daniel J. Schultz, interview by Robert Beadles, 5:58.

29 Minuteman Project: Sonia Scherr, "Top Minuteman Group Announces Breakup," Southern Poverty Law Center, April 30, 2010.

29 Dan found a meeting: Daniel J. Schultz, interview by Zak Payne, 9:30.

29 As the story went: Daniel J. Schultz, interview by Chuck B, 19:30.

30 Dan remembered: Daniel J. Schultz, interview by Chuck B, 20:15.

30 It reminded him: Daniel J. Schultz, "Interview by Dan Schultz" (with Chris Moore), *The Common Sense Show*, March 18, 2021, (video) 46:35.

30 Dan showed up: Daniel J. Schultz, interview by Tracy Diaz, 9:35.

30 Dan's assumption Daniel J. Schultz, "Precinct Nuts and Bolts," *Network America*, June 9, 2015, (video) 1:07:35.

30 a bad premise: Daniel J. Schultz, author interview, October 20, 2023.

30 Marxist: Daniel J. Schultz, interview by Chuck B, 20:15.

30 "not one of us": Daniel J. Schultz, interview by Zak Payne, 12:00.

30 early Tea Party event: Anjanette Riley, "Arizonans Take a Lesson from 1773, Hold Their Own 'Taxpayer Tea Party,'" *Arizona Capitol Times*, March 6, 2009.

31 Dan told the speakers: Daniel J. Schultz, interview by Zak Payne, 12:28.

31 He imagined: Daniel J. Schultz, interview by Robert Beadles, 41:19.

31 such a high price: Daniel J. Schultz, interview by Robert Beadles, 15:33.

31 Plato quote: Daniel J. Schultz, interview by Steve Bannon, "Governed by Inferiors," *War Room*, no. 720, February 10, 2021, (audio) 37:01. More precisely: "The chief penalty is to be governed by someone worse if a man will not himself hold office" (Plato, *Republic* 1.347c, trans. Paul Shorey).

31 Phyllis Schlafly: Daniel J. Schultz, "Precinct Committeeman Meeting," *Network America*, August 8, 2021, (video) 37:58.

31 "I can't guarantee": Daniel J. Schultz, interview by Zak Payne, 15:11.

31 Chicken Little: Daniel J. Schultz, interview by Bill Martinez, "Under Biden, Our Southern Border Has Become a Crime Scene, Has the MLB Gone Too Far, and a Strategic Approach Toward Defeating RINOs," *The Bill Martinez Show*, (audio) 52:45.

31 broken record: Daniel J. Schultz, interview by Robert Beadles, 7:57.

31 county attorney: Daniel J. Schultz, interview by David K. Clements, "Take Over the Republican Party," *The Professor's Record*, June 8, 2021, (video) 29:56. "Justice William G. Montgomery," Arizona Judicial Branch.

32 "what a real schmuck": Daniel J. Schultz, Rumble, August 8, 2023.

32 if it could work: Daniel J. Schultz, interview by Tracy Diaz, 23:02.

32 ten orders: Anti-Defamation League, "Oath Keepers," June 26, 2017.

32 intelligence assessment: "Rightwing Extremism: Current Economic and Political Climate Fueling Resurgence in Radicalization and Recruitment," U.S. Department of Homeland Security, Extremism and Radicalization Branch, Homeland Environment Threat Analysis Division, April 7, 2009.

32 DHS secretary apologized: Ed O'Keefe, "Napolitano Comments on 'Right Wing Extremist' Report," *Washington Post*, April 15, 2009.

32 The firestorm inspired: Daryl Johnson, author interview, October 18, 2021. Seyward Darby, *Sisters in Hate: American Women on the Front Lines of White Nationalism* (New York: Little, Brown, 2020), 75–6.

32 When Dan heard: Schultz, "Precinct Nuts and Bolts," 1:24:49.

32 It resembled: Daniel J. Schultz, "The 'Pre–Oath of Office,'" *The Liberty Pole*, ed. Steven A. Silver, vol. 3, no. 3 (June 1996).

32 he hated: Daniel J. Schultz, interview by Brannon Howse, 7:26.

33 Dan considered himself: Daniel J. Schultz, text message to the author, March 2, 2022.

Notes

33   Bundy: Schultz, "Precinct Nuts and Bolts," 1:21:39. *United States v. Cliven D. Bundy et al.*, 968 F.3d 1019 (Ninth Cir. 2020).

33   AR-15: Schultz, "Precinct Nuts and Bolts," 1:24:03.

33   He feared: Daniel J. Schultz, interview by David Clements, 3:49.

33   "me and the other Oath Keepers": Daniel J. Schultz, post on Oath Keepers forum, January 31, 2014. Obtained by an anonymous hacker and provided by the nonprofit group Distributed Denial of Secrets.

33   tried calling into: Daniel J. Schultz, "Precinct Nuts and Bolts," 1:23:16. Dan said he never formally joined the organization. Daniel J. Schultz, text message to the author, March 2, 2022.

33   big enough microphone: Jim Condit, "Neighborhood Precinct Committeeman Meeting," *Network America*, July 11, 2021, (video) 9:13.

33   iPad: Daniel J. Schultz, interview by Brannon Howse, 43:18.

33   handwritten note cards: Daniel J. Schultz (ColdWarrior1978), "Precinct Committeeman Strategy," Rumble, July 28, 2014.

33   He blogged: Daniel J. Schultz (ColdWarrior), *RedState*.

33   *"conniving libturds"*: Daniel J. Schultz (ColdWarrior), "The Solution to Political Pollution Is Dilution — But, It Takes YOU," *RedState*, July 14, 2010.

34   He wasn't sorry: Daniel J. Schultz (ColdWarrior), "What ColdWarrior Would Like to See at *RedState* — Bluntly," *RedState*, September 4, 2011.

34   screen name: Schultz, "Precinct Committeeman Meeting," 2:08:14.

34   Dan swore: Daniel J. Schultz, interview by Brannon Howse, 11:27, 14:18.

34   assigned his kids: Schultz, "Neighborhood Precinct Committeeman Meeting," 2:16:22.

34   signed up three: Daniel J. Schultz, interview by Chris Moore, 39:02.

34   "a mouth to feed": Schultz, "Neighborhood Precinct Committeeman Meeting," 2:10:59.

34   He saw it: Daniel J. Schultz, interview by Brannon Howse, 14:30.

34   "I'm going to a camp": Schultz, "Network America Conference Call," 1:54:18.

34   clickbaity parlance Daniel J. Schultz, interview by Elizabeth Nader, 4:34.

34   variation on the same theme: Daniel J. Schultz, "The 'Hobbits' Plan to Take Over the GOP," *Breitbart News*, August 12, 2015. Daniel J. Schultz, "One Weird Trick About How and Where Conservatives Should 'Rally' Against the Iran Nuclear Deal," *Breitbart News*, September 2, 2015.

34   "secret and dangerous missions": Daniel J. Schultz, "ColdWarrior Has a Secret and Dangerous Recon Mission for Every Conservative — and You Can Do It!," *Breitbart News*, August 14, 2015.

34   "I'll grow the party": Daniel J. Schultz, interview by Rob Maness, 16:19.

35   cheap and short: Danield J. Schultz, interview by Tracy Diaz, 41:06.

35   on the toilet: Daniel J. Schultz, "NPE Strategy," *Network America*, April 11, 2021, (video) 1:00:40.

35   the socialists did not want: Schultz, "Neighborhood Precinct Committeeman Meeting," 1:49:58.

35 copies to President Trump: Daniel J. Schultz, interview by Tracy Diaz, 44:05.

35 "basic American civics": Daniel J. Schultz, "2020 01 28 Trump Precinct Committeeman Recruitment & GOTV Strategy," YouTube video, February 8, 2020.

35 bused in from California: Daniel J. Schultz, interview by John Fredericks, "Outside the Beltway with John Fredericks," *The John Fredericks Show*, September 27, 2021, (video) 16:47.

35 "why is Arizona blue?": "Fox News Democracy 2020: Election Coverage," Fox News, November 3, 2020.

35 "This is a fraud": "President Trump's Election Night Remarks," *ABC News*, November 4, 2020.

35 "everybody and their dog": Daniel J. Schultz, interview by Rob Maness, 38:17.

36 governor of Arizona: Jonathan J. Cooper, "Arizona Governor Silences Trump's Call, Certifies Election," Associated Press, December 2, 2020.

36 state legislators: Daniel J. Schultz, "Neighborhood Precinct Committeeman Meeting," June 13, 2021.
Footnote: *Moore v. Harper*, No. 21-1271, June 27, 2023, 21.

36 too scared or too stupid: Daniel J. Schultz, interview by Chris Moore, 12:14.

36 Mark Finchem: Mark Finchem, interview by Steve Bannon, *War Room: Pandemic*, no. 616, December 28, 2020, (audio) 36:42. "Statement from Representative Mark Finchem," January 11, 2021.

36 Dan messaged Bannon: Daniel J. Schultz, interview by Chris Moore, 13:25.

36 "A beloved figure": Steve Bannon, "The Great Awakening," *War Room*, no. 619, December 29, 2020, (video) 36:22.

38 Dan reappeared: Daniel J. Schultz, "How to Win," interview by Steve Bannon, *War Room*, no. 712, February 6, 2021.

39 breakdown of community bonds: Robert D. Putnam, *Bowling Alone: The Collapse and the Revival of American Community* (New York: Simon & Schuster, 2000), 27.

39 Bannon knew: Steve Bannon, author interview, August 6, 2022.

Chapter 3: Nobody, but Somebody

41 In Miami: Rene Garcia, author interview, July 6, 2021.

41 In Polk County: JC Martin, author interview, July 14, 2021.

41 In Fort Worth: Rick Barnes, author interview, July 28, 2021.

41 Outagamie County: Matt Albert, author interview, February 8, 2022.

42 Cobb: Jason Shepherd, author interview, December 9, 2021.

42 far from the only: Greg Bluestein, *Flipped: How Georgia Turned Purple and Broke the Monopoly on Republican Power* (New York: Viking, 2022), 195.

43 "release the Kraken": Sidney Powell, interview by Lou Dobbs, "Detroit Judge's Voter Fraud Ruling Will Be Appealed," *Lou Dobbs Tonight*, Fox News, November 13, 2020.

43   the complaint: *Pearson et al. v. Kemp et al.*, United States District Court for the Northern District of Georgia, no. 1:20-cv-04809, November 27, 2020. The voting machines' manufacturer, Dominion, sued Powell and other Trump advisers for defamation.

43   Jason did not think: Jason Shepherd, author interview, December 9, 2021.

      his county committee voted: Larry Felton Johnson, "Cobb Republican Committee Votes to Join Sidney Powell Lawsuit Against Georgia Presidential Election Certification," *Cobb County Courier*, November 27, 2020.

43   Even Trump: Maggie Haberman and Alan Feuer, "Trump Team Disavows Lawyer Who Peddled Conspiracy Theories on Voting," *New York Times*, November 22, 2020.

43   using a video: Salleigh Grubbs, Facebook, March 7, 2021.

44   ran for Congress: Gene Britton, "Rep. Landrum, Mrs. Blitch Win," *Atlanta Constitution*, September 15, 1960, 12.

      Marietta city council: "J. Milton Grubbs, Lawyer, Former Marietta Official," *Atlanta Constitution*, September 25, 1987, 16E.

44   stuck with Salleigh: Hunter Riggall, "Cobb Countians Reflect on Lessons from Their Fathers," *Cherokee Tribune*, June 18, 2021. Don Hicks, "Matthew Trial Begins Monday," *Atlanta Constitution*, October 22, 1979, C2.

44   "old Marietta": Jason Shepherd, author interview, December 9, 2021.

44   She bounced around: CCAI, "Meet the Members," YouTube video, November 5, 2020, 7:15.

44   shotgun: Salleigh Grubbs, Facebook, March 15, 2021.

44   three rescue dogs and a pet tortoise: Salleigh Grubbs, Facebook, March 14, 2021.

44   "keyboard warrior": Salleigh Grubbs, interview with Monica Matthews, "Newly Elected GA GOP Official Receives Call from President Trump," *Red Voice Media*, April 21, 2021, (video) 2:50.

44   "regular voters": Salleigh Grubbs, interview with Todd Piro, "Breakfast with 'Friends': Marietta Diner," *Fox & Friends*, November 21, 2019.

45   mailed Pelosi: Salleigh Grubbs, Facebook, February 5, 2020.

45   wiped down her groceries: Salleigh Grubbs, Facebook, March 30, 2020.

      prayed: Salleigh Grubbs, Facebook, March 31, 2020.

      watched the briefings: Salleigh Grubbs, Facebook, March 31, 2020.

      grateful: Salleigh Grubbs, Facebook, March 31, 2020.

      She even supported: Salleigh Grubbs, Facebook, March 31, 2020.

      Salleigh figured: Salleigh Grubbs, Facebook, May 17, 2020.

45   She read a column: Salleigh Grubbs, Facebook, May 17, 2020. Andrew P. Napolitano, "Why Americans Must Stop Acting Like Sheep and Tell the Government to Take a Hike," *Washington Times*, May 13, 2020.

46   popular with most Americans: "AP-NORC Poll: Rising Support for Mail Voting Amid Pandemic," Associated Press, April 27, 2020.

46   cherished her memories: Salleigh Grubbs, Facebook, May 11, 2020.

46   Salleigh saw: Salleigh Grubbs, Facebook, June 14, 2021.

46   Rayshard Brooks: Brad Brooks and Dan Whitcomb, "Protesters Burn Down Wendy's in Atlanta after Police Shooting," Reuters, June 13, 2020.

Fox 5 Atlanta Digital Team, "3 Indicted for Arson of Wendy's Following Death of Rayshard Brooks," *Fox 5 Atlanta*, January 28, 2022.

46   not alone: *Morning Consult*, National Tracking Poll #2005131, May 31–June 1, 2020.

47   saw Trump post: Salleigh Grubbs, Facebook, August 19, 2020.

47   upside-down flag: Salleigh Grubbs, Facebook, June 8, 2020.

47   gotten married: Salleigh Grubbs, Facebook, October 25, 2018.

47   "not in God's plan": Salleigh Grubbs, interview with Monica Matthews, *Red Voice Media*, April 21, 2021, (video) 2:50.

47   "status shock": Diana C. Mutz, "Status Threat, Not Economic Hardship, Explains the 2016 Presidential Vote," Proceedings of the National Academy of Sciences, vol. 115, no. 19, April 23, 2018. Eduardo Porter, "Whites' Unease Shadows the Politics of a More Diverse America," *New York Times*, May 12, 2018.

47   did not even bother: Jason Shepherd, author interview, December 9, 2021.

47   Salleigh's main concern: Salleigh Grubbs, author interview, February 10, 2022. The state election director, Chris Harvey, did not respond to requests for comment.

48   asked all her friends: Salleigh Grubbs, Facebook, August 3, 2020.

48   brave and patriotic: Bobbi VanHorn, Facebook, July 6, 2020.

48   beautiful inside and out: Mary Jo Forster, Facebook, March 22, 2021.

48   an inspiration: Tina Parsons, Facebook, December 30, 2020.

48   they'd vote for her: Barbara Riker Phillips, Facebook, November 2, 2020.

48   profile picture: Salleigh Grubs, Facebook, August 12, 2020.

48   natural brunette: Salleigh Grubs, Facebook, August 23, 2017.

48   growing out her roots: Salleigh Grubbs, "'Unbelievable': Dozens of Georgia Witnesses Step Forward to Expose Election Irregularities — Part 1," interview by Susan Knox, *NTD News*, December 26, 2020, (video) 55:12.

48   "WARNING": Salleigh Grubbs, Facebook, September 1, 2020. Natalie Winters, "WARNING: Democrat Data Firm Admits 'Incredible' Trump Landslide Will Be Flipped by Mail-In Votes Emerging a Week After Election Day," *National Pulse*, September 1, 2020.

48   Republicans lost: Michael King, "Seismic Political Shift Takes Place in Cobb County Offices," *11Alive*, November 4, 2020.

49   should not have lost: Salleigh Grubbs, author interview, July 14, 2021.

49   thought about traveling: Salleigh Grubbs, Facebook, November 11, 2020.

49   recount procedure: Janine Eveler, interview by Claire Simms, "Cobb County Nears Finish Line of Presidential Election Audit," *Fox 5 Atlanta*, November 16, 2020.

49   had to see this: Salleigh Grubbs, author interview, April 11, 2022.

49   recalled a memory: Salleigh Grubbs, author interview, April 12, 2022.

50   "a total Karen": Salleigh Grubbs, author interview, April 11, 2022.

50   would have needed binoculars: Susan Knox, "Election Witnesses Speak," *NTD News*, November 16, 2020.

50   Salleigh thought she could see: Grubbs, "Unbelievable," 55:12.

50   454: Susan Knox, "Poll Watcher, Cobb Co. GA Speaks Out on Witnessed Election Fraud," *Monkey Savant*, November 29, 2020. Video, 2:37.

50   Exhibit Hall B: Salleigh Grubbs, testimony to Georgia State Senate Judiciary Subcommittee, December 30, 2020, (video) 1:58.

51   "no need to be rude": video provided by Susan Knox.

51   Salleigh wondered: Salleigh Grubbs, author interview, April 11, 2022.

51   "This is a fraud": Susan Knox, "'Unbelievable': Dozens of Georgia Witnesses Step Forward to Expose Election Irregularities—Part 1." *NTD News*, December 26, 2020, (video) 56:44.

51   "Nigeria": Susan Knox, author interview, January 14, 2022.

51   "not being judgmental": Susan Knox, author interview, April 12, 2022.

51   "Black as spades": Susan Knox, author interview, January 14, 2022.

51   "Oh. My. God.": Knox, "Unbelievable," 62:10.

52   felt a surge: Susan Knox, author interview, April 12, 2022.

52   called 911: Knox, "Unbelievable," 64:06.

52   Salleigh was in her office: Salleigh Grubbs, author interview, April 11, 2022.

52   someone in her family had died: Salleigh Grubbs, interview by Donna Fiducia and Don Neuen, "Cowboy Logic Radio," Donna Fiducia Productions, January 12, 2021, (audio) 39:14.

52   *Starsky and Hutch*: Salleigh Grubbs, interview by Rocci Stucci, "Restoring Republican Principles with Salleigh Grubbs," *The Situation Room*, May 25, 2021, (audio) 8:03.

52   "Who called you?": RedKudzu, "Salleigh Grubbs, Testimony of Voter Fraud and Irregularities in Georgia's 2020 General Election" BitChute, December 12, 2020.

53   what was he hiding?: Salleigh Grubbs, "If Nothing Is Wrong—Why Hide Your Face?," Facebook, December 13, 2020.

53   cookies: Grubbs interview, April 11, 2022.

53   Fifteen minutes: Susan Knox, affidavit, December 3, 2020, 4–5. Obtained through a public records request to the Georgia Secretary of State.

53   dialed 911 again: Knox, "Unbelievable," 66:16.

53   eleven miles: Salleigh Grubbs, author interview, August 30, 2021.

53   at a RaceTrac: Salleigh Grubbs, interview by Rocci Stucci, 10:30.

53   "Get in, girl": Salleigh Grubbs, author interview, April 11, 2022. Susan Knox, author interview, April 12, 2022.

53   SoulTown: Knox, "Unbelievable," 69:35.

53   Thelma and Louise: Grubbs, "Testimony of Voter Fraud and Irregularities in Georgia's 2020 General Election," 9:34.

53   Lucy and Ethel: Salleigh Grubbs, "When it's during an election recount and you're chasing a shredding truck," Facebook, February 3, 2021.

53   Hollywood car chase: Grubbs, "Testimony of Voter Fraud and Irregularities in Georgia's 2020 General Election," 9:34.

53   ran a red light: Susan Knox, affidavit, 5.

54   she started to worry: Susan Knox, author interview.

54   camp out all night: Salleigh Grubbs, interview by Rocci Stucci, 11:45.

54 911 call log: Cobb County 911 Incident Report no. CO-2020-11-20-00237888, November 20, 2020.

54 At the station: video provided by Susan Knox.

55 what a coincidence!: Susan Knox, Facebook, November 2, 2021.

55 FBI: Salleigh Grubbs, author interview, August 30, 2021.

55 Now Salleigh wondered: Salleigh Grubbs, "How far does the corruption go?," Facebook, December 21, 2020.

55 Lin Wood retweet: Jude Joffe-Block, "Georgia County Destroyed Election Waste, Not Ballots," Associated Press, November 21, 2020.

55 two Black election workers: Amy Gardner, "Election Workers Describe 'Hateful' Threats After Trump's False Claims," *Washington Post*, June 21, 2022.

55 inspired three people: Holly Bailey, Amy Gardner, Patrick Marley, and Jon Swaine, "Here's Who Else Was Charged in Georgia (Other than Trump)," *Washington Post*, August 15, 2023.

55 people were calling: Cobb County 911 Incident Report.

56 "routine" disposal: Cobb County Elections, "Document Shredding at the Jim R. Miller Park," November 20, 2020.

56 would never know for sure: Salleigh Grubbs, text message to author, September 3, 2021.

56 there was no way: Salleigh Grubbs, author interview, July 14, 2021.

56 subcommittee hearing: "Georgia Senate Subcommittee Holds Hearing on Election Issues," *NTD News*, December 30, 2020, (video) 2:52:00.

57 "Those continuing to claim": Gabriel Sterling, Facebook, December 26, 2020.

57 dump truckload: Grubbs, "Cowboy Logic Radio," 21:25.

58 *Rudy gets it*: Salleigh Grubbs, interview with Donna Fiducia and Don Neuen, 19:02.

58 so many texts: Salleigh Grubbs, Facebook, December 30, 2020.

58 "I'm just nobody": Salleigh Grubbs, "What's going on, America?," Facebook Live, January 9, 2021.

59 Justice Department: Richard Donoghue, "Mtg w/ DAG + Jeff Clarke—6th Fl.," January 2, 2021. Bailey, "Here's Who Else Was Charged in Georgia."

59 "find 11,780 votes": Amy Gardner and Paulina Firozi, "Here's the Full Transcript and Audio of the Call Between Trump and Raffensperger," *Washington Post*, January 5, 2020.

59 so many friends: Salleigh Grubbs, Facebook Live, 48:15.

59 their whole lives: Salleigh Grubbs, interview with Donna Fiducia and Don Neuen, 37:22.

59 made a plan: Salleigh Grubbs, Facebook Live, 6:06.

60 Salleigh hadn't been: Salleigh Grubbs, author interview, April 11, 2022.

60 Ginni Thomas: Kevin Daley, "EXCLUSIVE: Ginni Thomas Wants to Set the Record Straight on January 6," *Washington Free Beacon*, March 14, 2022.

60 Her seat: Salleigh Grubbs, Facebook Live, 7:15.

60 fighting for her: Salleigh Grubbs, Facebook, August 9, 2020.

60 She was the one: Mike Crane, "4 Salleigh Grubbs," YouTube video, July 5, 2021.

61 By the time he finished: Salleigh Grubbs, author interview, April 11, 2021. Salleigh Grubbs, Facebook Live.

61 time-stamped, geo-tagged photo: provided by Grubbs.

61 Salleigh called a friend: Salleigh Grubbs, author interview, April 11, 2022.

62 The screen was split: "The Daily Briefing With Dana Perino," Fox News, January 6, 2021.

62 chyrons: "Bill Hemmer Reports," Fox News, January 6, 2021.

63 her friends burst through: Salleigh Grubbs, Facebook Live, 15:56.

63 "Antifa coopted": Salleigh Grubbs, Facebook, January 6, 2021.

63 third party: Salleigh Grubbs, Facebook, February 5, 2021.

63 She would mobilize: Salleigh Grubbs, author interview, July 14, 2021.

63 "I'm a dedicated woman": Cobb County Republican Assembly, "Video of the 2021 Cobb RA's Candidate Forum for Cobb GOP Leadership," YouTube video, April 1, 2021, 30:54.

64 "mad as hell": Salleigh Grubbs, author interview, July 14, 2021.

64 "great day in Georgia": Salleigh Grubbs, Facebook Live video, March 23, 2021.

64 connected her with Dan: Salleigh Grubbs, author interview, April 12, 2022.

65 "perfect phone call": Salleigh Grubbs, author interview, April 12, 2022.

Chapter 4: A Hundred and Thirty-Two Coffees

66 deluged: Kathy Petsas, interview with Zoe Chace, July 31, 2022.

67 "child labor": Kathy Petsas, author interview, August 9, 2021.

67 Bob's Big Boy: Kathy Petsas, author interview, November 1, 2023.

67 Kathy's family: "Community Roots," *Kathy Petsas AZ* (campaign website), 2018.

67 Her grandfather: Kathy Petsas, author interview, August 3, 2022.

67 she joked: Kathy Petsas, author interview, July 31, 2022.

67 her uncle: Kathy Petsas, author interview, August 3, 2022.

67 sleep thirty: Kathy Petsas, author interview, November 1, 2023.

67 uncle's death: Kathy Petsas, author interview, August 3, 2022. Randy Cordova, "Thomas Pappas, Former Chief of State GOP, Dies at 49," *Arizona Republic*, November 26, 1989, 20.

68 past and present Republican icons: "LD 28 Officers," LD 28 GOP website.

68 Kathy sifted: Kathy Petsas, author interview, March 23, 2022.

68 answers disturbed: Kathy Petsas, author interview, August 9, 2021.

68 was to elect a Democrat: Arizona Secretary of State, "State of Arizona Official Canvass," November 30, 2018, 4.

68 radicalized: Kathy Petsas, author interview, November 1, 2023.

68 extreme: Kathy Petsas, author interview, August 9, 2021.

never called her back: Kathy Petsas, author interview, August 9, 2021.

69 wouldn't engage: Kathy Petsas, author interview, November 1, 2023.

69   "No, ma'am": Associated Press, "McCain Counters Obama 'Arab' Question," YouTube video, October 11, 2008.

69   39 percent: Karlyn Bowman and Andrew Rugg, "Public Opinion on Conspiracy Theories," American Enterprise Institute, November 2013.

69   Operation DeKookification: Laurie Roberts, "Precinct Races Key to DeKookification," *Arizona Republic*, June 9, 2012, B1.

69   "bitch session": Mackenzie Weinger, "Ariz. GOP Spox Derides 'B — Session,'" *Politico*, June 14, 2012.

70   briefly entertained: Jeremy Duda, "Push to Reject Trump at Convention Extends to Arizona," *Arizona Capitol Times*, June 22, 2016.

70   feared surrendering: Dan Nowicki and Yvonne Wingett Sanchez, "Can GOP Unite?," *Arizona Republic*, July 17, 2016, A6.

70   "Trump tourniquet": Kathy Petsas, interview by Scott Pelley, *CBS Evening News*, July 21, 2016.

70   Kathy ran: Kathy Petsas, author interview, November 1, 2023.

70   rudeness: Kathy Petsas, author interview, June 14, 2022.

70   cult of personality: Kathy Petsas, author interview, July 31, 2022.
     list of issues: Kathy Petsas, author interview, March 23, 2022.
     people believed him: Kathy Petsas, author interview, August 9, 2021.

71   By 2020: Kathy Petsas, author interview, November 1, 2023.

71   "1776": Jen Fifield, "Phoenix Candidate Posts of Revolution Before Capitol Riot," *Arizona Republic*, January 23, 2021, Z7.

71   trounced her: Kathy Petsas, author interview, August 25, 2022.

71   coffee after coffee: Kathy Petsas, author interview, July 31, 2022.

72   After each coffee Kathy Petsas, author interview, August 9, 2021, July 31, 2022.

73   new blood: Johnny Melton, author interview, August 11, 2021.

73   they didn't care: Sandra Dowling, author interview, August 10, 2021.

73   He was convinced: Derrick Rochwalik, author interview, August 2, 2022.

74   "adventure in never-never land": Rosalind S. Helderman, "Maricopa County Defies State Subpoena Seeking to Expand GOP Ballot Review, Calling It an 'Adventure in Never-Never Land,'" *Washington Post*, August 2, 2021.

74   "audit" "proved": *War Room*, no. 1,268, September 24, 2021.

74   asylum seekers: Renata Cló, "Hundreds Protest Scottsdale Hotel Turned Holding Facility for Families Seeking Asylum," *Arizona Republic*, June 2, 2021.

74   "a normal group": Kathy Petsas, author interview, September 15, 2022.

74   RSVPs: Kathy Petsas, author interview, August 9, 2021.

74   Derrick asked Kathy: Derrick Rochwalik, author interview, August 2, 2022.

74   counted the takeover as a victory: Kari Donovan, "America First Has Taken Over the GOP in Arizona — Those Not on the Train Are Being Replaced or Resigning," *Gateway Pundit*, June 6, 2021.

74   self-destructive for the party: Kathy Petsas, author interview, August 9, 2021.

75   did not even get a coffee: Kathy Petsas, author interview, July 31, 2022.

75 registered Republican: Sierra Ciaramella, Maricopa County Recorder's Office, email to the author, November 6, 2023.

75 Merissa felt: Merissa Hamilton, interview by Zoe Chace, August 1, 2022.

75 which belonged to her late mother: "Woman Who Cast Deceased Mother's Ballot in 2020 Election Sentenced," Arizona Attorney General, May 3, 2022. Jeremy Duda, "Scottsdale Woman Indicted for Casting Dead Mother's Ballot," AZ Mirror, July 13, 2021.

75 abusive ex: Merissa Hamilton, interview by Zoe Chace, August 1, 2022.

76 "weaponized against me": Merissa Hamilton, "Election Protection Initiative Training," Zoom, August 31, 2022.

76 "firing Petsas": Hamilton interview. Farley declined to be interviewed.

Chapter 5: The Virginia Model

77 "CPPPDS": Daniel J. Schultz, interview by Rob Maness, "America First Republicans: Winning in 2022 and Beyond," Lifezette, March 25, 2021, (video) 30:49.

77 "a little dry": Steve Bannon, author interview, September 30, 2023.

77 "Your wealth": Network America, "Precinct Committeeman Strategy Call," YouTube video, May 16, 2021, (video) 1:47:00.

78 feel some wins: Steve Bannon, author interview, September 30, 2023.

78 Bannon snapped: Steve Bannon, author interview, August 6, 2022.

78 cryptocurrencies: Chuck B, "Live Interview by Dan Schultz from precinctstrategy.com," RTT Nation, YouTube, (Video) 16:15.

78 inside job: Chris Gala, "Red Pill Reality Show," Rumble, May 15, 2021. Audio, 3:30.

78 Beanz: Tracy Diaz, "THIS Is How We Win," Dark to Light with Frank & Beanz, February 12, 2021, (Audio) 2:03.

78 guys in a basement: Network America, "The {NA} Network America NEIGHBORHOOD PRECINCT COMMITTEEMAN Week," YouTube, April 18, 2021, (Video) 1:58:06.

78 Myrtle Beach: David Gilbert, "One of QAnon's Earliest Influencers Just Got Elected to South Carolina GOP," Vice, April 26, 2021.

78 "not the marketing guy": Steve Bannon, author interview, September 30, 2023.

78 most ambitious eighty-year-old: Steve Bannon, author interview, August 6, 2022.

78 "Happy Clappy": Steve Bannon, author interview, September 30, 2023.

78 Talk radio reached: Paul Matzko, "Talk Radio Is Turning Millions of Americans into Conservatives," New York Times, October 9, 2020.

79 Bannon considered Fredericks: Steve Bannon, author interview, August 6, 2022.

"gross bad-boy banter": Sarah Ellison, "Trumpworld Has Converted the Nation's Regional Talk Radio Hosts into a Loyal Army," Washington Post, January 23, 2020.

"not about race": John Fredericks, interview by Don Lemon, CNN Tonight, CNN, January 11, 2018.

79　Fredericks grew up: Patrick Wilson, "John Fredericks, Who Predicted Trump's Rise, Overcame a Stutter to Host His Radio Show in Chesapeake," *Virginian-Pilot*, October 10, 2016. Rodney Ho, "John Fredericks Creates Freedom 1690 on AM Dial and Adds Doug Collins Radio Show," *Atlanta Journal-Constitution*, March 3, 2021. Ellison, "Trumpworld Has Converted the Nation's Regional Talk Radio Hosts into a Loyal Army." Myra Kahn Adams, "One of the Most Influential Talk Radio Show Hosts You Probably Don't Know," *Townhall*, June 15, 2020. John Fredericks, "Take Back Virginia Rally," Real America's Voice, October 13, 2021, (video) 1:32:56.

79　"Maybe we can": Wilson, "John Fredericks, Who Predicted Trump's Rise."

80　saw a business opportunity: Ho, "John Fredericks Creates Freedom 1690."

　　In 2011, he landed: Wilson, "John Fredericks, Who Predicted Trump's Rise."

80　Godzilla of Truth: Ellison, "Trumpworld Has Converted the Nation's Regional Talk Radio Hosts into a Loyal Army."

80　*Oh my God*: Real America's Voice, "Take Back Virginia Rally," Rumble, October 13, 2021, (video) 1:32:56.

81　In 2019: Real America's Voice, "Take Back Virginia Rally," Rumble, October 13, 2021, (video) 1:32:56.

81　He told the White House: *War Room*, no. 635.

81　The lesson John Fredericks learned: *War Room*, no. 635.

82　"Salleigh Grubbs": John Fredericks, "Salleigh Grubbs Speaks with John Fredericks About Her Election to Cobb County GA GOP Chair," Real America's Voice, June 5, 2021.

82　Terry McGenius: Ellison, "Trumpworld has Converted the Nation's Regional Talk Radio Hosts into a Loyal Army."

82　"total globalist": Steve Bannon, author interview, August 6, 2022.

82　"We're going to lose": Steve Bannon, author interview, August 6, 2022.

83　A parallel conversation: Isaac Arnsdorf and Josh Dawsey, "GOP Spends Millions on Election Volunteers to Search for Fraud," *Washington Post*, June 15, 2022.

　　"restore confidence:" Republican National Committee, "Report of the Temporary Committee on Election Integrity," August 11, 2021, 5, 18–20.

83　chartering their own: Meagan Flynn and Shawn Boburg, "An Army of Poll Watchers—Many Driven by GOP's 'Election Integrity' Push—Turns Out Across Virginia," *Washington Post*, October 27, 2021.

84　"weird and wrong": Laura Vozzella, "Youngkin Distances Himself from Controversial Rally Featuring Trump and Bannon," *Washington Post*, October 14, 2021.

84　censured by her colleagues: Laura Vozzella, "After Ducking the Question, Youngkin Says He Would Have Voted to Certify the 2020 Election," *Washington Post*, September 27, 2021.

84　"politely" correcting: Laura Vozzella, "Youngkin's Tricky Dance with 'Election Integrity' Complicates Run for Virginia Governor," *Washington Post*, August 6, 2021.

84　"brilliant": *War Room*, October 14, 2021.

85 counting problem: Rachel Chason, "Delays in Fairfax County Related to Technical Issues with Four Early-Voting Machines, Spokesman Says," *Washington Post*, November 2, 2021.

85 "why the delay?": Statement by Donald J. Trump, Save America PAC, November 2, 2021.

85 "shout-out": John Fredericks, interview by Steve Bannon, *War Room*, no. 1,385, November 3, 2021.

Chapter 6: Red Wave

86 developed barometers: Daniel J. Schultz, interview by Chris Gala, *Red Pill Reality Show*, May 15, 2021, (audio) 1:21:04.

87 private debate: Alex Eisenstat, "Trump's Secret Sit-Down with Ohio Candidates Turns into *Hunger Games*," *Politico*, March 25, 2021.

87 going rate: Michael Scherer and Josh Dawsey, "Trump Endorsements Slow and Prompt a Scramble by Candidates, Advisers," *Washington Post*, March 24, 2022.

87 two hundred thousand: Federal Election Commission records and a source familiar with the Jim Lamon campaign for Arizona Senate.

88 Dan imagined: "Neighborhood Precinct Committeeman Meeting," *Network America*, YouTube video, June 27, 2021, 2:15:18.

88 a different tack: Steve Stern, author interview, February 14, 2022.

89 Dan drafted: Daniel J. Schultz, "Precinct Strategy Helps Trump Defeat RINOs," Rumble, November 21, 2022.

89 "Just heard": Statement by Donald J. Trump, Save America PAC, February 27, 2022.

90 She wore a name tag: photograph provided by Salleigh Grubbs.

90 "homage to treason": Patricia Murphy, Greg Bluestein, and Tia Mitchell, "The Jolt: The Cobb 'Homage to Treason' Planned for Jan. 6," *Atlanta Journal-Constitution*, January 3, 2022.

90 Salleigh hated: Salleigh Grubbs, author interview, April 12, 2022.

90 "radicalized": Nicholas Bogel-Burroughs and Evan Hill, "Death of QAnon Follower at Capitol Leaves a Wake of Pain," *New York Times*, May 30, 2021.

90 She thought: Salleigh Grubbs, author interview, April 12, 2022.

90 Salleigh meant: Salleigh Grubbs, author interview, April 12, 2022.

91 "no uncertain terms": Statement by Salleigh Grubbs, January 2, 2022. "Fake News": Statement by Donald J. Trump, Save America PAC, January 5, 2022.

91 recently resigned: Jason Shepherd, author interview, December 9, 2021.

91 she didn't expect: Salleigh Grubbs, author interview, April 12, 2022.

91 caught COVID: Salleigh Grubbs, Facebook, July 9, 2021.

91 thought about her grandson: Salleigh Grubbs, author interview, April 12, 2022.

91 cheered Salleigh up: Salleigh Grubbs, Cobb County GOP Monthly Breakfast, Facebook Live, January 7, 2022.

92 "legitimate political discourse": "RNC Resolution to Censure Cheney, Kinzinger," *Washington Post*, February 3, 2022.

92 "Outside of the DC bubble": Josh Dawsey and Felicia Sonmez, "'Legitimate Political Discourse': Three Words About Jan. 6 Spark Rift Among Republicans," *Washington Post*, February 8, 2022.

93 wake-up call: Navin Nayak, author interview, June 16, 2023.

93 won or lost in the 2022 midterms: Michael Scherer, "Liberal Groups Devote Millions to Blocking GOP Election Deniers," *Washington Post*, June 22, 2022.

94 Navin's analysis: Navin Nayak, author interview, June 16, 2023.

94 To Matt: Matt Canter, author interview, July 20, 2023.

95 conducted research suggesting: Global Strategy Group, "Defining the Opponent," October 1, 2013.

95 early yet clear findings: Hart Research survey of 1,200 voters nationwide excluding strong Trump supporters, January 2022. Global Strategy Group survey of 1,200 voters nationwide excluding strong Trump supporters, February 2022.

95 presented an opportunity: Navin Nayak, author interview, June 16, 2023.

On a conference call: Navin Nayak, author interview, June 16, 2023.

Chapter 7: Karizona

96 had a feeling: Kathy Petsas, author interview, August 25, 2022.

97 "bunch of jackasses": McKenna Ross, "Hillsdale Republicans Censure Sen. Mike Shirkey for Departing from 'Conservative Values,'" *MLive*, February 8, 2021.

97 Piscataquis: David Marino Jr., "Piscataquis GOP Censures Susan Collins, Saying She 'Continuously Muddles Her Opinions,'" *Bangor Daily News*, May 5, 2021.

97 "or whatever": Dave Ball, interview with Jon Delano, *KDKA News*, February 15, 2021.

97 "irresponsible": "Nevada GOP Votes to Censure Nevada Secretary of State," Nevada Republican Party, April 11, 2021.

97 Dorchester County: Schuyler Kropf, "US Sen. Lindsey Graham Censured by Dorchester County Republican Party," *Post & Courier*, November 11, 2021.

97 Pecos County: Benjamin Wermund, "Republicans in Pecos, Medina Counties Censure Rep. Tony Gonzales over Votes on Gay Marriage, Guns," *Houston Chronicle*, August 15, 2022.

97 Jessamine County: Ana Rocío Álvarez Bríñez, "Jessamine County Republicans Censure Mitch McConnell for Support of Gun Control Bill," *Louisville Courier Journal*, July 23, 2022.

97 Kathy and her allies: Kathy Petsas, author interview, August 25, 2022.

98 Kathy said she knew: Jen Fifield, "Phoenix Candidate Posts of Revolution Before Capitol Riot," *Arizona Republic*, January 23, 2021.

98 Kathy was disgusted: Kathy Petsas, author interview, August 25, 2022.

98 She couldn't imagine: Kathy Petsas, author interview, August 25, 2022.

98 she understood exactly: Kathy Petsas, author interview, August 25, 2022.

99 how fitting: Kathy Petsas, author interview, August 25, 2022.

99 executive session: Recording obtained by the author, March 16, 2022.

101 wore a microphone: Ruby Cramer, "On Kari Lake's Campaign for Arizona Governor, the Mic Is Always Hot," *Washington Post*, October 16, 2022.

101 Trump would joke: Kyung Lah, Kate Sullivan, and Paul LeBlanc, "Trump Told Arizona GOP Senate Nominee 'You'll Lose if You Go Soft' on Election Fraud Claims," CNN, October 26, 2022.

101 emergence as a MAGA superstar: Cramer, "On Kari Lake's Campaign."

102 First up was Dan Farley: speeches by Farley and Mishkin, transcribed from a recording obtained by the author.

102 about to expire: Arizona Department of Real Estate, certified license history for Daniel G. Farley.

103 expected him to win: Kathy Petsas, author interview, March 23, 2022.

103 like a lunatic: Kathy Petsas, author interview, April 5, 2022. Farley declined to be interviewed.

103 Kathy thought surely: Kathy Petsas, author interview, April 5, 2022.

103 she thought the joke: Kathy Petsas, author interview, April 5, 2022.

104 challenged in court: Hearing recording obtained by the author, April 22, 2022. Kathy Petsas, author interview, April 26, 2022.

105 eighteen million: Karrin for Arizona, campaign finance report, Arizona Secretary of State, January 11, 2023.

105 Kathy went out knocking: Kathy Petsas, interview by Zoe Chace, July 31, 2022.

108 primary night: Kathy Petsas, author interview, August 2, 2022.

Chapter 8: Suspicious Minds

112 "Live from CPAC": *War Room*, no. 2,053, August 4, 2022.

113 convicted: U.S. Department of Justice, "Stephen K. Bannon Found Guilty by Jury of Two Counts of Contempt of Congress," July 22, 2022.

113 "that jail thing": Steve Bannon, keynote address delivered at the Conservative Political Action Conference in Dallas, Texas, August 5, 2022.

114 "peoples of mixed race": David Weigel and Isaac Arnsdorf, "Amid 'Mixed Race' Speech Blowback, Orban Echoes Trump in Dallas," *Washington Post*, August 4, 2022.

114 woman from Trinity County: Kathy Scofield, author interview, August 4, 2022.

114 he knew there were listeners: Steve Bannon, author interview, August 6, 2022.

114 "As people get older": Steve Bannon, author interview, September 30, 2023.

115 "hobbits": Steve Bannon, author interview, August 6, 2022.

115 Bannon was convinced: Steve Bannon, author interview, August 6, 2022.

115 "We're at war": Steve Bannon, keynote, CPAC, August 5, 2022.

116 "up their ass": Steve Bannon, author interview, August 6, 2022.

116 "hopeful": Description of "555," by Tiger Gang, on Soundstripe.

116 "This fight before us": Kari Lake, speech delivered to CPAC, August 6, 2022.

116 new video: Donald J. Trump, "A Nation in Decline," Rumble, August 6, 2022.

116 marketed as "uplifting": Description of "Mirrors," by Will Van De Crommert, on Artlist.

117 Trump liked: Isaac Arnsdorf, Josh Dawsey, and Michael Scherer, "How a Trump Soundtrack Became a QAnon Phenomenon," *Washington Post*, September 23, 2022.

118 "Q-U-L-T": Kelly Heath, author interview, September 23, 2022.

118 JFK Jr.: Meryl Kornfield, "Why Hundreds of QAnon Supporters Showed Up in Dallas, Expecting JFK Jr.'s Return," *Washington Post*, November 2, 2021.

118 apply gematria: Kelly Heath, author interview, September 23, 2022.

118 hidden meanings: Eileen McDermott, author interview, September 23, 2022.

118 "The truth": Julie McDaniel, author interview, September 23, 2022.

118 "We're standing": Melissa Cole, author interview, September 23, 2022.

119 "I know things": Alan Andrews, author interview, September 23, 2022.

119 "Military tribunals": Micki Larson-Olson, interview by Vaughn Hillyard, September 23, 2022.

119 "traitors": U.S. Department of Justice, "Texas Woman Sentenced to 180 Days in Jail After Jury Verdict Related to Capitol Breach," September 30, 2022.

119 "domestic terrorists": Larson-Olson, interview by Vaughn Hillyard, September 23, 2022.

119 McDaniel pointed: Julie McDaniel, author interview, September 23, 2023.

120 "That's why he says": Kelly Heath, author interview, September 23, 2023.

120 Trump didn't want: Arnsdorf, "How a Trump Soundtrack Became a QAnon Phenomenon."

120 "Look at those cameras": Donald Trump, at a rally in Latrobe, Pennsylvania, on November 5, 2022.

121 The law: Nick Corasaniti and Reid J. Epstein, "What Georgia's Voting Law Really Does," *New York Times*, April 2, 2021.

122 Salleigh's own heart: Salleigh Grubbs, Facebook, December 14, 2020.

125 To talk to Susan: Susan Knox, author interview, April 12, 2022.

125 This feeling of helplessness: Salleigh Grubbs, author interview, April 11, 2022.

126 Salleigh wasn't troubled: Salleigh Grubbs, author interview, April 12, 2022.

Chapter 9: The Abyss

128 The results: CAP Action, "Core Slides on GOP Branding," 7–9. Geoff Garin, "New Polling on MAGA Republicans," Hart Research Associates, September 22, 2022.

128 "really well known": Navin Nayak, author interview, June 16, 2023.

129 Garin, the pollster: Geoff Garin, author interview, June 15, 2023.

129 baby babble: Brad Komar, author interview, July 25, 2023.

129 arranged for Navin: Navin Nayak, author interview, June 16, 2023.

129 "MAGA Party": Remarks by President Biden at a Democratic National Committee Fundraiser, Portland Yacht Club, Portland, Oregon, April 21, 2022.

129 "deplorable": *CNN New Day*, May 5, 2022.

129 Navin saw it resonating: Navin Nayak, author interview, June 16, 2023.

130 polling found: Geoff Garin, "New Polling on MAGA Republicans," Hart Research Associates, September 22, 2022.

130 remained unpopular: Megan Brenan, "Steady 58% of Americans Do Not Want *Roe v. Wade* Overturned," Gallup, June 2, 2022.

131 poured resources into ads: House Majority PAC, "Makes Me Sick," YouTube video, October 24, 2022. House Majority PAC, "Values," YouTube video, September 15, 2022. House Majority PAC, "Warrior," YouTube video, October 31, 2022.

131 "we were hunting": Brad Komar, author interview, July 25, 2023.

132 Confederate uniform: Phil Stewart and Jarrett Renshaw, "Exclusive: Pennsylvania Candidate Mastriano Posed in Confederate Uniform at Army War College," Reuters, August 27, 2022.

132 "Hitlerian putsch": Greg Jaffe, "Doug Mastriano Warned of Left-Wing 'Hitlerian Putsch' in 2001 Paper," *Washington Post*, May 20, 2022.

132 Christian nationalism: Michelle Boorstein, "Christian Nationalism Shapes a Pa. Primary—and a GOP Shift," *Washington Post*, May 16, 2022.

132 charged with murder: Katie Glueck, "Mastriano Said in 2019 That His Bill Would Treat Abortions as Murder," *New York Times*, September 27, 2022.

132 *had* to win: Shapiro campaign official, author interview, July 11, 2022.

132 campaign kickoff: Josh Shapiro, Facebook Live, May 26, 2022.

132 "I'm only saying": Morgan Boyd, interview by New Castle News, "New Castle News interview with Josh Shapiro, Democrat for Pennsylvania governor," YouTube video, September 19, 2022.

133 "In a more normal world": Craig Snyder, author interview, August 22, 2022.

133 "feel alienated": Sarah Longwell, author interview, October 5, 2022.

133 Longwell herself grew up: Susan Glasser, "The Trials of a Never Trump Republican," *The New Yorker*, March 30, 2020.

134 voters in her ads: Republican Accountability Project, "Former Republican." Republican Accountability Project, "The Big Lie."

134 "that's the message": Sarah Longwell, author interview, October 5, 2022.

135 state-specific efforts: Steve Neavling, "Prominent Republicans Join Coalition to Support Whitmer for Reelection," *Detroit Metro Times*, September 12, 2022. Keith Ridler, "Idaho Republicans Supporting Democrat for Attorney General," Associated Press, October 11, 2022.

135 In Nevada: Pete Ernaut, "I've Spent My Whole Life Working to Elect Republicans. I'm Backing Catherine Cortez Masto," *Reno Gazette Journal*, August 2, 2022.

135 In Tennessee: Randy Stamps, author interview, October 28, 2022. Glenn Kessler, "Tennessee Congressman Andrew Ogles's Résumé Is Too Good to Be True," *Washington Post*, March 10, 2023.

135 In Washington State: David Nierenberg, author interview, October 14, 2022.

137 In Mesa: John Giles, author interview, October 15, 2022.

137 her phone pinged: Kari Lake War Room (@KariLakeWarRoom), Twitter, August 7, 2022.

137 Kathy was stunned: Kathy Petsas, author interview, October 3, 2022.

138 campaign-season routine: Kathy Petsas, author interview, August 25, 2022.

138 "pinot grigio": Kathy Petsas, author interview, August 3, 2022.

138 needlepointing: Kathy Petsas, author interview, September 14, 2022.

138 not the type of prayer: Kathy Petsas, author interview, November 1, 2023.

139 physical scuffle: Video and police records obtained by the author.

139 she was confident: Kathy Petsas, author interview, September 14, 2022.

139 she was ready: Kathy Petsas, author interview, August 25, 2022.

139 The movie claimed: Ali Swenson, "Fact-Checking *2000 Mules*, the Movie Alleging Ballot Fraud," Associated Press, May 8, 2020.

139 amounted to nothing: Philip Bump, "Discussing the Gaps in *2000 Mules* with Dinesh D'Souza," *Washington Post*, May 17, 2022.

139 dogs: Nicole Grigg (@NicoleSGrigg), Twitter, October 19, 2022. Yvonne Wingett Sanchez, "Alleged Voter Intimidation at Arizona Drop Box Puts Officials on Watch," *Washington Post*, October 20, 2022.

139 guns: Yvonne Wingett Sanchez and Adriana Usero, "Video Offers Rare Glimpse of Police Enforcing Arizona's Election Laws," *Washington Post*, March 9, 2023.

139 Mardi Gras mask: Kathy Petsas, text message, October 19, 2022.

139 in all seriousness: Kathy Petsas, author interview, September 30, 2022, and October 3, 2022.

140 She didn't really want: Kathy Petsas, author interview, September 14, 2022.

140 Kathy got a call: Kathy Petsas, author interview, October 7, 2022.

140 personal hero: Kathy Petsas, author interview, October 5, 2022.

140 privately saying: Paul Kane, "Liz Cheney's Political Life Is Likely Ending—and Just Beginning," *Washington Post*, August 15, 2022. Paul Kane, Josh Dawsey, and Jacqueline Alemany, "Rep. Liz Cheney Tells Americans Why Jan. 6 Should Terrify Them," *Washington Post*, June 10, 2022.

140 Her role bolstered: Sarah Longwell, author interview, June 30, 2022.

141 J. Michael Luttig: "Hearings Before the Select Committee to Investigate the January 6th Attack on the United States Capitol," U.S. House of Representatives, 117th Congress, Second Session, Government Printing Office, serial no. 117-10.

141 saw Cheney as an inspiration: Kathy Petsas, author interview, October 5, 2022.

141 she was worried: Kathy Petsas, author interview, October 7, 2022.

141 most memorable: Kathy Petsas, author interview, October 5, 2022. Tim Miller, text message, November 8, 2023.

141 public speech: Liz Cheney, interview by Sofia Gross, McCain Institute, October 5, 2022.

Chapter 10: The Trump Machine

143 "Trump machine": Kathy Petsas, text message, November 8, 2022.

143 not ready to celebrate: Kathy Petsas, text message, November 12, 2022.

143 tweet: David French (@DavidAFrench), Twitter, November 9, 2022.

143 felt vindicated: Kathy Petsas: text message, November 9, 2022.

144 thirty points: Josh Kraushaar, "How Kari Lake Lost Her Bid for Arizona Governor," *Axios*, November 20, 2022.

144 Kathy understood something: Kathy Petsas, author interview, September 15, 2022.

144 streaming: AZFamily, "LIVE: Maricopa County set to certify 2022 election," YouTube video, November 28, 2022.

145 Richer understood: Stephen Richer, author interview, August 24, 2022.

146 Joe Oltmann: Hearing video, 31:40.

146 Kathy Roscoe: Hearing video, 49:00.

146 Ben Bergquam: Hearing video, 1:10:29.

146 Chris Hamlet: Hearing video, 1:31:55.

146 real glitches: Yvonne Wingett Sanchez, Isaac Stanley-Becker, Reis Thebault, and Josh Dawsey, "Problems with Voting Machines in Arizona's Maricopa County Trigger Unfounded Fraud Claims," *Washington Post*, November 8, 2022.

147 no malfeasance: Yvonne Wingett Sanchez and Isaac Stanley-Becker, "Printer Glitches in Ariz. Election Not Due to Malfeasance, Review Finds," *Washington Post*, April 10, 2023.

147 One man cited: Hearing video, 1:11:16.

147 Book of Psalms: Hearing video, 41:07.

147 demanded a revote: Hearing video, 1:24:30.

147 played a clip: Hearing video, 1:35:00.

147 thick accent: Hearing video, 1:43:00.

147 Kathy thought: Kathy Petsas, author interview, November 28, 2022.

147 go into hiding: *Fox 10* Staff, "Maricopa County Chairman Moved to 'Undisclosed Location' for Safety after Midterm Elections," *Fox 10 Phoenix*, November 20, 2020.

147 broke down in tears: Kathy Petsas, text message, June 1, 2023.

148 "true believers": Kathy Petsas, author interview, November 28, 2022.

148 "I am now": Merissa Hamilton, text message to Zoe Chace, December 1, 2022.

148 County meeting: recording obtained by the author.

149 That was it: Kathy Petsas, author interview, January 28, 2023.

149 Friends would ask: Kathy Petsas, author interview, January 28, 2023.

150 Kathy told him: Kathy Petsas, author interview, January 28, 2023.

150 *Just keep smiling*: Kathy Petsas, author interview, January 28, 2023.
her courage: Kathy Petsas, author interview, January 14, 2023.
150 He was there: Daniel J. Schultz (@ColdWarrior1978), Rumble, January 20, 2023.
150 people coming up to him: Daniel J. Schultz (@ColdWarrior1978), Rumble, November 23, 2022.
150 Dan believed: Daniel J. Schultz (@ColdWarrior1978), Rumble, January 3, 2023.
150 "I want my kids": Daniel J. Schultz (@ColdWarrior1978), Rumble, January 12, 2023.
150 The teacher had asked: Daniel J. Schultz (@ColdWarrior1978), Rumble, November 1, 2022.
151 Dan hoped: Daniel J. Schultz, Rumble (@ColdWarrior1978), January 16, 2023.
151 "what the hell": Daniel J. Schultz (@ColdWarrior1978), Rumble, January 20, 2023.
151 "go Galt": Daniel J. Schultz (@ColdWarrior1978), Rumble, July 4, 2023.
151 He asked himself: Daniel J. Schultz (@ColdWarrior1978), Rumble, July 18, 2023.
151 so many reasons: Daniel J. Schultz (@ColdWarrior1978), Rumble, June 21, 2024.
152 "the mechanism": Steve Bannon, author interview, January 22, 2023.
153 Grundoons: Hadas Gold, "Steve Bannon's 'Tough Love,'" *Politico*, September 2, 2016.
153 Bannon's vision: Steve Bannon, author interview, January 22, 2023.
153 Bannon knew: Steve Bannon, author interview, January 22, 2023.
154 South Dakota: *War Room*, no. 2,446, January 16, 2023.
154 Nebraska: *War Room*, no. 2,408, December 31, 2022.
154 Washington State: Kira Gilbert, "The Conservative Revolt within the Republican Party," Convention of States, April 14, 2023.
154 Kansas: Red Pill News, "Precinct Strategy in Action—Taking Back Kansas with Thad Snider," Rumble, 2023.
154 Texas: *Bannon's War Room*, "'Replace Politicians with Patriots': Steve Stern Calls for the Deplorables to Get Involved," Rumble, 2023.
154 Pennsylvania: Charles Homans, "Will the Real G.O.P. Please Stand Up? A National Power Struggle Goes Local," *New York Times*, January 24, 2023.
154 "massive sea change": Steve Bannon, author interview, January 22, 2023.

Chapter 11: The Waldorf and the Nuthouse

156 at Trump's request: Michael Scherer and Josh Dawsey, "Trump Calls Romney 'a Great Man,' but Works to Undermine Him and Block Senate Run," *Washington Post*, December 8, 2017.
156 thirty thousand poll watchers: Ronna McDaniel, interview by Steve Bannon, *War Room*, October 11, 2022.

156 breakfast was included: John Fredericks, author interview, January 25, 2023.

156 block rate: An RNC official who wasn't authorized to speak publicly.

156 to Fredericks: John Fredericks, author interview, January 25, 2023.

157 Candidate forum: John Fredericks Media Network, "OTB 1/26/23: Replay of RNC Chairman's Candidate Forum on Jan 25 in Dana Point, CA," Rumble, January 26, 2023.

157 depending on whom you asked: John Fredericks, interview by Steve Bannon, *War Room*, December 2022.

157 uninvited: A Trump aide who spoke on the condition of anonymity.

158 "most insane": John Fredericks, author interview, January 25, 2023.

158 Fredericks did not blame Trump: John Fredericks, author interview, January 25, 2023.

159 inside game: Ben Proto, author interview, January 26, 2023.

159 Kaufmann Email obtained by Josh Dawsey.

159 She went around: Caroline Wren, author interview, January 27, 2023.

159 "fucking sellout": Interviews with two people present.

160 By Friday: There was one vote for former New York congressman Lee Zeldin, who'd decided in December not to run for chair.

160 Fredericks never really expected John Fredericks, author interview, January 25, 2023.

160 high-performance seat belts: LinkedIn.

161 "America First army": Isaac Arnsdorf, Doug Bock Clark, Alexandra Berzon, and Anjeanette Damon, "Heeding Steve Bannon's Call, Election Deniers Organize to Seize Control of the GOP — and Reshape America's Elections," ProPublica, September 2, 2021.

161 America First delegates: 2022 Michigan Republican candidate evaluation form.

161 criminal referral: Michigan Senate Oversight Committee, "Report on the November 2020 Election in Michigan," June 23, 2021.

161 Karamo swore: Jeremy Herb and Sara Murray, "Trump-Backed Michigan Secretary of State Candidate Spread False Election Claims and January 6 Conspiracy Theories," CNN, November 16, 2021.

161 finished high school: Craig Mauger, "Meet the Candidates to Redraw Michigan's Political Boundaries," *Detroit News*, July 21, 2020.

162 had run the earlier convention Terry Camp, "Infighting in Saginaw County GOP as America First Wing of Party Takes Control," *WJRT*, November 30, 2022.

162 He felt pained: Curt Tucker, author interview, February 17, 2023.

162 tonight's meeting: Geno Phillips, "Sag. GOP Convention," YouTube video, January 26, 2023.

163 All but one: Isaac Arnsdorf, Josh Dawsey, Hannah Knowles, Yvonne Wingett Sanchez, Patrick Marley, and Ashley Parker, "Trump's Grip on the Republican Base Is Slipping — Even Among His Fans," *Washington Post*, February 23, 2023.

164 willingness to say out loud: Josiah Jaster, author interview, Feburary 17, 2023.

164   protests in Lansing: David D. Kirkpatrick and Mike McIntire, "'Its Own Domestic Army': How the G.O.P. Allied Itself with Militants," *New York Times*, February 8, 2021.

164   helped mobilize: Paul Egan and Clara Hendrickson, "Activist Who Organized Buses to DC About to Take Mich. GOP Role," *Detroit Free Press*, January 7, 2021.

164   phony certificate: David Eggert, "Michigan AG Asks Feds to Investigate Fake GOP Electors," Associated Press, January 14, 2022.

164   some older party officers: Paul Egan and Clara Hendrickson, "Activist Who Organized Buses to DC About to Take Mich. GOP Role," *Detroit Free Press*, January 7, 2021.

164   won overwhelmingly: Samuel Dodge, "Emails Reveal Tension Among University of Michigan Regents amid Ron Weiser's Capitol Riot Controversy," *Ann Arbor News*, December 28, 2021.

166   "It's a vote": Josiah Jaster, author interview, February 18, 2023.

167   "fucking hillbillies": Marla Braun, author interview, February 18, 2023. footnote: Chris Gautz, "Republican National Committee No Longer Lists Jackson as Birthplace of Republican Party," *Michigan Live*, March 24, 2011.

167   Josiah was more sanguine: Josiah Jaster, author interview, February 17, 2023.

167   "We definitely believe": Andrea Paschall, author interview, February 17, 2023.

167   "Not really": Meshawn Maddock, author interview, February 18, 2023.

Chapter 12: Complete MAGA Takeover

168   "Happy": Salleigh Grubbs, text message, May 17, 2023.

169   "hot mess": Salleigh Grubbs, author interview, June 9, 2023.

169   independent analyses: Maya King and Nick Corasaniti, "A Georgia Mystery: How Many Democrats Voted in the G.O.P. Primary?" *New York Times*, June 2, 2022.

169   Salleigh wasn't sure: Salleigh Grubbs, author interview, June 9, 2023.

169   She cracked up: Salleigh Grubbs, text message, November 16, 2022.

169   news reports: Roger Sollenberger, "'Pro-Life' Herschel Walker Paid for Girlfriend's Abortion," *Daily Beast*, October 3, 2022.

169   Salleigh took seriously: Salleigh Grubbs, author interview, December 9, 2022.

170   "rattled": Geoff Duncan, interview by Don Lemon, *Don Lemon Tonight*, CNN, October 5, 2022.

170   she demanded: Salleigh Grubbs, text message, October 6, 2022.

170   "TKO": Salleigh Grubbs, text message, October 14, 2022.

170   at the campaign's party: Salleigh Grubbs, author interview, December 9, 2022.

170   Salleigh had to decide: Salleigh Grubbs, author interview, February 21, 2022.

170   she felt blessed: Salleigh Grubbs, author interview, February 21, 2022.

170 grisly photos: Salleigh Grubbs, author interview, June 8, 2023.

170 a rumor went around: Salleigh Grubbs, author interview, June 11, 2023.

170 moved to tears: Salleigh Grubbs, author interview, March 23, 2023.

170 by acclamation: Salleigh Grubbs, author interview. June 11, 2023.

171 two priorities: Georgia Republican Assembly, "GRA President Alex Johnson: Proposed Accountability Rule," YouTube video, June 3, 2023.

171 Salleigh was all for that: Salleigh Grubbs, author interview, March 23, 2023.

171 Salleigh, though, was skeptical: Salleigh Grubbs, author interview, June 6, 2023.

171 The other drama: Salleigh Grubbs, author interview, June 6, 2023.

172 Even though Salleigh was an insider: Salleigh Grubbs, author interview, June 9, 2023.

173 "I have been Indicted": Donald Trump, Truth Social, June 8, 2023.

173 Friends were texting Salleigh: Salleigh Grubbs, author interview, June 8, 2023.

173 She felt like: Salleigh Grubbs, author interview, June 11, 2023.

174 It made her think twice: Salleigh Grubbs, author interview, June 8, 2023.

175 "Here we go again": Laurie Wood, author interview, June 8, 2023.

175 "Trump tries": Sam Carnline, author interview, June 8, 2023.

176 "I'm not surprised": Jim Tully, author interview, June 8, 2023.

176 "Don't start me": Orien Roy, author interview, June 8, 2023.

176 commissioners' rejection: Kate Brumback, "County Leaders in Georgia Reject Election Board Nominee Who Challenged Voters' Eligibility," Associated Press, June 7, 2023.

176 "Literally nothing": Jackie Harling, author interview, June 8, 2023.

178 "Meatball goon squad": Preston Parra (@The PrestonParra), Twitter, March 30, 2023.

178 reminded her: Salleigh Grubbs, text message, March 30, 2023.

178 She viewed DeSantis: Salleigh Grubbs, author interview, June 11, 2023.

178 Captain K: Miles Parks, Allison Mollenkamp, and Nick McMillan, "Election Deniers Have Taken Their Fraud Theories on Tour — to Nearly Every State," NPR, June 30, 2022.

181 new "it" thing: Josh Dawsey and Isaac Arnsdorf, "Republicans Plan Efforts to Tout Early Voting Tactics They Once Vilified," Washington Post, July 12, 2023.

181 lip service to mail voting: Republican National Committee, "Former President Donald Trump Asks You to Bank Your Vote," YouTube video, July 26, 2023.

181 in interviews: Donald Trump, interview by John Fredericks, American Sunrise Show, Real America's Voice, July 28, 2023.

185 "I've never felt so loved": Salleigh Grubbs, author interview, June 9, 2023.

185 Salleigh got up at five: Salleigh Grubbs, author interview, June 11, 2023.

187 football field: "South Exhibit Hall," Columbus Georgia Convention and Trade Center.

187 sharp stick: Salleigh Grubbs, text message, June 10, 2023.

187 voting down: Amy Gardner, "Georgia Is Likely Next Ground Zero for Trump's Battle with Law Enforcement," *Washington Post,* June 12, 2023.

187 furious and disappointed: Salleigh Grubbs, author interview, June 11, 2023.

188 But now Salleigh: Salleigh Grubbs, author interview, June 11, 2023.

189 "I'm just a girl": Salleigh Grubbs, text message, June 19, 2023.

189 gift box: Salleigh Grubbs, text message, June 10, 2023.

189 Some day she planned: Salleigh Grubbs, author interview, June 11, 2023.

189 Salleigh told Trump: Salleigh Grubbs, author interview, June 10, 2023.

190 She hoped: Salleigh Grubbs, text message, June 10, 2023.

190 She wished: Salleigh Grubbs, text message, June 19, 2023.

190 chatted with Greene: Salleigh Grubbs, author interview, June 11, 2023.

190 happiest days: Salleigh Grubbs, author interview, June 10, 2023.

190 like the teacher: Salleigh Grubbs, author interview, June 11, 2023.

191 FINISH WHAT WE STARTED: As delivered, Trump said, "finish the job that we started." (He apparently soured on the line, because in subsequent speeches he finished the passage with, "and we will Make America Great Again" or "we will finish the job once and for all.")

Epilogue: The People's Republic of MAGA

194 during sex: Matt Gaetz, Firebrand: Dispatches from the Front Lines of the MAGA Revolution (New York: Bombardier Books, 2020).

194 told Bannon: Steve Bannon, interview with the author, September 30, 2023.

196 Bannon gestured: Bannon's War Room, "Sign Up To Become A Precinct Committeeman TODAY," Rumble, September 30, 2023.

196 Dan Schultz, meanwhile: Dan Schultz, "Precinct Strategy 93 Days. 403 Days. Royce White's Latest Podcast," Rumble, September2 9, 2023.

197 Frank argued: Thomas Frank, *What's the Matter with Kansas? How Conservatives Won the Heart of America* (New York: Picador, 2004), 1–12, 75.

197 he'd noticed: Thomas Frank, "Are those my words coming out of Steve Bannon's mouth?," *The Guardian,* October 6, 2017.

198 In Nevada: Maeve Reston and Michael Scherer, "Trump gains advantage as states set delegate selection rules," *Washington Post,* July 30, 2023.

198 Michigan Republicans: Ibid.

198 The California Republican Party: Ibid.

198 In Florida: Kimberly Leonard and Gary Fineout, "Florida Republicans reject DeSantis for Trump in loyalty pledge fight," *Politico,* September 15, 2023.

198 voted to suspend him: Georgia Senate Republicans, "Statement Regarding the Indefinite Caucus Suspension of Senator Colton Moore," September 28, 2023.

198 sympathetic to Moore's cause: Salleigh Grubbs, interview with the author, October 3, 2023.

199   She thought Republicans: Salleigh Grubbs, author interview, November 9, 2023.

200   privately telling advisers: Isaac Arnsdorf, Josh Dawsey, and Devlin Barrett, "Trump and allies plot revenge, Justice Department control in a second term," *Washington Post*, November 5, 2023.

200   "suckers": Jake Tapper, "Exclusive: John Kelly goes on the record to confirm several disturbing stories about Trump," CNN, October 3, 2023.

200   "very petty": Bill Barr, interview by Bob Costa, "Face the Nation," CBS, June 18, 2023.

200   "wannabe dictator": Mark Milley, Farewell Ceremony, Joint Base Myer-Henderson Hall, Arlington, Virginia, September 29, 2023.

200   Cobb: Ty Cobb, email to the author, November 3, 2023.

200   "significant irregularities": United States v. Donald J. Trump, D.D.C. 1:23-cr-257 Docket no. 1, 30.

200   Insurrection Act: Isaac Arnsdorf, Josh Dawsey, and Devlin Barrett, "Trump and allies plot revenge, Justice Department control in a second term," *Washington Post*, November 5, 2023.

201   He did get it: Edward-Isaac Dovere, *Battle for the Soul: Inside the Democrats' Campaigns to Defeat Trump* (New York: Viking, 2021), 86.

201   "democracy will save itself": Franklin Delano Roosevelt, "Radio Address on the Election of Liberals," FDR Presidential Library and Museum, November 4, 1938.

201   He felt the people's need: Richard Ben Cramer, *What It Takes: The Way to the White House* (New York: Vintage Books, 1993), 370.

202   thought he did great: Kathy Petsas, text message, September 28, 2023.

202   She still found: Kathy Petsas, author interview, November 1, 2023.

203   "stitch his mouth closed": Kathy Petsas, text message, October 1, 2023.

203   "MAGA extremist": Jaime Harrison, Democratic National Committee statement, October 25, 2023.

      "MAGA Mike": Ammar Moussa, Biden-Harris 2024 statement, October 25, 2023.

      "MAGA MIKE": Donald Trump, Truth Social, October 25, 2023.

Index

About the Author

Isaac Arnsdorf is a national political reporter for the *Washington Post* who covers former president Donald Trump, the MAGA movement, and the elected officials, activists, donors, and media figures on the right who are powering the Republican Party. He was previously an investigative reporter covering national politics at ProPublica and a money-in-politics reporter at *Politico*. His reporting on President Trump's agenda for veterans won the Sidney Hillman Foundation's Sidney Award and the National Press Club's Sandy Hume Award. *Finish What We Started* is his first book.